Life Changing Events:
Who We Are Now

An Anthology
Basil B. Clark

Waldenhouse Publishers, Inc.
Walden, Tennessee

LIFE CHANGING EVENTS: WHO WE ARE NOW

All scripture quotations, unless otherwise indicated, are taken from the Holy Bible, New International Version C, NIV C 1973, 1978, 1984, 2011 by Biblica, Inc. TM Used by permission of Zondervan. All rights reserved world-wide. www.zondervan. com. The "NIV" and "New International Version" are trademarks registered in the United States Patent and Trademark Office by Biblica, Inc. TM
Cover photograph by Basil B. Clark (South River, Riva, Maryland)
Compiled by Basil B. Clark 606~205~5243 www.clarks-cove.com
ISBN: 978-1-947589-44-5
Library of Congress Control Number: 2021948980
A collection of interviews examining the aftermath of life changing events, be they losses, abuse, inner and/or outer woundings, or other events, negative and positive. Looks at pathways people have traveled as they ask, "Since the eventful turning point, who am I now?" ~ provided by Publisher
Published by Waldenhouse Publishers, Inc.
100 Clegg Street, Signal Mountain, Tennessee, USA 37377
423-886-2721 www.waldenhousepublishers.com
Printed in the United States of America
SEL043000 SELF-HELP / Post-Traumatic Stress Disorder (PTSD)
SEL021000 SELF-HELP / Motivational & Inspirational
SEL023000 SELF-HELP / Personal Growth / Self-Esteem

DEDICATION #1
CORA LARSON

For a long time I walked around with a yellow backpack slung over one shoulder. In it I carried several folders containing draft manuscripts to some eight or nine book projects. The evening of March 22, 2009, Cora and I were discussing all these unfinished scripts, and she suggested that maybe it was time to prioritize, and complete some. She wondered if maybe I kept working piecemeal on different ones (and listing ideas for new ones) because I was afraid of success. I agreed, but also knew it was hard to just set old habits aside. The next morning I was reading my Bible, and in Isaiah 28: 24, and 28a saw "When a farmer plows for planting, does he plow continually?" and, "Grain must be ground to make bread; so one does not go on threshing it forever."

I immediately made a note beside them with the date, and that, to me, was just a confirmation of what Cora had been saying the night before. I stopped carrying all the folders around, and started to concentrate on *Marvel's Mistake*, and *Barabbas*, two short stories that would be the easiest to complete. They actually moved down on the priority scale when I took a Sabbatical in 2013 and wrote and published *War Wounded: Let the Healing Begin*; then B*arabbas: Son of a Father* was published in 2015; *Massacre at Hill 303* in 2018, and now I think I have taken a little backslide from Cora's advice, as along with this book, *Marvel's Mistake* is in final draft stage, along with *No Rest for the Wicked: And I Ain't Slept Lately*. And there are other drafts on a shelf now that I truly want to get to in the future; but, one (or two) at a time, so thank you Cora! (Cora's story, Chapter 18)

(Cora and I connected on eHarmony in November 2008, corresponded for a while and met in person January 3, 2009, and dated two years before our marriage on March 13, 2011. More of the background on that appears in Chapter 45: "A Truly Life-Changing, Most Positive, Climb Ever.")

DEDICATION #2:
DEMON CHASERS. SCOOTER AND LITTLE BIT

They adopted us. True. In 2012 Cora and I were at our local PetSmart Store looking for a shelter cat to adopt. There were many candidates, and as we looked, and re-looked, and wondered, at one point I reached around and patted Cora on the hip. Or so she thought. When she looked down she realized it was a black paw belonging to a large cat touching her. That was all it took. At first we called him Panther, as in a Black Panther cat. However, in short order we discovered that Scooter would fit him much better.

Scooter was an "only child" until about four years ago when we decided to go to PetSmart again in search of a pal for him. There was the usual array of cats and kittens in cages, and there was a large box on the floor where a couple felines were being transferred in to a cage. I looked at them, and one reached up and hooked both her little paws around my left arm and pulled it toward her. She was about half the size of Scooter, so Little Bit she became.

I have post-traumatic stress disorder, and it can be triggered by many things, sometimes without warning; in the following case, it was no surprise. My surprise was Scooter. It was around 2 a.m. and I was in bed, Scooter lying at my feet. I was reading a book, *The War Still Rages*, written by a friend, Chuck Matheson. I was at the place where Chuck was describing the first firefight he was in, and abruptly I was overwhelmed with January 1st, 1969, my first firefight. I just lay there staring through the page, no longer reading, but caught in the sounds and sights of that bloody New Year's Day as if they were occurring in real time.

Suddenly Scooter did something he had not done to that point in the five plus years he had been with us. He jumped up on my chest and started bumping against the book until I finally just set it on the dresser beside the bed and turned off the light. Then he stretched his paws up, one on each side of my neck, tucked his head tight against my bearded chin, and lay there until I was asleep (I guess, I don't remember him leaving). Now, frequently, he curls against my chest and puts his head up toward my face. He waits for his reward, a kiss on the head.

And as far as Cora, Scooter does not allow her any space to do anything by herself; he is right there, helping (we would never dare call it hindering.) Sometimes if she is bent over doing something, Scooter puts his front paws on her shoulders and peers over, supervising.

About a year after we got Little Bit, I was real restless one night, and she got into bed under the covers, stuck her head back out, and cuddled into my arm. I eventually drifted off to sleep and did not know when she left, presumably to run around the house with Scooter. She maintained that routine for about a year, and then switched to sometimes lying on my chest, other times curled up either against my back or legs. Now every night she comes and cuddles in my arm, I guess sensing I need more settling down.

And I'm not at all sure "what is what" when Little Bit cuddles in my arm while Scooter curls up at my feet. Guess they're just saying, "Between us two Angels, Dad, we've got you covered."

(Anthology Compiler)

ENDORSEMENTS

Trauma's primary effect is to isolate us from ourselves, our loved ones, our communities and spiritual practices. Trauma insists on taking everything from survivors, and leaves the individual in a state of constant horror, re-experiencing a moment frozen in time over and over again until someone reaches out and helps establish a safe, secure connection beyond all the suffering. Basil Clark's latest work does just that. By telling the stories and allowing survivors to share their hurt and healing in their own words, Clark allows for those primal and necessary components of connection to regenerate--contact, comfort, safety, shared narrative and shared healing.

C.J. Robinson, Ph.D.

These are stories that deserve to be told, from the only people who could tell them. We all reach a Robert Frost moment – you know, "Two roads diverged in a yellow wood." Sometimes we get to choose a road, sometimes we just limp down it with nothing but hope. This collection by Basil Clark shows not only a glimpse into those moments, but a beautiful mosaic of the many leaves picked up along the way. -

Buddy Forbes, Big Sandy Bureau Reporter at WYMT TV

LIFE CHANGING EVENTS: WHO WE ARE NOW

The day started out like any other, normal, positive, and then … it … … … everything changed. It was vicious … tearing me to pieces to the nth degree … finding its way into the very core of my being … causing me to … I mean … before this traumatic event I at least had some idea of who I was and what I wanted … but now the question is … Who *am* I now?

Although the above paragraph is indicative of a negative situation, another thing to keep in mind regarding life-changing events, some are positive.

Compiler

....

"The future keeps telling us what the past was about. You make the past mean different things by the way you use the time that comes after."

Lt. ARTHUR FANCY, NYPD Blue,
12/10/96. Season 4, Episode 8

CONTENTS

FOREWORD

I have been emotionally swept away by these courageous souls who have contributed to this anthology of "HOPE." These personal, told from the heart, stories are more about the heroic survival of the spirit than about loss and grief. Each contributor adds another painful life experience, but even though it appears to be great sadness, each story is blessed with insight and compassion. In the end, you will realize that this is all about love.

I was touched by all of these people. I could feel their pain and struggle to maintain a continuing life purpose. Most have endured huge life changing events that would stop most normal people from going on with their lives. These people however, looked deeper within themselves for greater meaning. It is in that search that these inner questions arise: What do I do now? What does it all mean? Why did these things happen? How do I go forward with my own life? Where is God?

In that pursuit of finding real meaning to all that has happened they evolve into something much greater and stronger than they were before. They have changed and will never be the same. They found themselves tested beyond compare, and yet, they still seek out that LIGHT of HOPE that shines from within us all. They never give up on life, or themselves. That is why these stories are so powerful and moving. Readers will be touched by their words and they will begin to find themselves changing as well.

We all enter this world and discover that in life "things do happen" to all of us, most of which we cannot control, or even prevent. This is the nature of mankind. But for those among us who are seriously tested, they have a choice to make, to either submit to the negative dark night of soul, or to learn whatever lessons and find whatever gifts these sometimes-horrible events bring us. The people who shared their personal pain with us in this collective of tears and suffering have found that they have been given a gift of compassion and love, even though it came at heavy cost. I pray for all of them and send them my spiritual hugs, and love, but I thank them for sharing these stories with me and all of you. I am a better person for having read them. I know that people can, do, and will, continue to emotionally survive and find that Divine purpose for their own life. There is always HOPE and LOVE awaiting us in the LIGHT!

Rev. Bill McDonald
Author of *Warrior: A Spiritual Odyssey, Alchemy of a Warrior's Heart, Purple Hearts,* and *I Still Can See Tomorrow*
Poet, Actor, Artist, Documentary Film Advisor, Vietnam War Veteran (The Distinguished Flying Cross, The Bronze Star, The Purple Heart, 14 Air Medals), International Motivational Speaker, Minister, and Veteran Advocate.

Acknowledgments

To all who allowed me to include their stories in this Anthology, and, especially to Cora, who not only helped with proofreading, but also encouraged me to get to the finish line.

INTRODUCTION

The title could imply this is an anthology about life after Covid-19; it is not. The compiling of these stories started months before we had ever heard everyday use of the words coronavirus, self-isolation, social-distancing, etc. Furthermore, the events of 2020 are not yet in our rear view mirrors enough for us to know who we are now.

But one thing that is for certain, people still have encountered individual traumatic events which leave their marks; loss of a loved one whether through death, divorce, or moving miles away; illnesses that hinder; physical, sexual, and emotional abuse; a sundry of addictions; rejection; bullying; oppressive attitudes; victims of natural disasters, random acts of violence, and loneliness, to name a few. These battles are usually very subjective, and the end results can be devastating. And some things are not a sudden life changing experience, but rather a series of life forming events.

Beyond the event, life goes on; but different, often very different.

So all these handicaps, along with many other things not listed, have impact on our lives and leave us questioning, "who am I now?"

This anthology is just a few of the many stories of people asking the preceding question. These people are heroes in their own right for their perseverance as they walk the often painful pathway of discovery and healing.

And we also discover that "in our diversity of experiences we find just how much we have in common." (Basil B. Clark, *War Wounded: Let the Healing Begin*)

(Compiler's Note) And while putting final touches on this, something else occurred that I'm sure all are familiar with, Tiger Woods was in a serious crash. I like Tiger Woods, he set remarkable records. And his accident was newsworthy. But, at the same time, many others were in car wrecks, suffered in other situations, bore losses, and in many cases, felt they were bearing these life changing events alone and unnoticed. Who cared? Aren't their lives and losses and pains just as significant?

The paradox is that while they may feel like they have less support, or people caring, they also experience the blessing of missing out on some of the insensitive prying questions that may come from an in-your-face press.

PROLOGUE

While a student at Eastern Kentucky University I was talking with one of my professors in his 50's about a basketball game my sons had re-cently played in. (They were still in grade school at the time.)

He said he was glad to see I enjoyed their games and that I seemed to enjoy doing things with them. Then he became real serious and told me that his father had gone to only one of his games when he was a young boy. My professor said that at one point in the game, the ball was passed to him, the floor was clear, and he took off running and made a basket – on the opposing team's end of the floor. He said his father stood up in the stands, hollered, "You stupid idiot!" stomped out of the gym, and never attended another of his games.

As he related this I could see the pain still on his face and hear it in his voice. Some 40+ years later he was still affected by that one in-cident, which actually was a microscopic definition of his relationship with his father; a life changing event. But he went through a question-ing process on the way to becoming a respected University professor.

Life after the event does not mean it is totally eliminated. The saying, "What happens in Vegas, stays in Vegas" does not apply to traumatic events. Try as we like, these things don't stay in the funeral parlor, the doctor's office, Iraq, Afghanistan, Vietnam, the playground, and other places where the traumatic events occurred. Some things will never fully leave us, nor should they. As humans we aren't con-structed this way, and to forget some things could be a disservice as we need to grow in the aftermath, and in some cases, avoid repeating what may have led up to the event.

CHAPTER 1:

BECOMING A SAD, SAD CHILD
SUSANNA DEANGELIS MARESCA

I turned eight years old thirteen days before my life changing event of October 31, 1969. But my family was unaware of anything until a day or two later. I recall that evening; it was either the first or second of November. My mother was doing dishes at the sink. She went into a panic because out the window she saw our priest and soldiers in uniform. They first went to a neighbor's house and became aware it was the wrong one, and then came to our door and knocked, and shattered our world. My father was serving in Vietnam with the 1st Battalion, 12th Cavalry Regiment, 1st Air Cavalry Division.

They told my mother my father had been on a helicopter that crashed; that there were ten men on board total. At that time eight bodies were recovered and two were missing; one of the missing was my father Captain Adamo E. DeAngelis. He was placed on the MIA list.

That evening a lot of relatives started to arrive and it was chaotic. I remember running around confused, excited, I guess just being an eight year old kid who didn't really understand everything going on. What does stand out in my mind is that a cousin, who was quite a bit older than me, slapped me across the face and said that this was not the time to run around. I think the reason the slap impacted me so was that really was the beginning of becoming a sad, sad child.

It took a long torturous six months for the military to determine my father had been killed. I just recently learned this was established by way of a process of elimination. One small bone unclaimed must have been his. I remember my uncles on my mother's side went to Washington, DC where a board convened and declared it was my father, Captain Adamo E. DeAngelis.

During the months from notification of the crash and the board's declaration, my poor mother lay in bed withering away. The officer assigned to notify her, perhaps unwittingly, caused her great heartache and stress, telling my mother my father must have been nothing more than "shard jelly."

In April 1970 we finally buried a bone not even really knowing for sure if it was my dad, but I believed, as did my whole family. At the funeral I had not yet made my first Holy Communion; that took place a couple of weeks later, but at the funeral mass I was shoved out of the pew to go receive communion. I recall being scared because I didn't know what to do, so I just went up and took it.

In 1970, as we all know, the Vietnam War was becoming very unpopular. I could never really say my daddy was killed in Vietnam because people were cruel, and often said all the wrong things. I felt like I was not able to feel proud of him. My mother didn't have support of any kind. She was a Gold Star wife but there was no respect back then, and you only could feel shame and receive pity. There was no grief counseling back then, at least none we knew of. No one talked about the war and it seemed like nobody cared.

In 1992 my youngest brother took us all to Washington for a wonderful event, Sons and Daughters of Vietnam Veterans. I was eight months pregnant with my beautiful daughter and that weekend helped us experience the beginning of a little bit of healing. I remember being at the wall and they were calling off names and my job was to touch that name with the Rose. That day I felt so many of our soldiers received the respect that they so well deserved. Bagpipes played, and you know what bagpipes can do to one's soul. But I truly don't know if I have ever healed from that day as there are still so many questions. My younger brother even went to Vietnam to look for closure.

October 2019 was 50 years since learning my father was in that chopper crash. Now that I reflect back on the time, I'm filled with sorrow for wasting so much of my life being hurt; truly and deeply hurt. My heart still longs for, and breaks for, my mommy who raised five children with a heart that was so deeply broken. The wounds from that day seemed bottomless for so many years. I've tried to close the chapter but when I look back, and, I'm human, I can't help doing so, it fills me with anger and sadness. Perhaps if it had been a different time and he was killed in a different war, and there had been help and respect, then maybe it would have been different. I still question till this day what really happened to my father Captain Adamo E. DeAngelis. It's hard and I even read some books that might account for that day and it says how happy some were that that helicopter crashed because they were not fond of some of the men aboard it. So I don't know if this was something I could have ever healed from.

I put my dad on a pedestal and I do admire him and commend him for his sacrifice. But I wish he did not go to Vietnam. He volunteered because he loved his country, and he had leadership skills and he wanted to help all those young men. But what happened was he left a beautiful wife with five children to suffer the consequences of his actions. But I will respect him, and I no longer want to chase his ghost. I guess through all this I have learned, love your country, respect your country, but be loyal to your family first.

In closing, I wonder every day who I could have truly been if he had survived. Don't get me wrong, I've had a good life, very good life, and my mommy, my dearest mother was incredible. I wish I could hold her one more time and tell her how proud I am to be her daughter, and that if any book should be written, it should be on someone like her.

(Compiler's note) Susanna then added, "Sorry probably not what you were quite looking for but I tried. I can go on and on and on." I told her that I also used to tell students when I taught at the University of Pikeville (KY) to never apologize for emotions you are feeling.

She responded, "Ok, thank you. It's so funny I guess the whole part of my life changing experience is I'm always saying sorry. I guess that's something I can work on, especially when I'm expressing my feelings. Thank you." I replied that is also something I still struggle with, apologizing, and feeling like I've screwed up. Susanna replied, "Ok, well at least I know I'm not alone."

And then I began to ponder. Did part of the "Who am I?" begin as an eight year old girl who was behaving normally in the given circumstances, with a face slap that left her feeling like she needed to be sorry for being?

(BIO:) I was raised in Ramsey, NJ, by my loving Mother of five children; I was the fourth. Life was happy until October 31, 1969 when all our lives changed forever when my Dad, Captain Adamo E. DeAngelis was killed in Vietnam. The challenges and struggles we faced were hard, so very hard. I really believe none of us ever truly healed from that day. My younger Brother and I have chased a ghost for 50 years, but we have finally put Dad to rest. My beautiful Mother passed April 25, 2012; she is now living her life with her beloved Adam.

In 1980 I choose a career in cosmetology, holding both my barbers and beauticians license. I first became interested in this area when my Mom asked me to help her as she was attempting to perm her own hair. I love my job where over the years I have built so many great relationships with my clients through the good times and the sad! Currently I am still working; just fewer hours.

I married my husband Ralph Maresca on July 18, 1992, and on August 3, 1993 I gave birth to my beautiful daughter Maria Nicole! She is my greatest gift in life. She followed in my footsteps and is in the hair industry. I felt so wonderful when she told me that was what she was going to do. She is super talented, and a kind, compassionate and awesome human being. When she married, I also gained an amazing son in- law Carey Puzo. I believe my greatest achievement in life is the love of my family!

CHAPTER 2:
LONGING FOR A PERSON I'VE NEVER MET
STACEY UNZICKER

My Dad, Gregory Unzicker, was killed approximately 9 weeks before I was born.

The earliest memory I have of talking about Dad was when I asked my Mom and step-dad why my last name was different from their last name. This happened before I began kindergarten in Fall 1975. They explained to me that I was special because I had two daddies… one here on earth and one in heaven. At that time, I don't believe I really understood the concept of death or what it really meant that I had one daddy in heaven. As time went on and I came to the realization of just what it meant – I was proud.

However, regarding feelings later still focused on the event, to this day, I still get angry, extremely sad and question… What exactly did he die for? For years, I was very bitter that Dad had been killed doing what his country asked of him. He wasn't the only one, but he was he only one that mattered to me. Now I see it much differently. Every name on the Wall matters!

I have a friend that lost her son in Iraq 17 October 2006. She refers to that date as the day her son was murdered. The first time she said it, it stopped me in my tracks. I had never thought of Dad's death as being murder. But what it boils down to is that another human shot him with the sole intent to kill him because he was the enemy. That day hurt my heart and soul before I had even taken my first breath. That man didn't just kill my father… he stole a large piece of me before I was even born. Regardless, I still have trouble thinking of it as murder. It was senseless and needless, but I'm not sure murder is the right description.

I would have to say that due to losing him before I was born, I never questioned, what will I do now? I never knew life with Dad –

only without. I only know the emptiness of my biological father not being in my life at the hands of another human. I remember dreaming of him once. In that dream, he was standing off to the side smiling and nodding his head. I'm hoping that was his approval of me. And so, because my life has always been without Dad, I also never wondered who I was without him as I have no comparison point.

I realize the Vietnam Era was another time and space. And I am grateful for the lessons our nation and military learned regarding the support of those left behind. Through things such as Snowball Express and Wreaths Across America, I have met many Gold Stars – Moms, Dads, Wives, Siblings and Children (I really dislike that the Grandparents get left out.) While we each know the pain, we know it from different perspectives and views. The pain is the same, yet completely different.

Participating in Snowball and with Wreaths Across America has been a double edged sword to my heart at times. I see all the wonderful things that are done for this generation of Gold Star children, to include the Snowball Express, and my heart swells. I was lucky enough to have the opportunity to participate one year as a volunteer in Dallas/ Ft Worth. It was a very emotional experience for me. It was amazing to see the love and support for these children, but… that little girl in my heart wanted to scream… "What about me??"   Where were the organizations or supporters when I was growing up? No one cared… we were just supposed to move on.

Regarding any aspect of, who I am now that probably would not have occurred had I not had the life changing event, there was never a before for me. His absence is all I have ever known. However, without his loss, I'm not sure I would have the same level of empathy or compassion towards Gold Star family members.

Further ramblings about my situation: I was born into an exclusive club; one in which no one really wants to have membership. On 17 July 1970, before I had even taken my first breath, I became a Gold Star. I was born 24 September that same year.

Mom remarried when I was just over a year old. I gained a wonderful bonus family (I don't like the term step.) Most of my early teen years – I was not a pleasant person. I had a lot of anger and resentment over Dad – but I was also a hormonal teen trying to figure myself out. For these reasons, some things were kept from me until just a few years ago. What I found out was that my bonus Dad had also received his draft card, but his eyesight was too bad and he was overweight, so he was turned down. Looking back, it was probably best that I wasn't told. That knowledge probably would have only fed my anger.

Growing up, people didn't talk about Dad much. When people would hear my name or figure out who my Dad was, the subject was quickly changed. This happened for various reasons… hate of the war, feelings of loss, of regret, of guilt and so on. Regardless of the reason, through the eyes of a child, it didn't matter. All I knew was that talking about Dad made people nervous or uncomfortable. As such, I stopped sharing and/or asking much about him. I didn't want to be the cause of someone's discomfort, but in the long run, it only hurt me.

This uneasiness included my own family. Some was my own do-ing - I always thought I would have time to ask my Mom questions about Dad, but I always put it off. I hated to see her cry for any reason. It felt wrong to ask someone about something so painful and I never want to make someone hurt to satisfy my curiosities. It wasn't that she wasn't willing to talk about him; I don't think I was emotionally ready to sit down with her. Unfortunately, I lost Mom when I was 26 years old.

My grandparents never really accepted his death. The casket was closed as his body was not viewable. Had it been open, they might have had some kind of closure.

I only remember two instances of Dad even being discussed in the family while Grandpa was alive. Once at Christmas, two of my un-cles who were Vietnam veterans were having a discussion and at some point Dad was brought up. I was sitting in the doorway to the next room, so they couldn't see me, but Grandpa could. I can still remember the anger in Grandpa's voice when he cut the conversation off.

The only time I remember Grandpa bringing Dad up was at another uncle's wedding. I must have been about 12 or 13 years old.

Grandpa had had a few drinks and was feeling pretty good. He told me that I reminded him of my Dad and that my Dad would be very proud of me.

Years after Grandpa passed, Grandma would occasionally talk about Dad if I brought him up. She told me that she felt like he just never came home. She also had a lot of regrets. Dad was the oldest and he delivered papers before and after school. Because of this, he had to give up sports and other activities. He was the only sibling to graduate from the local Catholic high school. This happened only because he delivered papers to pay his own tuition. With a family of nine, there were many times Dad had to contribute to the household funds. At least one Christmas, the only reason his siblings even received gifts, was because Dad had given Grandma the money.

Each of Dad's siblings struggled with his death in their own way. Over the years, one by one, they began to talk to me about him. But there is still so much I don't know.

Family not discussing Dad was hard. I didn't understand why the topic of Dad was so taboo. I thought they should be proud and want to talk about him, but it didn't happen. Years later, as an adult, I understand now that it was heartbreaking for Grandma and Grandpa to lose their first born child. I believe not talking about him was a coping mechanism for them, but I don't think they ever realized how hurtful it was for me. Sadly, I didn't spend much time around them even though they only lived a couple miles from me, and I regret that now.

For years, I felt let down by the military and our government. When my dad was killed, there were no welcome homes; there was no thank you, or support groups. My Mom was given some paperwork and then never heard from the military. We were on our own. Mom did receive a small check each month to help with my care. Once I turned 18 that money continued to come to me until the age of 22 while I was still attending college full time. If I remember correctly, the last check I received was for just under $400. We had no idea that I was entitled to health and dental care until I was just a couple months shy of my college graduation. These things were not explained to us.

I see the support given to the families of today's military and I find there are still things that I am bitter about. I thought I had gotten past most of it, but occasionally it hits me all over again; the lack of compassion, the lack of consideration, the lack of common decency of the military and the powers that be. They weren't prepared. Especially for those who were drafted like Dad. As far as I'm concerned, they didn't know what to do with us so they walked away.

The draft... Dad was 19 when he was drafted. He was married, working full time and going to college full time. He never asked for a deferment. He did what he was called to do. He would not live to see his 21st birthday or the birth of his only child.

My Mom became a widow at the ripe old age of 21 and she was seven months pregnant. In return, the United States gave her a "we're sorry telegram" and a check for $10,000. One time I figured up that in total Mom received less than $60,000 in life insurance and monetary support for me. Somehow that never seemed like an even trade. Right or wrong, I think there will always be a part of me that feels cheated and bitter.

I have worked for a military insurance company since 1996. Very few people knew my story. Out of habit, it wasn't a topic that I discussed unless I was very comfortable with people. I had a small 1st Cavalry lapel, or hat pin, hanging at my desk. No one really noticed it for a long time except for two amazing gentlemen. One was a retired Colonel, Tom Dials, who had become the president of the company. The other was a retired Sergeant Major, Larry Smith, who worked with marketing and military relationships. Each asked about it at different points in time as both had been 1st Cav. In talking with Larry, I learned that his outfit was pulling out of Cambodia about the same time that Dad was coming in country. According to several of Dad's letters home, he was pretty sure they were in Cambodia even though "officially" they weren't there.

A few years ago, one of the travelling Walls came to Leaven-worth, where I live now. I volunteered at different times to help find names and take people to them. One day, I saw a couple slowly moving from panel to panel, nearing 8W, and scanning the names on each.

I walked up and asked if I could help them locate a name. They said they were looking for a name of a school friend of the gentleman. They knew they were close and they would just keep looking. The gentleman then asked if I worked for the travelling Wall. I told him no, I was just volunteering. He then asked if I knew anyone on the Wall. I told him yes – my Dad was on the Wall on a nearby panel. The couple asked me to show them my Dad's name. I took them maybe ten feet and pointed to my Dad's name. The guy got a strange look on his face and asked me to point again. I reached up and pointed again and said Dad's name out loud. When I looked back at him, he had tears in his eyes and just kept saying that he couldn't believe it. The name he was looking for was actually my Dad's name. Chills ran down my spine.

After a big hug and more tears... we introduced ourselves and talked for a little while. He went on to tell me that he hadn't been back from Vietnam for very long, just two or three days, when the announcement hit the papers about Dad's death. He remembers sitting at the kitchen table with a bowl of cereal, opening the newspaper to find a picture of Dad. He knew Dad had a child on the way, but he never knew if it was a girl or a boy.

I've had bad experiences as well when I would tell people that my Dad was killed in Vietnam. Occasionally, the stupidity of some humans astounds me.

When I was in high school, there was one English teacher that would tell students about her escapades as a protester at the airports and other rallies during Vietnam. She talked about carrying signs to show how terrible Vietnam was... you know; the "baby-killer" signs. I begged and begged to be put in one of her classes, but one of the vice principals remembered my Mom from her high school days and had attended my Dad's funeral. He made sure that I was not in any of her classes. He couldn't fire her – freedom of speech and all, but he did his best to keep us apart.

As an adult, I was working as a bartender at a local hole in the wall. You know; the type of place where everyone knows everyone else. One Saturday morning I was working and only one other person was in the bar. He was a usual customer and a friend. We were talking about nothing in particular and a stranger walked in. He sat down at the bar and ordered a glass of beer. Nothing unusual about it and pretty soon he joined in our random conversation.

I honestly don't remember how the topic of war came up (this would have been early 1992) but it did. My regular customer got up from the bar to go to the bathroom. The stranger asked me if I knew anybody that had been to war. I answered that my Dad was killed in Vietnam. He set his beer down on the bar, looked at me and said, "Well he got what he deserved." I was dumbfounded and was convinced that I had misheard him. I took a couple steps down the bar, directly in front of the guy and asked him, "What did you just say"? He looked at me and repeated, "Your Dad got what he deserved."At the same time my friend was coming out of the bathroom, I grabbed the glass of beer and threw the beer directly in the guy's face and told him, "Get the @#(!)$&@) out of my bar!"

The guy started yelling, "You are a crazy $*$&# bitch and started to lunge at the bar towards me – my friend flew across the room, grabbed the guy and started shoving him towards the door telling him that he didn't know what happened, but if I dumped beer on him and told him to get out he had better get the hell out and never come back. Had there not been anyone in the bar with me, I think there would have been an all-out brawl between the two of us. I still had the heavy glass mug in my hand and had every intention of hitting the guy with it… repeatedly! Consequences be damned, that guy was going to eat his words! It took hours and hours for me to calm down. That day reminded me that there still are stupid people alive and well.

Another instance of human stupidity in a place I never thought I would run into it… I was on my very first marketing trip for work at some type of military convention in Colorado Springs. I think it was 1999. I was gung-ho and eager to do well. We had a booth and of course the dreaded "sign up for a chance to win a prize" opportunity. During one of the convention's working sessions, traffic was almost non-existent in the booth area so my co-worker went to wander around. An officer walked up to our booth and I greeted him and asked him if he would like to sign up for our raffle. He looked at me and said, very rudely, something to the effect of, "No, I won the lottery once… I'll never do that again." I was extremely naïve and said "Really? What did you win?" He laughed at me and said, "An all-expense paid round trip." Again, me being naïve still wasn't catching on to his meaning and said something back to him like congratulations. He then laughed at me again, leaned across the table and as nasty as you please said, "You obliviously don't have a clue about life little girl. I won a trip to Vietnam."

Without thinking, I stood straight up and said, "Well you obviously didn't win the grand prize like Dad. My dad won the same trip, but he won the grand prize – a metal box to return in under our flag." The guy just looked at me, immediately turned and walked away. I was so furious! (It wasn't until later I cried.) But, for the rest of the convention, he wouldn't come anywhere near our booth. I don't know where I got the nerve to stand up to him, but I figured if he complained about me, he'd have to admit to what an ass he was to his military superiors. I hope he felt like the ass he was.

I don't think I've run into anyone for a long time that measured to the levels of stupidity described above. Maybe people have gotten smarter, maybe Iraq/Afghanistan have made war more present and personal, maybe people have found their hearts, maybe it is something else entirely. I don't know. What I do know is that you can hate the war, hate the politics and all that surrounds war. But you must remember, there are soldiers and family members left behind that will never be the same.

Over the last seven or eight years, I have talked about my Dad more than ever. As far as I can recall, there wasn't anything in particular that made me start opening up about Dad again. Maybe my heart finally started to heal. It is hard to explain to someone that hasn't walked the same path what it is to long for a person I never met. Many people don't understand that his loss hurts me. I was born with a broken heart. They think since I never met him, it shouldn't be that painful. How do you miss someone you never met? I have done it every day of my life.

Geez, so I did a lot more rambling than anything else. But, I must thank you. Whether you can use any of it, or not, it was cathartic for me. Always, Stacey

(With her permission, from a Facebook post Stacey made December 14, 2019.)

I participated in Wreaths Across America at Fort Leavenworth National Cemetery this morning. It is always an incredibly moving experience! But this year was a little more amazing …

I was getting into my car to leave and noticed a couple behind my car looking at my Families of the Fallen license plate. I got out asking if something was wrong and this very nice lady asked me about the symbols on the plate. I proceeded to tell her I am a Gold Star child, but before I could say much more the gentleman with her asked my name … I tell him and he says, "Of course you are," with tears in his eyes. His wife is tearing up at the same time and I'm just standing there with I'm sure a very puzzled look wondering what was wrong with these people … LOL! It turns out the gentleman, Harold Lett, knew/knows my Uncle Leon Unzicker from school. He told me a story of when they were younger and Leon had spoken of Dad and it always stuck with him. We had mutual friends on FB and he had seen my posts about Dad from time to time and had wanted to reach out to me to let me know the impact the story of my Dad's death made on him, but wasn't sure how to do it without seeming to be "stalker-ish" … LOL !! Come on … What are the odds that we would park next to each other at a Wreaths function??? Somebody had a hand in this meeting!!! Lots of tears were shared and new friendships forged … All in honoring our fallen heroes!

(BIO:) I am CPCU, API, Senior Quality Assurance Specialist Armed Forces Insurance. Also, I recently (January 2020) was able to take ownership of one of my dad's most cherished possessions, his 1965 Gibson electric guitar and Fender amplifier. I think it is one of the most beautiful things I have ever seen in my life, to the point I'm almost afraid to touch it. I am taking it to a specialty music store to have it looked at, restrung, and appraised. The day I pick it up will be the first day I will have EVER heard it played.

CHAPTER 3:

I IDOLIZED HIM
LEON UNZICKER

There were seven of us siblings; my brother Greg was the oldest, I was the youngest. I've heard about situations where older siblings didn't want a younger one around, but my early memories and understandings of our relationship were that he kinda looked after me. He let me tag after him. When he took me fishing, just him and me, that made me feel good. Greg liked to play guitar, and sometimes he would have me sit between him and the guitar, and have me strum the instrument while he played chords. He treated me like I was important.

When he joined the Army, I was vaguely aware there was a war going one, but of course, at my age, the concept was more restricted to playing soldiers, that kind of stuff. But when Greg graduated from boot camp and the guys were marching in and then out together, I thought he was leaving and that it was the last time I would ever see him. I started crying, and my folks asked why, and then reassured me that I would see him again.

I was nine when he was home for leave before going to Vietnam, and when it was time for him to leave, I didn't want to walk out with him to say goodbye. But I did watch him get in the car from outside, behind the house. I'm not sure; I think there was a fear that I really wouldn't see him again. I didn't cry then, perhaps because of my crying at his boot camp graduation; perhaps I'd worked through a certain grief. However, as it turned out, watching him get in the car was the last time I saw him. That was June 1970.

On July 17, 1970, while serving with Delta Company, 1/12th Cavalry, 1st Cavalry Division (Airmobile), while moving down a jungle trail in Vietnam carrying his M-60 machine gun, my brother was caught in an ambush and instantly died. Along with my siblings, parents, and other family members, he also left behind a wife who gave birth to their baby girl, Stacey Unzicker, nine weeks later.

Sometime after that, a man and woman showed up at our door and informed my parents of Greg's death. They let us kids know about it, and there was a funeral later, but no one really spoke about his death after that. I know I didn't cry when we received the news, nor at the funeral.

I think at the funeral I was probably in shock, in disbelief, and numb. At times I didn't believe what was happening was real, and since it was a closed-casket funeral, I remember a part of me thinking that maybe it wasn't him in the coffin, that maybe there had been a mistake. I do remember my oldest sister, who was closest to Greg in age crying hard; I know she really loved him and took his death hard. But as I mentioned, no one after the event really spoke about his death. I guess everyone was afraid that it might hurt someone if the subject was mentioned.

I mentioned his daughter, Stacey, who was born nine weeks after he was killed. As she got older she would ask me questions about her father whom she had never known, and I hope I've been able to help her. I think that sharing with her helped me a lot in my own healing process. You see, I was a shy and quiet person before Greg's death, and afterwards I became a severely quiet and shy person! I think sometimes it's harder when you're young; you don't have the same understanding as when you are more mature. I became less trusting and that made it very difficult for me to get close to anyone. Now I'm sure that my perspective and memories are different from my brothers and sisters, but for me, perhaps because I idolized him so much, I never felt safe again after his death, my innocence was forever lost.

No one at school ever said anything about Greg, except in high school once a history teacher was talking about Vietnam and then mentioned that I had lost a brother there in the war. That caught me off guard, and really hit me hard.

I feel most peaceful when I am listening to music. For me, music expresses what I am unable to put into words; music talks for you. I said I didn't cry at the funeral, but as I've gotten older I have shed more tears. Sometimes I have wondered if we all would have turned out to be different people if it never happened. It's been over fifty years and the pain is still there under the surface. Sometimes I can talk about it and other times I can't, especially if caught off guard. It's difficult to explain to someone how I feel if they have never been through it.

Three years ago I was able to go to the Vietnam Memorial Wall in DC and that was a moving experience for me. I've been involved in some Gold Star Family events over the past few years. And in Bellevue, Nebraska, Bellevue University has a Remembering Our Fallen exhibit which includes Tribute Towers with pictures of those who have died since 911. Bellevue University has been designated as an official Purple Heart University because of their support of military personnel and veterans, and their families. I've gone down there for a dinner and parade that they host. This helps with knowing that I'm not alone in my feelings.

This may sound funny; I will say thank you to Vietnam Veterans, but I'm almost afraid to, I feel unworthy. Over time I've gotten so I can talk more about my brother, but one thing I don't want to hear is if people try to inject politics. I don't want to hear that it was a waste of lives, or that the soldiers over there never should have been there. Some people can be so insensitive and just don't think before opening their mouth.

Before Greg went into the Army I didn't know anything about war, but I learned quickly, and the hard way. But I watch movies that increase my understanding and help me to be more aware of history.

(BIO:) We have a daughter and three grandsons, and I'm also very aware of the importance of time with family. I hardly knew my own grandparents growing up and I have told my wife that I want our grandchildren to know us. My daughter lives in Omaha, so they are just a couple hours away and that makes visits and keeping in touch easier. I'm aware of the fragility of life, and see it as a gift. I do spend time in reflection over how quickly things can change.

CHAPTER 4:

A RESCUER
KAREN OFFUTT

(Compiler's note.) I am starting this chapter with my commentary. Karen exemplifies many who suffer greatly themselves, but continue to live a life of service.

I'm including the background story regarding the award of the Soldier's Medal to Karen some thirty years after the initial event. In January 1970 as she served in Vietnam, while off-duty, Karen saved several Vietnamese families from a fire in their hamlet. The hamlet chief wrote documents, after talking to all the witnesses and those who were saved, and presented his documents to the US Army. A request for the Soldier's Medal was submitted through channels, but denied with the reason given that she was a woman and women didn't usually receive the Soldier's Medal for heroism. The request was downgraded to a Certificate of Achievement.

I hope you caught the reason for the downgrade, that she was a woman, and women usually didn't get such an award for heroism.

The citation for the Soldier's Medal later awarded to her on April 2001 is as follows:

(Then) Specialist Five, United States Army For heroism not involving actual conflict with an armed enemy: Specialist Karen I. Offutt, Women's Army Corps, United States Army, assigned to Headquarters Military Assistance Command Vietnam, J47, distinguished herself by heroic action on 24 January 1970 while in an off-duty status. Observing a fire in Vietnamese dwellings near her quarters, she hurried to the scene to provide assistance. Without regard for her personal safety and in great danger of serious injury or death from smoke, flames, and falling debris, she assisted in rescuing several adults and children from the burning structures. Without protective clothing or shoes she repeatedly entered the buildings to lead children that had reentered their homes to safety. She continued to assist the Vietnamese residents in removing personal property and livestock, although danger increased until fire-fighting equipment and personnel arrived. Specialist Five Offutt's heroic action reflects great credit on herself, the United States Army, and the United States mission in Vietnam.

(Now, Karen.)

My grandparents had a farm, so animals have always been a part of my life; I still smile recalling some of our chickens, my horse, and my pet gopher. Because of that, I have always loved and cared for animals, and the sense of caring was strengthened when I helped care for my younger brother, when I was all of three years old.

I was a volunteer Candy Striper, Havens Angels, while in high school, and I believe that was a turning point in deciding to later go into nursing school at age seventeen. I left at eighteen, went into the Army and was assigned to the Pentagon. While there I was a victim of attempted rape. That affected me in such a way that I really didn't trust anyone. When I went to Vietnam, I was actually as afraid of some of our men and women, as of the Viet Cong.

I went to Vietnam as a stenographer and, mistakenly, was initially taken to Long Binh where we were mortared my first night there. I finally was able to contact Saigon and MACV (Military Assistance Command, Vietnam) had a Sergeant Major come pick me up. I served on General Creighton Abrams (Commander of US Forces in Vietnam) staff with MACV from July 1969 to June 1970 in Saigon, with occasional chopper trips to other areas, and because of my position, was in Top Secret Eyes Only meetings.

At the time I was in Vietnam, I was the youngest and lowest ranking enlisted woman in Saigon. In Long Binh, I realized that although there was a fear factor playing in my head, the fear of dying was not at the top of the list. However, after I got home, I listened to a tape I had sent home to my parents, and I was aware of how much of a monotone I was speaking in, like there was deadness already in my spirit. By the way, when that particular tape was made, I had been there all of about twenty days; I still had about 345 left until my DEROS (Date Estimated Return From Overseas.)

When I was leaving Vietnam, I guess what I was experiencing is now termed Survivor's Guilt. I cried all the way home. I'm sure there was some relief mixed in over having survived, but I was also awash with thoughts and feelings of the myriad of experiences mingling together in ways that made little to no sense. How was this past year going to affect my future? What did it mean, and why?

While serving as a WAC in Vietnam from July 1969 to June 1970 with MACV, I was exposed to Agent Orange, and I have paid for this dearly. I had twin sons; Kevin had ADHD, and Justin was diagnosed with kidney cancer when he was fifteen months old. Later, in 1975, Kristin, my daughter, was diagnosed with epilepsy. I also have grandkids with juvenile diabetes and grand mal epilepsy. Around 2000, I testified at a Congressional hearing with Senator Arlen Specter about a bill for children born with birth defects to women Vietnam Veterans. It was said these effects would last in a family for seven generations.

I started having breast lumps in my 20's or early 30's, and have undergone some ten or eleven lumpectomies. Colon polyps began showing up in my life in my 30's, and I have now had somewhere around thirty polyps, of which quite a few were pre-malignant. I developed a hiatal hernia, which was incorrectly diagnosed as cancer, along with peripheral neuropathy in my feet and part of my legs, which became evident in my 50's, along with peripheral vascular disease. I have problems with my balance and fall frequently.

Normally a tonsillectomy is not a big deal, but I had a procedure in 2004 because doctors thought one was malignant. Their concern over this was heightened by the fact I had two surgeries for cancer in 2000.

For a long time, I had severe anxiety and couldn't leave the house, because of PTSD. To this day I still avoid crowds, and if I go to a restaurant I sit with my back to the wall. I just don't like being around a lot of people or loud noises.

I deal with Fibromyalgia, Osteoarthritis, Degenerative Disc Disease, bone spurs in my feet and shoulder, an ulcer in my esophagus which has caused acid reflux for years, and extremely low iron for which I take daily iron meds. Geez, looking over this paragraph, I'm thinking, I could continue with more "stuff", but isn't this enough? (Hey, I do try my best to keep a sense of humor.)

I also deal with tinnitus. Anyone who suffers from severe tinnitus knows exactly what kind of hell that puts you through. Some days the noise just wants to take over and dominate. It was in late 1974 when I became aware of this loud, high pitched ringing in my ears.

I'm not telling my story for pity, but hopefully to open some eyes to what some of us have dealt with, in the aftermath of going to war, doing what we believed we should do at the time. I understand that to some, they don't get why I worry so over the things I mentioned in the preceding paragraphs. Some have called me a hypochondriac and many other names. I've learned not to worry about what others say. My only wish is that my body had not been exposed to Agent Orange and that I had been told of its usage and effects prior to volunteering for Vietnam.

There is also what PTSD has done to my life. Interestingly, an October 2019 article in The Washington Post stated that women are more than twice as likely as men to suffer from PTSD, and that research has shown that PTSD raises the danger of heart disease, obesity, diabetes, blood clots, certain cancers, and autism in their offspring. My medical conditions have been overwhelming, but the PTSD has literally destroyed much of my life, including the ability to trust, form close relationships, and the desire to mingle with others. I lead a pretty solitary life, except for my animals.

In my situation, much of my PTSD has to do with the fire mentioned in the Soldier's Medal citation. I mentioned to a former comrade of mine how sometimes I could hear the sounds of bullets whistling by, and I couldn't place why, and she said, "Have you blocked out New Year's Eve, 1969? We were up on our rooftop and fired at by a sniper." The thing that bothers me, at times, is how there are blank spots in my memory, as if under certain conditions my mind blocked out whatever was happening. It's like some pieces to a puzzle are missing. Then there are events I can vividly recall, for example, my rides on a Huey helicopter, although, again, I only remember a couple times and my friend said we went on several.

Again, back to PTSD, and such things, I'm lucky to be able to sleep four to five hours in twenty-four and I need a sound machine to do that. I isolate, etc., but I think you get the picture. As my body gives out, I struggle to do the work I do, taking care of my home, car, lawn, animals, alone for twenty years. Yep, I've been told that I'm just fine, that I can do it, that I'm a nut for worrying, even when so many of my Vietnam Veteran Brothers and Sisters have passed already. I rarely ask for help. I only ask for support, prayers, encouragement and positive thoughts. I've never thought that was asking too much, but, because of the list of maladies that keep piling up, I guess I really can't expect others to understand. I once had a minister's wife tell my one of my friends I must be a hypochondriac. I must seem like a freak to have all this crap going on! Everyone has an opinion, but we each walk in only our own shoes.

Vietnam changed me forever; it stole my youth. I volunteered at an orphanage my half day off and I saw what war did to children and tiny babies. I saw what evil does. When I returned to the States everyone was going about their business as usual, like I'd been on a vacation. My family never asked me what I saw or did, even though they could sometimes hear attacks when I was taping to them.

Another thing regarding PTSD, there were no Vietnam veteran groups just for women dealing with it. I discovered a lot of male Vietnam veterans who treated us as if we were nothing, like we didn't deserve recognition.

It has been hard going for me, period. Most of my Vietnam friends and acquaintances are dead or dying. Our government betrayed us. War changes everyone who witnesses it. It is the gift that keeps on giving.

So who am I? Well, I've known many who have gone through so much more than I, and, unfortunately, many who have ended their lives. I'm seventy now, and lucky to have made it this far, even though

I've been alone for a good part of those years. Every kind word, I cherish. Every prayer for me, I am strengthened.

I do feel at times like I am a walking time-bomb. Recently, I've had this thought occur, that the only reason I was placed on this earth was to save those people from the fire and to give birth to my children.

(Compiler's note) Let's just imagine a bigger picture where Karen is met (in whatever form an afterlife may take) by several adults and children who greet her with, "Because of you, I was able to ..." My thoughts are, what a life worth living!
(Back to Karen)

I do a lot with animals and my love of animals and nursing have saved me. Rescue has always been important to me. I recall an incident one night when I was going out at midnight to feed some animals, and as I approached a Burger King it looked like a field next to it had dozens of little lights. Closer examination revealed they were cats' eyes. I got out of my car with a bag of cat food, put some nuggets in my hand and headed toward them. One of the cats came to eat out of my hand, and I took him home. I have trapped cats, taken them to the veterinarian to be fixed, and if they were not adoptable, then returned them to their colony. I always have some food in my car for cats and dogs, even birds, and, yes, believe it or not, I once performed CPR on a frog. As a labor of love, I have given out raincoats to the homeless and sweaters for their dogs.

Again, who am I? An Arkansas born woman, who would be as happy as hell if I could be in the woods with some foxes and deer. I love gardening and working the dirt. A few years ago I bought over 2000 pounds of cinder blocks, and moved them myself to make a raised garden. Don't know if I could do that anymore, but I'd sure give it a try. I'm a lot slower now, but I still love nature; I love mowing the yard on my riding mower and walking barefoot in the grass. Yeah, I'm just a Nature Girl (woman?)

I've always loved music; I started playing the clarinet when I was ten years old. I also play guitar some. In Arkansas I played with the Hot Springs Concert Band. I'd love to play with a group here, but so far haven't been able to. Playing with a band is about the only time I tolerate being with a group of people.

I became an RN in 1984 and worked until PTSD and medical issues became too much.

The following is a poem I wrote in 1999; just a tattoo on an old woman's brain.

Memories – And The War Goes On

Don't show them you're afraid.
Smile - get on the plane.
Go on over there, wherever "there" is.
You'll probably come back.
I don't feel like I'll come back.
I'm scared 'cause ahead is the unknown.
My family is crying. They're making this worse.
Go home. Let me do this. I have to.
Long flight. I am tired.
Already miss my brother – My best friend.
I'll show my parents I am strong and brave and, and
And can do anything a boy can do.
Plane full of men – no women – what am I doing?
What am I trying to prove?
You know it won't be good enough anyway.
You'll die and it still won't be good enough.
They'll say, "We told her not to go."
"We told her to marry, stay home and sew,
Raise babies, take care of a man."
Act like a girl! What's wrong with you?
Finally, I am here, but I don't know where.
I want to go home but can't.
Need to sleep and try to figure this out.
Pick a bed, any bed, not that bed, this one.
Monsoon rains pouring outside and in the room.
Hitting metal pans with giant "plunk", "plunk", "plunks"
Everything is hot and the earth red as blood.

Click your heels together and you'll be home.
You are home, silly girl. Rest now.
What's wrong? Being hit with powerful concussions,
As though a giant's fists are pounding them.
My bed is shaking and I'm afraid.
More afraid than I've ever been.
There is nowhere to hide … to run to.
Someone says there's a bunker somewhere.
What's a bunker? Where is it?
I'm lost and new here. Why won't anyone help me?
I am paralyzed in my little bed. It continues all night.
I wait to die. Well, that is why you came.
Give your life for your country.
Make them proud as they drape the flag
Over your empty casket, because you're in pieces
Somewhere in a place far from home.
Pray. Tell God to let your family know you love them.
Prepare to die. I am 19. I haven't learned how to live.
And I don't know how to die.
How do I do this right? Can't I do this one thing right?
Fall asleep from the drumbeat. It pounds steadily,
Louder than my heart. What music is that?
It's a rocket and mortar symphony. It's the music of war.
How can I sleep when someone is trying to kill me?
This is insane.
I awake and it's morning. The music has stopped.
I am alive. I am dead. I am a kid. I am old.
Home Ec, Honor's Biology, Basic Training,
All of it worthless. No class prepared me for this.
Naked children playing in the mud.
Beer can and cardboard houses.
Children selling their sisters to the soldiers.
Working 9 – 5, what a way to make a living.
Just like a song, only this is real.
Children touching my skin, teenage girls feeling my eyelashes,

GI's taking my picture.
Strange sounds, penetrating smells that will never leave.
Snipers firing, barely missing my head.
Don't flick your lighter – it'll explode.
Don't pick the kids up – they may be booby-trapped.
Claymores and barbed wire, mama-sans and black pajamas.
Time to go home, but I am home.
I don't want to leave. I'm on the edge of life and death.
Fear and excitement mix. Pride and guilt intermingle.
I'm confused again – still.
Parents meet me at the airport.
Seems they think I've been on vacation.
They have suffered they say.
Mom shows me her white hair and her limp from
Where a tumor is pressing on her uterus.
I feel guilty. I have failed again.
I haven't brought them honor - only pain.
Why didn't I die there?
Maybe I can go back and try again.
What am I afraid of? Of not measuring up?
Of not doing life right even though there
Seems to be no "right" way of doing it?
Afraid to die but wishing I could, quickly, painlessly.
Scared of not being loved. Frightened of the dark,
When all the bad people out there
Wanted to hurt someone with their war toys and evil hearts.
Afraid of myself and the rage inside.
Afraid of the dark side of myself,
The war words that can come from within
To push others away so that I am alone
As I deserve to be. Alone and afraid. Afraid to live, afraid to die.
That year of war changed me. Made me see the evil in mankind.
Took my youth and trust and naivety,
Grinding them into the red mud of Vietnam.
You can't see the scars...I look as good as new,

But they're there - inside.
Vietnam is alive and well.
And the war goes on. . .
Karen Offutt   Copyright ©August 1999

(BIO:) Karen Offutt was born in Arkansas, lived in many places, is a Vietnam Veteran, Mother, Grandmother, Registered Nurse, and Animal Rescuer and Advocate.

CHAPTER 5:

THE DAY IT ALL CHANGED
ADRIENNE GEARHEART

This has been the hardest thing I have had to write, ever. You would think I would be able to put a few facts about my husband on a sheet of paper, but I have had mild, and sometimes not so mild, panic attacks whenever I got close to my computer to jot things down.

I recently for the first time heard the song; I'll Never Love Again by Lady Gaga from the movie A Star is Born and within the first verse I was in tears. I cannot think of any other words that were more apropos than those I heard in that song. I wondered if I would be a constant walking pile of open nerves breaking down every time I heard a love song. Although the lady sitting next to me was probably wondering what was wrong with me, I'm glad this song led me to a cathartic breakdown. Afterwards, I had a little more clarity as far as what I need to convey to you concerning Wayne. I know this may sound dramatic; Wayne would often say I dramatized things, but the words, the emotions, the memories I'm about to reveal are very dear to me and I both guard and cherish them.

"Are you okay?" asked Wayne looking intently at me. He stood in front of me, cutting off my steps as I left the kitchen. "I don't mind taking you to work today."

"I'm okay, I guess" I said.

"I don't mean to be cruel, but you don't look so good. Are you sure you're feeling okay?"

"I'm a little sluggish, but I'll be okay."

"I don't have any meetings or classes for a few hours; besides, I can tell you need to vent a little bit more before you get to work," he said looking somewhat worried and agitated. "I wish you didn't let these people get to you. You are a good teacher and you care about those kids more than some of their own families do, so you should stop second guessing yourself and go into that building and just be you".

It was the first Monday of September, we had just gotten back from celebrating our daughter, McKenzie's, 20th birthday in Lexington Kentucky, I was completing the final class in graduate school, and I was in the beginning of starting teaching at a new school in Eastern Kentucky. I was feeling a bit lethargic and my husband wanted to give me a ride to school; he didn't like the idea of me driving on those curvy roads when I wasn't feeling well.

"No," I said, "I don't want to put you behind in your day. I'll be okay."

I liked having my husband take to me to work, sick or not. We would enjoy music together, current events, the scenery, whatever. We legitimately loved being together.

After approximately 15 minutes, I changed my mind. "You know, on second thought." I said "that would be nice. I would like for you to take me to work today. Blowing off a little steam would do me good. Let me fix you a cup of coffee; it will be my payment for your services today." We laughed and I patted him on his butt as he exited the kitchen on his way to our bedroom.

I really did like having him take me to work. It was my first-year teaching at this school and as the only African American in the building, it was alarming sometimes hearing some of the comments the people in the building made. Wayne wanted to make sure I was safe. He wanted everyone to know that I had him in my corner.

This was not anything uncommon. This was not the first time Wayne had offered to take me to work. As a matter of fact, he and I spent a lot of time together. He helped me coach the varsity boys and girls track and field teams when I worked at Pike County Central High School, he helped organize events when I was the PTO president at West Middle School in Oakland TN. He would drive me to my classes at Morehead University on Saturday morning when I was working on my master's degree. I traveled with him when he went to Kent State to meet a Nobel laureate; I traveled with him when he had to go to Chicago to work on writing questions for the MCAT. I rode with him evenings when he worked as an adjunct at Big Sandy Community College. Wayne and I authentically loved being with each other.

The ride to East Ridge High School was noneventful. The roads were not overly crowded, the sky a bit cloudy, but I don't remember the roads being treacherous. Wayne dropped me off at the back door of the wing where I taught high school English.

"I'll be here to pick you up after my meeting".

I said, "Don't forget, I will be meeting with a couple of teachers this afternoon".

"No problem," he said. "I'll bring my tennis shoes back with me and walk a couple laps around the track. I love you". I smiled at him, exhaled, and said, "I love you too".

Then we kissed, I got out of the truck he rented for our trip to Lexington and walked into the building.

These were the last words my husband, Dr. Walter Wayne Gearheart spoke to me and the last words he heard me speak before everything changed. Before my reality became a living, breathing, and constant nightmare.

Mondays have changed for me. I don't think of them in the same manner as people dreading to go to work. Monday is the one day of the week I genuinely do not like. To be more specific, I don't like Mondays at 7:30 am. That was the time in which my husband last told me he loved me. That was the last time he smiled at me. Damn it!!! No matter what day or time this fateful moment occurred, I wouldn't like it.

Although I don't like Mondays at 7:30 am, I hate Mondays at 4:30 pm. I hate that day and that time because that was the day and time my husband passed away. The day and time a part of me permanently dissipated into nothing but a dark, pounding abyss of hurt, loneness, confusion, fear.

(Compiler's Note.) Wayne was fatally injured when a coal truck

crossed the dividing line and rolled onto its side and crushed the car he was driving. The accident occurred in the morning, and Wayne died that afternoon.

(Back to Adrienne.) Wayne was born on Wednesday January 18, 1956. His dad was Walter Fred Gearheart and his mom was Dottie Sizemore Gearheart. He was their first born and their pride and joy. Walter's family owned, and still does, a telephone company in Eastern Kentucky.

Wayne loved his family incredibly and when his mom and dad got a divorce, he was devastated. He took on the job of protector of his mom. If she had a problem with a tradesman, Wayne wanted to help. If she had a problem with a waiter, he would want to help. If she had problems with someone she was dating, Wayne wanted to help. At an early age Wayne developed a desire to help those that he felt were being taken advantage of. This quality would only get stronger and stronger as he grew older.

Although Wayne's family, one of the most affluent families in the area that was not affiliated with coal, wanted every member of the family to enter the family business, Wayne wanted to go another route. He wanted to carve his own path for not only his self, but also his future family. Therefore, he decided to go into the world of academia.

Yes, Wayne was a great husband, but that wasn't all. He was a devoted father. There was never a school performance of any kind that he missed and would travel any length at any time of the night in order to be with McKenzie, our daughter. He loved and supported her beyond measure. When McKenzie was a freshman at Transylvania University, she was elected to be a state officer in 4-H, secretary. Early in her tenure she and the other officers were staying at the Crown Hotel in Louisville while they completed some duties at the state fair. Well, McKenzie's roommate decided to get drunk and let her boyfriend stay in the room with them. This unwanted arrangement made McKenzie feel extremely uncomfortable, so she called her dad for help. We immediately packed our bags, left Pikeville, and made lodging arrangements for our daughter at another hotel in Louisville. McKenzie's well-being was paramount to him. It didn't matter at all what time of the day or night he would get to his daughter and help.

Wayne's passing has been devastating to McKenzie as well. For the first two years after his passing, I worried a lot about her. She experienced a bout with obsessing over the most morbid things. She worried about my health and well-being.

(BIO:) Adrienne is still teaching.

CHAPTER 6:

A BLESSING IN DISGUISE
NATALIE JUSTICE

I remember when the Achalasia set in, and at the age of eighteen I realized something was wrong. I had just begun college and was out with some friends when I choked with no explanation on sesame seed chicken. At that moment I knew something was not right, and it gradually got worse.

At the age of thirty I was underweight, having never made it past 100 pounds, and I could eat barely anything. Even soup was starting to cause a great deal of difficulty. Then I found a lump that concerned me, went to see my doctor, and was diagnosed with cancer. This turned out to be a blessing in disguise because later, thanks to hospitalization for the cancer, I was diagnosed with Achalasia.

Achalasia is defined as, "a rare disorder making it difficult for food and liquid to pass into the stomach. Achalasia results from damage to nerves in the food tube (esophagus), preventing the esophagus from squeezing food into the stomach. It may be caused by an abnormal immune system response."

And so my life changed again. The cancer was a devastating life change, but the Achalasia was what was going to kill me, and now the thing that felt like an invisible illness had a name and doctors were telling me how they could alleviate (not cure) some of the symptoms of Achalasia. And I was thrilled. At age eighteen it seemed like everything was going downhill, and when things changed again at age thirty via cancer, my life was saved.

After the initial incident at age eighteen I experienced a lot of confusion and loneliness. The Achalasia made it difficult to be social with people, and so I did not eat with people. It also caused havoc on a dating relationship with a guy I had been hoping to marry. It isolated me. I felt like God had made me wrong. And I was on a desperate quest to be normal.

Once the Achalasia had a name, and I knew I was not the only one in the world dealing with this, unexplainable disease (until this time,) my loneliness eased. During a transition to a position as Associate Pastor at Ooltewah United Methodist Church, I became friends with two wonderful people in Chattanooga who were always loving and supportive, Brett and Amanda Hyberger. Over the years I felt so stigmatized in the area of social dining, and it was such a joy to eat dinner with them, and if I had issues, to not feel ashamed about it.

I must admit, at times I still have questions about, what will I do? I have a high risk for cancer to come back. Regarding Achalasia, I was told I could have a surgery, Heller Myotomy, where the muscles of the cardia are cut so food and liquids are able to pass to the stomach which would alleviate the problem and help me have a healthy weight gain. In that moment I became so excited, I knew it was the right decision, and having the procedure saved my life. So now swallowing is not as bad as it used to be but is still a problem. I know I am at risk for things to get worse and I still question what I will do if it does. I did struggle greatly for some time with who I was as a person, but later recognized that the illness does not define me; that since I am a child of God, who can make me feel inferior?

When thinking about how time, or what specific activities, have helped me heal and/or discover who I am now, friendships have been a big part of this, and through these special relationships I have experienced God in an incredible way. Brett and Amanda Hyberger taught me a lot about love, including, but not limited to, loving and accepting people for who they are. And by example they taught me that Someone greater loves me despite the Achalasia, that I was not a mistake. God loves me, and I am a child of God. The illness or people's perspective of that illness does not define me. My identity resides in God, and once I accepted that, it helped me further heal.

I have thought about if there is an aspect of who I am now that probably would not have occurred if I had not had these life changing events, and I definitely realize that I have drawn much closer to God. Every moment over the last few years has strengthened me and brought me closer to him. It recently hit me, that that has been a healing process in itself, and I believe it came about because of the relationships God placed in my life to open my eyes, and my heart to accepting it. I now see who I am in Christ, and it is an incredible and freeing moment to realize that no one else can define me but God. Just because I struggle with Achalasia and am a cancer survivor does not mean I am worth less. I am priceless. And I think this one moment changed everything for me to realize that. Mind you, it took five years of experience and God bringing in people in my life to open my eyes.

I think I've learned that life changing moments are just moments in an overall big picture of time. We think that crisis last forever, but they are just moments. None of the stuff that has happened to me was my fault. It has taken a long time to accept that, but it is the truth. The cancer was genetic and the Achalasia was genetic. I did not cause any of it. But it happened. And it shaped me to be the person that I am today. It opened my eyes to things I would have otherwise never seen, and then God brought people in my life like Brett and Amanda Hyberger who were tools to open my heart to loving God more.

Another point of interest. I was prayed over by several pastors before I was diagnosed. I did not know if I had cancer at the time or not. The prayer was powerful and I believed that I would not hear bad news. But then I heard the words "you have cancer". The pastors who prayed over me were shocked and heartbroken. They thought I would experience healing (and I did too). And I got angry with God. I look back on that now and finally get it. My healing came over a long journey triggered by one event, one moment; a moment I would not wish upon anyone but a moment that changed my life for the better. I found out I had Achalasia. I met people who accepted the autoimmune disease and did nothing but support me. You would be surprised how many people actually made fun of me when I was choking. But people like Brett and Amanda Hyberger did not. Janet Coughlin did not. They supported me and loved me through it. They didn't coddle me, but they also did not judge me for something I could not help. And through those relationships the bitterness and anger I felt with God disappeared and I found healing. I opened my heart to God and surrendered my life fully to his will and it has changed me completely. I am healing. Healing in a way that I believe those prayers by the pastors were meant to heal me. That moment changed my life but helped me find overall healing, the healing I could only find with God.

(BIO:) I went to Carson-Newman College where I majored in religion. Next I received a Masters of Divinity in pastoral care and counseling from Gardner-Webb School of Divinity and I did additional coursework but did not receive a degree from Asbury Theological Seminary to go towards my ordination.

My first appointment was associate pastor at Jefferson City, NC, and then I was appointed lead pastor at the Greene County, VA circuit, having to discontinue my ministry there after a year to go on medical leave.

After I came off medical leave I received my third appointment at Ooltewah UMC, which is where I was blessed to meet Brett and Amanda Hyberger. Then I was assigned at Smyth County, VA circuit as lead pastor.

In 2021 I started a journey that was unexpected. I am now appointed to the newly formed Russell County Cooperative Parish. My role is three-fold: I am associate pastor at Lebanon Memorial United Methodist Church; new executive director at Elk Garden School Community Ministries; and working with and serving as pastor of Church Hill UMC, Dennison UMC, and Munsey UMC in Lebanon VA.

CHAPTER 7:

QUITTING IS NOT AN OPTION
AMY HOTELING

I was 27 years old and it was a Sunday morning in March of 2010 when I awoke not able to see out of my left eye and had pain that was just excruciating. I am not one to go to the doctor unless it is a dire emergency and for some reason I didn't feel like this was. I worked for a physician at the time, so in my mind I thought I would just run it by him or one of the nurses in the morning. I was sent for testing: MRI's, spinal taps, lab work and some test that I cannot remember the name of, but I am sure it is used on individuals to get them to give up government secrets. I was told that I might have a brain tumor. Now when you hear those words you freak out a bit. My thought was I could do without an eyeball but if my brain has a tumor in it that is a little more difficult to fix. Other options that it could have been were a pseudo tumor, optic neuritis, iritis, or Multiple Sclerosis. I will say that after some research none of them sounded appealing.

It took six different specialists and five months to finally diagnose me with Multiple Sclerosis. In the five months that I waited I went through episodes of not being able to trust my legs to get me where I needed to go. I had times where I had wet the bed or myself without realizing that I even needed to go to the restroom. I still had trouble with my vision and the pain in my limbs was almost unbearable at times. I had muscle spasms that felt like someone was trying to use the same technique for wringing out a washcloth but using my legs. I felt sensations of what I can only describe as having an electrical current run through my body. I did not have anything for pain or inflammation but the trusted Ibuprofen. When I was finally given my diagnosis, we were living in a small town in Kentucky, not the most advanced area with regard for healthcare, and furthermore I did not know anyone else who had MS (multiple sclerosis).

Prior to my diagnosis I was a very independent, goal oriented, free spirited young lady who only wanted to do things her way and on her own time. I was disciplined, determined and full of life. I loved to go on adventures, sometimes getting in my car just to see where I would end up. I have always enjoyed seeing new places and meeting people. I am always looking for individuals who need a helping hand. I love to run; running was my mental health therapy. Had a bad day, extra energy or just mentally exhausted? Go for a run. I had dreams to become a nurse or microbiologist. I was in school, worked full time and was an Army wife with two wonderful bonus children. I was busy. And I felt that Sunday morning like my life came to a screeching halt.

I found myself being extremely fatigued and struggling to remember what I was reading or what I was supposed to be doing. I couldn't concentrate, I couldn't see. Getting the energy to go to work and be a functioning adult became a challenge. I will admit I have never been a morning person and I have been practicing it now for 37 years, but I struggled finding the energy to get out of bed. Now the struggle was even worse. Inside I was having a storm of emotions that I could not understand but on the outside, I wanted everyone to think I was ok. I felt I had to be strong for them because I had always been the strong one that everyone leaned on. I couldn't let anyone know how I was feeling on the inside, I could not show weakness. I have spent years suppressing these feelings, bottling them up and hiding them away. I guess part of me thought that if I didn't address them that they didn't exist. I started treatment, and at times I didn't know what was worse, the side effects or the disease itself. Imagine taking a medication that is supposed to suppress having an MS flare but in return you feel like you have the flu every week. I would take my injection on Saturday, and Sunday I felt like I had been hit by a bus. I had chills so bad that my husband would hold me to try to keep me from shaking so bad. He would top me with layer after layer of blankets to try to get me warm. After a year or so, I started to feel better, still fatigued but I was running again.

Two years after my diagnosis my husband was on orders to transfer to Seattle, WA, and I was so excited. I had always wanted to Go West; as crazy as it sounds my soul has always yearned for a place that I had never been to. When we finally got settled in our new home, new jobs, new routine everything seemed great. I was a receptionist at a family practice, and this was when things took an emotional turn for me. I finally saw a patient who had MS, and she was in a wheelchair, could not talk, and her disease was far more advanced than mine. Then, and now, most days when you see me you would never know I have MS. I get around pretty good, although sometimes it is difficult for me to put thoughts together, concentrate and my balance isn't great. My memory is terrible, just ask my spouse. I have the most trouble with my legs. Other than that, I am good. I try not to complain because let's be honest, no one really cares, and you can drag yourself down a dark path that is hard to return from. If I do tell someone that I have Multiple Sclerosis, they tell me I don't look sick. I am not sure how I am supposed to look, but I take it as a compliment and move on.

But back to seeing the MS patient in the wheelchair; I was starting to see what my future could be at any time. I was told that six months prior, this lady was doing great, but her MS became aggressive and now she was in bad shape. I was trying to keep my composure. This could be my future; how would I cope. I will never forget my ride home; all those feelings I was suppressing came flooding back like a tsunami. Prior to me meeting this young lady, my husband and I, with some of our friends, signed up to do an MS Walk. It became something I was dreading, but when I commit to something, I do everything in my power to complete it. It was so damn difficult. Seeing all these individuals that were in wheelchairs, having crutches, not able to move their bodies or speak, I was devastated. I felt guilty. It wasn't fair that I was doing this good and they were dependent on someone else for everything. I struggled with guilt and nothing has been more difficult to deal with than my own mind. See, I have always been my own worst critic. When I don't feel like doing something or I end up laying in bed an extra hour, I will tell myself, Hey, you are being lazy. You could be doing all these other things but here you are laying in bed. You are not sick, get up.

I decided to go see a counselor as at this point in my life I had not dealt with the fact I had a chronic disease that was not curable. I was still trying to convince myself and my neurologist that they had this all wrong; that it was a mistake someone had made. I went to this counselor for two sessions and all she could talk about with me was how I was overweight. Yes, I was aware of that, but I needed help dealing with this disease not being reminded that I am overweight. After being highly disappointed with counseling I decided to stick to my own therapy. I tried to be nicer to myself, let myself rest when I needed to. I tried to not over commit myself and tried to let go of things I could not control. I didn't have to be a super woman all the time. I have always held myself at a high standard, I am harder on me than anyone could ever imagine.

Things have become more difficult now that I have MS; I have tried to find a different way to do them. I am learning, this year specifically, the hard part of trying to accept not being able to do something at all. I have been researching and fighting my physicians for nine years now, saying repeatedly, that this is a mistake. Of course, they tell me that is not the case. Why after all these years, all the scans, am I still having a hard time accepting this diagnosis? Recent years have been getting harder. I have not been able to run for a couple years now. I am not able to do squats, jumping jacks, or go on a hike. Trying to work out these days seems impossible. I spend a large part of my day thinking about when I am going to be able to lay down again. I have this theory that if I come home and hurry up and do my chores I can just go to bed. I do not like to make plans because I do not know how I will feel that day. Every day is a battle that I fight with myself; if it isn't my body trying to kick my own ass then it is my mind trying to fight me. I put on this brave face day in and day out; I am constantly fighting a battle that most of my friends and family know nothing about. I have a pep rally in my head telling me you can take one more step, or you can stay awake one more hour. My friends plan outings and I do not want to commit because I don't know how I will feel that day. If I do decide to go, I know I will pay for it the next day. I spend most of my hours trying to hide the fact that I am hurting, my body is so fatigued, and I have all these different sensations running through my body that I cannot control. I cannot tell you how many times a day someone will ask me, "how are you?" I give them the "I am doing fabulous" speech, when honestly I am driving my struggle bus.

The mornings are the worst, your alarm clocks starts to ring and you lay there trying to convince yourself that you can get up, after an hour of debating you make it to the shower, only to get out of the shower and lay back across the bed trying to find the strength to do your hair and get dressed. Every day is a war, some days it is won and some days end in defeat. I try to keep my feelings to myself; I don't like for people to feel sorry for me. Now don't get me wrong, I have my own pity parties every now and again. I struggle, I feel sadness and I get down, but I allow myself to feel those emotions, process them and carry on. You feel the pain physically and emotionally, it's a tell-tale sign that you are still alive, still fighting, and still able to make a difference in the world. It's a vicious cycle but I just don't choose to reside in a place where my self-pity consumes me.

I often wonder how my life would be had I not been diagnosed. Would I have finished school; would I have been a good nurse? Would I be running my first marathon? How many more adventures would I have been on had it not been for my illness. The one thing I have learned about myself is that I am strong, I fight, and I keep going, even when I feel like I can't. I find the courage and strength; I tell myself multiple times a day that there are people in this world that have it far worse than I do. I try to take each day and rejoice in it. I feel like I have had to mourn the person I was before MS. I am still learning to love this complicated body and the new me. You will see me do a lot of crazy things, but quitting is not one of them.

(BIO:) My husband David and I are also involved in volunteer work with Tilted Tavern Animal Sanctuary, a farm animal rescue located in Jonesborough, TN where rescued animals live out their days peacefully. My favorite is a goat named Skittles. Skittles was used as bait in a dog fighting ring. She is my favorite because she is resilient; she has

scars on her neck, and she came to the sanctuary with mastitis requiring her to have a mastectomy.

December 2020. I've dreaded this day since I fell in love with Skittles. That's the hard part when you love someone, one day you will have to say goodbye, it's the same thing when you fall in love with an animal. They become part of your family and they grow to trust you and love you back. Skittles and I had an understanding, I was her servant! I accepted this title and the great responsibility and high standard she set for me. I held her bowl while she ate, didn't show up without lettuce; peanut butter crackers were cool but make sure it was Ritz, and always bring the cuddles. She had the best facial expressions. She has always been willing to tolerate me for our selfies, even on her last day she allowed me one last photo op. She was my Queen! I feel like Skittles was the matriarch of The Tilted Tavern Animal Sanctuary. She was one of the originals, rescued from a dog fighting ring, and what we would learn about Skittles was that she was a warrior herself! She was resilient and although she had those battle scars, she loved everyone she met. Humans had failed her and yet she let us be a part of her life. Every Tuesday on my lunch break consisted of me running to Food City to get her lettuce, I have never bought myself organic romaine lettuce but I would buy my girl some anytime I knew I was going to see her. I became such a frequent flyer at Food City that even the cashier came to expect me and she learned why I bought lettuce and often asked about Skittles. This Tuesday will be different, it will be hard and I feel a void. I will miss that sweet face running to the fence to greet me and to check to see if I was carrying extra bags. She ran a tight ship. I find comfort that she is no longer in pain and I am sure she ran faster than ever across the rainbow bridge. I think I can speak for all of us at TTAS when I say our hearts are broken, the tears fall like rain but it has been our pleasure to take care of our Queen. Please keep us in your prayers as we adjust to the new normal.

CHAPTER 8:
MY MOTHERS' LOVE:
ANNA KOWALOK

I never really knew who I was, and I don't know if I'll ever know. I guess that's part of growing up. When I look back on my life so far, I always tend to come back to one, pivotal moment in my life and what is has taught me. Here is my story. Here are my lessons. Here is my truth. When I was six months old, my life changed forever. A woman, who knew it was her time to have a baby, made her way to Guatemala with her father. After a few days in the country, she finally got to meet her baby girl. All the waiting, paper work, and constant worry that it would not have happened had finally paid off. She was able to hold her daughter for the first time and bring her home. To clarify, that baby was me, and that woman is my mom.

Now, let me tell you a little bit about my mother and her journey. She is a highly educated woman. She has loved. She has been heartbroken. She has lived life to her fullest. My mother is, without a doubt, one of the strongest and most selfless human beings on the planet, and I am not just saying this because she is my mother. She really is. When she was going through the process of adopting a baby, she actually received another phone call before I had come into the picture. She went full circle with the process, but that time it was not meant to be. Unfortunately, the birthmother of this particular baby decided to keep her. My mother was crushed. Why wouldn't she be? She had gotten her hopes up that she was going to be a mother, but that dream was shattered in a matter of seconds. However, little did she know that in a few months, she would receive another phone call, and this time, it would work out. This time, she was going to get a baby. She and my grandfather were in Guatemala by the end of that week. Her prayers had been answered, and she was a mother! She has always been a mother.

My mother has always been honest and truthful with me. Before I could completely comprehend what had actually happened to me, my mother would tell me constantly that I was adopted and I was loved. I remember her telling me that all the time. Ever since I could open my eyes, she would remind me that I was loved. Of course, as I grew up, I didn't really understand the concept of adoption. If anything, I correlated adoption with purchasing a pet. Never in a million years did I think that people were able to have children in a different way other than through biology. But as I grew up and asked more and more questions I began to fully understand what the term adoption meant. She told me that my birthmother was someone who knew that her baby needed and deserved a better life than the one that she could provide, that she made the difficult decision to say, "My baby deserves a chance." As I look back now, I cannot seem to wrap my head around that notion that someone could love that much. Maybe it's because I'm not mother yet. I don't know, but I still have time to learn.

When I think about the event that happened to me, I begin to remember what it felt like from my point of view. Let me paint a picture for you. When I was young, let's say six, my mom and I would go to the grocery store. I would be holding her hand and sitting in the seat of the grocery cart. Like people do, they look. I didn't think anything of it at the time, but there were some times in which I noticed a glare in our direction. To a six year old, I didn't care. I was getting attention, so I smiled. Little did I realize that my smile wasn't being returned. Why was this? At that time, I didn't see any difference between my mother and myself. As I have grown up and learned the meaning of discrimination and oppression, I can't help but think that these folks were judging my mother. They were judging me. They were judging us. Why? I wish I had an answer, but I don't. Some people say that they don't see color. Well, I'm here to tell you that that is not possible. Not one person looks exactly like another. Some might say, "Well, what about identical twins?" My answer is, "Yeah. They might look alike, but they are not identical. They have different values or beliefs. They are their own person."

Ever since I was a little girl, my mother always told me that family does not have to be the same. Family can be created in a multitude of ways. For instance, we have people that come into our life and change it—good and bad. It doesn't matter where they come from. They changed your life. From this, I am reminded that anyone looking in on my family does not and should not affect the way I see myself and the family that God created for me. I can confidently say that I don't care who judges my family. Worry about your own. My family is mine, and that's the way God intended it to be.

As I reflect on how my life has been created, I remember thinking frequently, what would my life have been like if I wasn't adopted? Thinking about it, I think of some distinct events that have happened to me that would not have happened if I had not been adopted. To start off, I would not have received the education that I have had (and continue to work on.) I had the opportunity and privilege of going to school and getting a holistic education. I wouldn't have been able to travel to DC, I wouldn't have received multiple positions on campus that helped build my resume, and I wouldn't have had the opportunity to learn and appreciate new cultures and become an open-minded person. If I hadn't been adopted, I do not think I would have met and married the love of my life. When Michael came into my life, it changed. Having someone who has seen you at your best and worst is a blessing that some people never get to experience. He, like my mother has said, keeps me grounded. We are each other's best friend and also give each other honest critiques. There is one characteristic that Michael holds that continues to amaze me and is the reason I fell in love with him, his acceptance. He accepts that my family is different. He accepts me for me. He accepts the notion that we, as a couple, will be judged because we are not "normal." He shows both of our families what it means to be open-minded and open-hearted. He and my mother are the two most important people in my life, and I would have never had this if I wasn't adopted.

There is one thing that I want to make perfectly clear. While I am forever grateful and blessed with everything that I have, there is one person that I cannot forget; my birthmother. Without her, I would not have the life that I have today. She made a choice; a choice that gave me the life that she knew I deserved. She asked for someone else to take care of her baby and to teach her what it means to love. There will never be a time in which I can express the gratitude and love I have for her. Her decision saved my life. She gave me that chance to grow into the woman that I am today. She is my hero, but my mother is my mama. It takes a special person to be a parent. They sacrifice time, energy, patience, and strength to give us a life that is great. My mama might not have given birth to me or held me in her uterus, but dammit she's my mom. She is my rock, my biggest supporter, and she is without a doubt one of the greatest women that I know. I pray that I can be a quarter of the woman that she is; a quarter of the mother that she is. I pray that I can continue to make her proud and show her how much I admire, cherish, and love her.

I leave you with some final thoughts. No matter where you come from, remember to embrace who you are. Try, every day, to be the best person that you can be. I challenge you to always stand up for your family and yourself. I challenge you to learn something new every day no matter how small. I challenge you to love your family, your friends, and, yes, even your enemies. I challenge you to love yourself. Always know that you are special, you are great, and most importantly, you are loved.

(BIO:) My name is Anna Kowalok. I was born in Guatemala (a country on the coast of Mexico), and I was adopted when I was six months old. I lived in Pikeville, KY for 20+ years, but then I moved to Pittsburgh, PA to pursue my Master's Degree in Higher Education Management. I am recently married. I enjoy cooking and baking, a nice glass of Moscato, and binge-watching Gilmore Girls or The Great British Baking Show.

CHAPTER 9:

FLY HIGH, MY SONS
ANDY RIOS

In 1969, at age twenty-two, in a senseless war in Vietnam in 1969, I experienced the death of buddies and friends that left an impact I've never been able to fully shake. I spent my year in the Infantry with Delta Company, 1st Battalion, 12th Cavalry Regiment, 1st Cavalry Division Airmobile. I survived with a few bumps and scars to civilian life, but have struggled with Survivor's Guilt over the years. I wonder often about the men who died, and my thoughts and prayers are with their families.

After Vietnam I got married to my best friend, Aurora, and in time we were blessed with three wonderful children, Arthur, Alan, and Amanda. I think that overall you would describe us as a fairly typical family with a strong love for each other. Then, when he was a young twenty-eight years old, Alan was diagnosed with a brain tumor, and died soon thereafter. I was shocked and in disbelief, and an emptiness filled my heart that I really can't even begin to describe. He was so young. I guess I went through the normal stages of grief; I just know that one factor that entered in was a deepening of the already existent guilt over being present in this life when he was gone; he and I had done so many things together.

Alan was so full of life; he was a jokester who loved to make people laugh, always selfless, putting others first, and an artist. He loved sketching, and music. He played the violin and viola, starting in the 7th grade.

Ten years later in 2013, at age forty-one, our son Arthur died in an auto accident. A positive thing that stays with me is that two days before the accident I had hugged his neck and told him how much I loved him. My message to all who read this is to cherish those close to you and don't be reluctant to tell them you love them. We never know what a day will bring our way.

Again, as with Alan, I was living in disbelief and limbo. Arthur lived closer to us and so I saw him more frequently. He was married and had two boys at the time of his passing. Arthur loved sports activities, especially soccer, and was an avid reader. After school he joined the Navy and served on an aircraft carrier for 4 1/2 years.

I think that for a while after this, Aurora's reactions may have been similar to mine – lost, angry at God, and a feeling of "here we go again", but she was much quicker to move to the belief that we were blessed to have had the time we did with our sons, and regarding God, say that sometimes we just have to accept things and move on. We did our best to do this; for some time we were able to go out dancing three times a week.

I believe my daughter Amanda's reactions were closer to those of her mother, consumed with grief, and then move on. She has two boys and two girls, so she had to keep going forward for their sakes. At one point she and her family moved to Colorado, but later moved back closer to us, still about four hours away. My mother, who is still alive as of this writing was in shock for the third time as my older sister had also lost a son a few years earlier.

In thinking about the question, "Who am I now?" I find myself sadder and lonelier; I see myself as a survivor, but only by God's grace and love. I live with the awareness that anything can happen, and I still frequently ask and wonder "Why?" I find myself in limbo and sometimes even find it hard to believe what has happened. Even now, as I think of all the great memories that I do have of times with my sons, tears flow, and I realize they will always be in my heart and never forgotten. I will always miss those smiles and hugs.

I find myself asking, "Is there any good news anymore?" I hope and pray to continue to hang out with family and friends, but I sometimes feel lost again and am not sure how that works. In Vietnam I know I became part of a Brotherhood that exists to this day, and I have become part of another Brotherhood, and am a Master Mason. It helps me out, gives me an outside source for a different perspective. It helps as I travel down the unknown pathway that I did not choose. I also like to golf, and being out on the course is calming for me and provides a certain sense of peace.

However, as a result of these life changing events, I now understand others and empathize with them in a way that I never could have before. We all wrestle with unseen things, pains, and sorrows. One time after I lost Arthur I saw one of my cousins crying and I found out she had recently lost her daughter. I felt a strong sense of camaraderie, just like in Vietnam.

One of my nieces has a daughter who is twenty one who has been sick for eleven years. She was an avid ball player, and when she was ten years was hit in the head with a softball. But as a result of examinations following the injury, doctors found a tumor for which she has to date had eleven surgeries. In some ways, for me, this has been a re-living of when it was discovered that Alan had a tumor. The triggers for flashbacks can be anywhere, and strike at any time.

I still have faith that here are good things that await in this life, and that we may even find out reasons for it all someday. In spite of doubts, sadness, and lonely times, I also have found faith to keep moving forward and persevering, and I know I will see Alan and Arthur again someday. So fly high, my sons. I will love you forever!

(BIO:) Andy retired in 2015 from Apache Oil Corporation and enjoys regular golfing and eating with friends at local restaurants. He and his wife also enjoy spending time with their daughter Amanda and their grandchildren.

CHAPTER 10:
THE HOLE IN MY HEART
RAMON RAMOZ

December 31st, 1968, I arrived with my Infantry unit in Vietnam, Delta Company, 1/12th Battalion, 1st Air Cavalry; by helicopter as the company was out in the field. I had seen the small opening in the jungle where the chopper was apparently landing and my thoughts as I scrambled off the chopper with my 75 pound pack on my back were, "Well, here we go." I was assigned to 3rd platoon, and met my squad leader SGT York, and also the platoon medic, DOC Hurley, nicknamed Fat Medic.

Of course everyone had to pull their turn on guard duty, and I don't recall if I was on an early or later shift, sitting behind the foxhole with legs dangling down into it; I do know I didn't hardly sleep all night as the Listening Post personnel were radioing back in that they could hear noises around them, some of it sounding like people were climbing trees.

The next morning, January 1st, 1969 I was told to go outside the perimeter to retrieve a claymore mine in front of our position as we would be packing up and moving out soon. There was a bomb crater a ways out in front of our sector of the perimeter and the claymore had been camouflaged near it. I was moving toward where the mine was located, rolling up the detonation wire as I went along. As I reached it I realized the wire had been cut where it connected to the claymore, and at the same time saw in the underbrush nearby that there was a Chi-Cong mine. The Chi-Cong mines were made so that when they were detonated the shrapnel would fly both to the front and back; I was standing to the side. When I saw it I said, "What the fuck –" and my sentence was interrupted by a loud explosion. I realized I had been hit with shrapnel as the blast threw me on my ass and then I momentarily lost consciousness. When I came to there was another blast of another

Chi-Cong explosion where shrapnel from it flew right over and past me; that may even be what awakened me to back to consciousness as I recall being aware that if the 2nd mine had been exploded first, I would have been standing directly in the kill zone of all that debris.

There was a slight pause in the action so I ran back to the fox-hole, dove for it, but overshot and landed on my back behind it. I was still in shock and suffering from a concussion, but I remember seeing an apparently wounded DOC Hurley lying nearby, being worked on by a couple guys. I myself had several holes in my shirt where shrapnel had penetrated my upper right shoulder, my right arm and elbow, and there was shrapnel damage to the stock and handguard on my M-16, but I was still able to engage with my Combat Brothers in the firefight. After about an hour more of fighting, the NVA were driven back by our company's firepower and support of artillery barrages. When the battle was over, I was medevaced with several others; just from 3rd platoon (of 25) there were 13 wounded, and 2 killed, Doc Hurley and "Jose" Isabelo Jimenez-Gonzalez.

However, all the feelings and shock and confusion of that day, and many days to follow in the next year, were nothing in comparison to November 29th, 2003, three days after Thanksgiving, when my 31 year old son Rico passed away. He had been wrestling with an addiction problem, had been in a few rehab programs, but could never get a handle on it. The evening of the 28th he took some pills while drinking, went to sleep, and never woke up. He was a Christian, and reading through some of his journals found after his death, he just couldn't find his way to break free, prayed for an ending, and was even asking God to free him by death if necessary.

At first I was engulfed in numbness and disbelief, and then anger began to mix in. I was angry at him, angry at God, hell, I was angry at the whole world. I could not imagine life without him; I saw no way of going on without him. It was a like a piece of my life was stolen and would forever be missing. You've heard the expression broken heart; I felt physical pain as if my heart was being ripped out. I can't even be-gin to describe how lost I felt, still feel a lot of the time. Even some 16+

years later, I sometimes still feel anger and an overwhelming sadness. Thoughts of the event still really piss me off. I guess there is a large part of me that has never healed; I don't know if it can. I wish there was a switch you could just flip off to end all these feelings.

After Rico died things deteriorated between me and my ex-wife; we didn't divorce immediately, but after a few years we did. During the years between his death and the divorce, my (now) ex-wife moved out, and I spent a lot of time running with my motorcycle friends.

In 2007 I was at a rock band concert, at a campground restaurant/bar near Daytona Beach, and my eyes landed on a pretty woman who I decided to talk with. Her name was Lauren and she worked in a local school system. I enjoyed our conversation, and so we met a few times to talk and eat; I was still desperately searching for peace of mind, and we were more just friends, and then after three or four years our friendship developed into dating, and then marriage. Lauren is my Rock; she is my guide and companion along my healing path.

Then again, I don't know one can ever truly heal from a traumatic event such as this. That hole in my heart is still there; will always be there. The VA put me on some meds that probably saved my life in the immediate aftermath. I believe in the value of pets when it comes to dealing with difficult times. Therapists and other VA programs offered relief. I went to a Florida RVN group in Melbourne (FL) and that helped me too. At one of the meetings I was talking to a Vietnam veteran who was a pastor, and he said something that got through to me. He told me, "You have got to get yourself straightened out spiritually before anything else; make peace with and get into fellowship with him." I took my friend's words to heart, and found out God was waiting patiently for me to finally turn to him. And, although I still struggle, I do find some peace when I am fishing, riding my motorcycle, or engaged in other outdoor activities. I have a dog, Pumpkin; I've had her since 2008. She's amazing. She knows when to come over and just lay her head in my lap.

It is still hard for me to talk about this, although I have found that a connection with others who have gone through similar circumstances helps. I recently connected via phone and FB with Andy Rios, a Vietnam Brother who I served a year with in Delta Company, and I have been able to share with him, and gain some comfort from that. Andy lost two sons, and I find that almost beyond comprehension, knowing how I felt and feel after the loss of Rico. In early October 2019 I went to a Delta Company, 1/12th Battalion, 1st Air Cavalry Reunion at in Columbus, Georgia, and Andy and I would go down for breakfast at 6 a.m. each morning and just sit there visiting for about three hours.

I've heard people say how they've been able to help others by what they've been through, and my initial answer to that question is that I haven't done that. But as I thought about it, maybe I have. Just last month I was at a small men's group where I attend church, and someone asked another man whose son had recently started court related rehab, "How's your son doing?" Since I knew first-hand about being a parent of a son who had struggled with drug addiction, the wheels of my mind started turning. Later I said to the man with the son who had been court ordered to rehab, "You don't really know what your son needs, but I can speak from experience, you need to be able to talk to someone; a counselor." He kind of brushed it off and I reiterated, "You really need to talk to someone about this."

It took me back a little as he said, "Why? I've got you." I realized I had made a connection with him without really trying. I guess all we can offer to others sometimes is hope, and I have come to realize that means a lot, offering hope.

(BIO:) Ramon Ramoz is retired and lives in Hendersonville, North Carolina where he and Lauren enjoy hiking, riding motorcycles, and just spending time together.

CHAPTER 11:

ANGEL KISSED ME GOOD MORNING
JOHN DUKE KEITH

I was in the car accident mid-January, 2008.

When I finally came to some three months later I remember lying in bed thinking, how did I get here; who did I come to see? Then I looked down and saw my body with wires, rods, and tubes coming out of it everywhere, and I started screaming and nurses rushed in to settle me down. I asked them to call my parents and they said they didn't have their number. I said, "I do!" Once they saw that my memory was coming back, I had some twenty doctors in my room; I was later told for the next hour no one within two floors of me got any service as all the doctors were with me.

In my mind, it was like someone had turned on a light switch, but now I was super scared and felt all alone. Then out of nowhere this little old lady with a mild glow emanating from her, pushed the doctors and nurses aside while walking over to me, kissed me on the cheek, and said, "Welcome back, Mr. Keith. We've been waiting for you." Her voice was so calming, I was flooded with peace, and then she walked right back out of the room.

The latter part of December 2007 I had gone on a two week vacation to Florida with my three children, Hannah, Johnny, Jeffrey, my parents, two sisters, a brother-in-law, and four nieces and nephews. Of course all vacations end, and I was on the first day back at the job in St. Louis, a Manager of Yard Operations (MYO) for the Union Pacific Railroad. I worked 12 hour shifts; one month nights, one month days, one month swing. I had just finished a night shift and left the office around 6 a.m.

I lived 45 minutes from work, and was within 5 miles from home when my life changing event occurred. The sun was bright on this snowy morning and the snow was gleaming in my eyes when I came to a curve in my Grand Am, and had a head on crash with some kind of SUV, which ran up my driver's side, and crushed the driver's door and hood on top of me. They brought the Jaws of Life to come and get me out, and although I have no recollection of this, the paramedics and fire department people on the scene said I was alert and told them where to cut into the car so I could crawl out, which I subsequently did.

I feel very blessed. I ended up with a ripped aorta (statistics are that 90% die on the scene, another 5% in the hospital), my hip bone was shoved through my pelvic bone, and every bone but three on the left side of my body from my collarbone to my big toe was fractured. The police called my parents who live about 45 minutes south of Chicago in Peotone, and told them, (very tactfully?) "Your son has been in a very bad car accident. Be careful and don't put yourself in danger by rushing to get here as he will be gone by the time you arrive."

Obviously, I made it past that day, and then doctors told my parents I would die, every day for the next two weeks. My parents brought my pastor from the Monee Free Methodist Church (just north of Peotone) down to pray over my soul, kind of like last rites, I guess, but I still lived on. The doctors kept telling my parents, "There is no medical reason he is alive; he will be brain dead and unable to walk the rest of his life." Again they were proven wrong.

I mentioned earlier I came to three months after the accident. Actually, I do have very minor glimpses of memory of doctor's faces and snatches of their conversations with my parents. My loving parents told their bosses they didn't know when they would be back to work, and stayed with me in the hospital, one time a month straight without going home. They told me they kept saying, "Don't give up son; you were in a bad car accident, and it will be okay."

Then, as I mentioned earlier, the little old lady with a mild glow emanating from her, kissed me on the cheek, and said, "Welcome back, Mr. Keith. We've been waiting for you." We sometimes talk lightly about our guardian angels; I have no doubt she was my Heavenly Angel watching over me, and giving me peace. When I said earlier my memory came back to me like a light switch and my angel gave me peace, it was then I realized God held my spirit in his hands until my mind and body were ready for it.

So I knew God was good, and I knew he was with me, but about a month later I was having issues and doubts about my faith, wondering why God would let me be in such pain and not answer any of my prayers. I remember lying in the bed yelling, nurses looking at me like I was nuts yelling at God, asking, "Why have you left me in this place with all this pain!?!" Just then I saw what looked to be either a small bird, or a large butterfly come out from my bed and fly toward the window. Then I really got mad and started yelling louder, "God! I come to you about my pain, and you left me in a hospital with bugs!" I asked two nurses to look for that bird, butterfly, whatever it was, and they asked me where it came from and I told them, "Down by my feet." Suddenly I realized that I was pain free and that my pain had been manifested in that bird and thrown out the window. I continued to have no pain the rest of the night; however, that was, and is to this day, the only time I have been completely pain free in my body.

But back to that instant when the pain disappeared, I recognized that I had just shared a moment with my Maker (my wish is that everyone at some point in their life gets to feel the overwhelming Love I did that day.) I just lay there and cried for several minutes, and then started singing, I didn't remember a lot of songs, but Jesus Loves Me came to mind, and I sang that song non-stop for an hour or so.

One of the nurses came back in and said, "Well it sure seems like you're doing a lot better."

I said, "Yes, Ma'am, I am; I just shared a moment with God." She expressed some doubt about that, so I explained to her my yelling and then my singing.

"So," she asked. "You really believe that was God?"

"Yes I do," I said, "with all my heart."

"Well," she replied, "if someone in your condition can believe like that, then I think I better start going to church again."

While in the hospital, I had to go to vocational and physical re-habilitation. One thing I vividly recall from this was they wanted me to do was write a letter to a family member expressing something I was feeling. So I wrote a letter to my parents telling them how sorry I was that I was in the accident.

One of the nurses said, "You mean you want to tell them 'thanks', and they would tell you they were sorry that you had to go through this."

"No," I said. "I want to tell them that I am sorry. I know there is nothing I can do about the accident, but they called off work, and came to stay with me, and worried about losing their only son. I don't want anyone to feel that, and I'm sorry that I made them go through that."

What a lot of people don't realize unless they've been through this type situation (and I don't wish this on anyone) is the sense of guilt that is on you. It weighs heavy because you are making loved ones change their lives for you. We would all sacrifice like that for a loved one, but the guilt of being the reason for that is something that stays a long time. I had a lot of built-up guilt; I never asked them to change their lives, but they did, and would do so again, and when I was in the hospital and then going through rehab there were many nights I just lay there and cried because I felt sorry for my family and friends and the sacrifices they made on my behalf.

So now the events just described are several years in my rearview mirror and I found there were ongoing areas of dealing with guilt. One was trying to prove to my kids that I wouldn't leave them again. At the time of the accident my daughter Hannah was 7, and the twin boys, Johnny and Jeffrey were 5. Not only was I in the hospital for several months, but I also had to move to my parent's house for over a year as I mended. I felt so bad not being able to be there for them. I made a promise to myself to do everything I can in whatever time the good Lord gives me to be the best father I can be. I've made mistakes along the way, but God is good all the time. I was able to gain full custody of my children when Hannah was 15 and the twins were 13. I am so blessed to have these wonderful children. I love sports, and have in-stilled in them the ability to love and play sports. It was a way for me to teach them about life. So far, it has worked out well for them. Hannah is currently a sophomore in college on a softball scholarship, and the twins are juniors in high school and both are being looked at for sports scholarships.

I have had to look at a different career path since I am unable to work for the railroad anymore (which I love to this day and wish I could still be there) due to no feeling or movement from my ankle to my toes in my left foot. I have been able to go back to college and earn three Associate degrees (all three Cum Laude.) A major motivation for me to return to school was to teach my children that no matter what happens in life, you still give it your best. I wanted them to see that if their dad could do well in college after some 60 plus surgeries, then they most definitely could succeed. I studied in front of them many nights to demonstrate that even if you don't feel like it sometimes, you give it your best shot and good things happen. I am very proud of my three children and want nothing but the best for them. As is the case with many parents, sometimes in wanting the best for them you may push too hard. I did a lot of thinking about that and never made them play a sport or play a musical instrument or join any group that they did not want to. The main way I encouraged them was in saying, "If you choose to do something, never quit, and do you best while you are obligated. If at the end of a school year or sport season you decide you don't want to continue, then you can opt out."

I am coming to a new time in my near future that I have been thinking on for some time. Once my sons graduate high school and go off to college, then I will encounter Empty Nest Syndrome. I'm fully aware that I will be going through some searching to find out the next steps in my life.

(Compiler's Note) Before John's story continues, I am inserting a Facebook message I received from John on January 30, 2020 (at 10:10 p.m.) I just found out yesterday I have cancer in my lower leg and they are going to have to amputate from the knee down ... so my thoughts are a little scattered now ... but I am hoping by the weekend I can organize them into words ... hope you and Cora are doing better too.

(Back to a series of FB updates by John)

February 2020

UPDATE UPDATE ::: Still in pain (who would've guessed losing weight n a leg this fast would be painful) I was up n moving in a walker today - tomorrow I get transferred to St. Mary's Hospital (it's also a top notch grade A rehabilitation facility...... thanks for the prayers God is Good n Worthy to be Praised.. thanks for Cards n dinners —-

March 2020

Physical Therapy today was Awesome .... went to St. Louis Zoo ... me and another patient Dave got out for a few hours (felt great after losing leg & being cooped up last 2weeks) ...(saw a red panda - looks more like raccoon)

May 2020

UPDATE: - pet scan showed cancer spread to lymph nodes by hip n pelvic ... so I start radiation on Wed. (25 sessions in 25 days M-F) then week off n back to 35 weeks of chemo ..... #CancerSucks but I'm #DukeStrong n will beat this giant.

June 2020

Got my new leg ..... can't wait for PT & OT to learn how to walk again ...... gonna push myself .... thanks for all the Support - Food - Love ...I am a Blessed Man

October 2020

WOW..... HOW THINGS CHANGE IN 1 YEAR .... No Football —- NO MOM (lost her fight with cancer) ...... No left leg for me (found out I have cancer n amputated) .... Been a real rough year ——- But there are still reminders of how BLESSED I AM

Dec 2020

UPDATE::::: today's the last chemo session for 3 weeks—— getting pumped with chemo for over 6 hours isn't fun (it's hard to sit still for 6 hours) ... get a new pet scan mid January to see if cancer shrinks or grows in left hip/pelvic.....(was really sick n weak for 3-4 weeks bout 2 months ago (100% better now) —— so I was going to therapy for

8 hours 2 days a week, but had to out on hold while sick .... so I start learning to walk again in January...... 3 weeks NO CHEMO —- I just might pack up n head to Florida . Thanks for all the prayers n gift cards for food I am blessed Love To You All

Closing Thoughts: One thing I think is that I have become a better coach since I've lost my leg; I watch a lot more. Sometimes as a coach it is easy to order players around rather than observe, and then teach. The second way you can learn yourself, and then realize there is even more you need to learn.

When I lost my Mom in June 2020 to cancer I saw firsthand how quickly things can change. I was told she asked for Johnny, and when I got there we kissed and hugged and then she gave a big sigh. She was alive a few more days, but that moment was really our goodbye.

But with my cancer I try to keep my mind off the "what ifs" and focus on the moments. I am blessed and have a lot to be thankful for. I was sick as a dog for a month, but I have learned I can find relief and cope better when I find the areas where I can laugh, yes laugh, about my condition. It is supposedly under control but it is still there in one lymph node in the pelvic/hip area. I told my doctor to just tell me the plain truth, good or bad, and I'll deal with it. In January 2021 we're supposed to talk about the pros and cons of surgery. I'm leaning that direction as the chemo is not having then desired reductions they had hoped for.

I'm fighting for my kids; I want them to know that. I want to take the necessary steps to win life. My life now has my kids as my top priority. I want to teach and support them in their lives, and follow the advice that has been in my family for years, passed from my grandfather to my dad to me: "I'll always stand with you and behind you and support your choices. However it will be easier to support your choices if you make the right ones."

(BIO:) John lives in Breese, Illinois, and is on long-term disability from the Railroad. He enjoys time with his children, and whenever possible as an assistant coach. He has always had a passion and love for sports.

CHAPTER 12:
SEE YOU WHEN I SEE YOU
HANNAH LUCAS

Jacob Mitchell Lucas was born on June 29, 1992, the middle child and only biological son to my parents. My brother and I were exactly 18 months apart. I was the oldest, but people thought we were twins growing up. You didn't have one without the other. Throughout our lives we went through so much together; our parent's divorce and then each remarrying someone else, sickness, high school, one of our parents having cancer, our heartbreaks, trials and successes, and we also helped raise our younger sister, Rachel. And then we started the journey into adulthood.

As I just stated, Jacob and I grew up together all through childhood and adolescence, and we were supposed to continue to go through life together, grow into adulthood together, watch each other get married to the love of our life, and start our own families. I moved away from home and he did as well. As young adults we had a routine where we talked every night on the phone on our way back home from our jobs, every night. Our conversations would last sometimes a few minutes to even hours at a time, depending on what there was to talk about. Jacob and I held each other to a higher standard than anyone else in our lives. We were each other's biggest cheerleader and each other's biggest critic. We told each other exactly what we thought when we thought it necessary. As a result, occasionally we fought, but honestly it didn't last but a day or two at most because Jacob would say, "Life is just too short."

August 16, 2013 my life forever changed. At the age of 22 I lost one of the most significant people in my life, the person who was supposed to be there for me my whole life, the person who was supposed to outlive me, the strongest and most dependable person in my life, my brother Jacob.

Jacob really and truly gave the meaning to the expression, "the good die young." Yes, he was a normal guy, including showing a streak of rebellion at times, but he had the biggest heart of anyone I know to this day. He stood about 5'9", was slender, had the brownest eyes to the point you could not see his pupils, and always, always had a rough beard. He called his beard an Indian beard, a patch here, and a patch there, he would say. You never saw Jacob without a smile, even on his darkest days. His smile and laugh were so contagious; he could make anybody's day better. His motto was you only live once, and he did his best to live up to that. Jacob was known to be an Evel Knievel type person who could withstand almost any injuries; every summer he had stitches and something in a cast. He experienced more life in his 21 years than most people do in a lifetime. He was also the type of guy to help someone change their tire on the side of the road no matter how he was dressed. He was the friend you would call when you needed bailed out of any situation. And as good as a friend he was, he was always a better brother. Even in his death, years later he continues to impact and help people; more on that in a minute. I still believe he loves the attention he gets to this day.

I remember everything about that hot and muggy August Friday. I was preparing for my last year of college to begin on Monday. I was a double major and had registered for a full load of classes. Jacob had mentioned that he thought he was coming home for the weekend but would let me know for sure later in the day. My OCD was going full blast. I had been cleaning my apartment top to bottom and before I knew it, I looked at the clock and it was 5:00 p.m. At 5:20 my phone rang and on the other side was my grandmother who was upset. She began to explain that Jacob had been in a car accident with a big truck while on his way home. I became sick to my stomach so I quickly gave the phone to my friend to get the rest of the details while I went to throw up. I tried to remain calm because he was still alive.

I quickly made my way to the hospital where the helicopter had flown him from the accident site. I will never forget getting off the elevator; when the doors opened over thirty of my closest family and friends were there. Of all these people, not one person said a word to me. It was like I was a ghost walking above the ground, like everyone knew something that I didn't, and all they could do was stand there staring at me. I quickly realized that my mother and father were not in this group of people. Finally someone came up to me and hugged me and said we are praying for Jake and your family. This weary feeling took over my body and I just knew that it was bad. I quickly asked, "Where are my parents?"

There was a little room with the door cracked open and I could see my parents were in there, along with my step parents. They were all holding hands and praying for their son, my brother Jacob. I was hesitant to knock on that door at first, but I did and I heard my sweet momma sniff and ask, "Who is it?" I replied, "Hannah" and I heard her sigh and say, "Come in." I sat in front of the four of them and none could find the words at first. Then my momma started to talk and explained how the accident occurred, but then she became so upset that my step-mom had to finish.

They explained that Jacob had hit the back of a large flatbed truck and was declared dead when the ambulance arrived. My step-mother continued to describe how the medical personnel revived Jacob multiple times while getting him on the helicopter and enroute to the hospital. All of Jacob's injuries were explained to me, and then my parents told me that they signed a Do Not Resuscitate order; their thought process being that my brother was so full of life that they did not want him to suffer and live off of a vent. I recalled it sinking in that if Jacob was declared dead again, he was truly gone from this world, but even at this moment of realizing how bad it truly was, I still had hope, in fact so much hope that I thought he would be a miracle.

Once my brother was out of surgery and stable I got to see him. I remember now, some almost eight years later, that long walk down the ICU hallway. I had so many thoughts racing through my mind, but never imagined what I would endure the next week. I got to his room and there he was. He was hooked to what seemed tons of machines. As I looked at him I could not believe it was my brother. It did not look like him at all; his body looked so fragile and thin. I told myself, this isn't my strong brother. I was truly in denial and still had so much hope that he would be ok. I can recall that evening being in his room with my sister and my paternal cousins praying and crying to God for a miracle, our miracle.

That next week was a blur and happened so fast. All of our family, friends, and community prayed hard for my brother, but eventually Jacob was considered brain dead as a result of strokes he endured after his accident. It turned out we never received our miracle, however, four other people did.

A little backstory; my paternal grandfather received a heart transplant over 20 years ago, given the gift of life by a young male. My grandfather got to watch his grandchildren and family grow because someone was selfless enough to make the decision to be an organ donor. Jacob had realized this at a very young age, and at age 16, with the consent of my mother, he registered to be an organ donor. After my brother's accident and injuries he became the perfect candidate to donate his organs, exactly what he wanted.

My parents and doctors discussed the process and completed the necessary paperwork to make my brother's wish true. All of the necessary tests took time to complete and this gave me the time I needed to say goodbye. I would set in his hospital room by his bed holding his hand and talk to him for hours at a time. I would talk about the memories of our past and laugh. I did plenty of apologizing and crying as well. To this day I believe he heard my every word. I am thankful for this time because I made sure I had no regrets.

That final day came. It was a Wednesday and I had had plenty of time to say goodbye but it didn't make it any easier. During that last visit with him and conversation I felt my heart literally aching. I just could not fathom that this is truly it, the last time I would physically see him, touch him, and talk to him. When time was up I just wanted more time. More time was my only wish. But my time was up and I helped the nurse push the hospital bed down the hallway and I just couldn't say goodbye so I said "see you when I see you". This was a country song that wasn't really popular at the time but it was the perfect saying. I just could not say goodbye. I don't think I have cried so hard in my life after the doors closed to that operating room where my brother would get his last wish.

Jacob's organs were donated to four people who were in need of a miracle; he was also able to donate bone marrow and tissue. My family and I personally know the young female who received my brother's heart, which the doctors described as a rocket for her. She lives less than an hour from our hometown to this day. The doctors told our family that my brother's organs fit perfectly for each person who received one and that they could not have found a better match for these individuals. The doctors explained these people were in their last days and that Jacob was truly their miracle and saving grace.

My view on life, decisions, and my life path changed drastically after the death of my brother. Life is too short to be unhappy. My plan before Jacob's death was to attend law school. Instead, I decided to finish college with a Bachelor of Arts in social work. I graduated a little later than expected due to all of the events, but nonetheless, I did graduate in December of 2014.

I think about the fact that my brother has missed out on so many events and, of course, he will continue to do so. Jacob was a man of many great qualities and all the women knew that about him. He was for sure a lady's man. He was handsome and had the personality to go with it. He was always afraid of ending up alone so he had plenty of women lined up.

I believe subconsciously he knew his life would be short. He lived every day like it was his last, never held a grudge, and was easy to forgive. My advice to anyone that is reading this is to live like Jake! Also, because he had a heart of gold, donate like Jake! Check out organ donation!

I can remember times when my brother would warn and protect me, many times in life. Now there have been many moments in my life where I could have been hurt physically, for example, zoning out while driving and something caught my attention to draw my attention back to the road. I truly believe that he is watching down on me and taking care of me still here on earth, just like he did when he was here physically. And I know he is in heaven laughing at me and my sister Rachel fighting over who will name their child Jacob.

I have flashbacks to the last time I saw him before the accident. I can see it so clearly. It is a memory I hold on so tightly to. Our family went to King's Island just a couple weekends before his accident. It was a perfect summer day. We waited in line for some rides an hour at a time and I remember him standing there with biggest smile on his face. He didn't mind standing in line like I did. The last ride of the day was a ride I swore I wouldn't go on, but Jake and my sister pushed "Come on Hannah!" "You know you want to." So I went. The whole ride my eyes were shut, and I was quiet, but my brother was laughing and having the best thrill of all. If I could freeze any moment in time it would be that day. When it ended we went our separate ways! I will never forget the hug, telling him that I was so proud of the man he had become and that I loved him so much! I never imagined that day and hug would be the last time I would see him as himself … before the accident.

My brother would celebrate every success of anyone he loved or cared for, and also would hold your hand or be a voice to help or to pick you back up and dust you off and if you had failed.

I have changed how I view life. I know that life is so fragile and short. I tell everyone I love how I feel. I ask myself is this something I will regret later on in life all the time? If my answer is yes then I make that choice count.

Eight years later I still can feel my heart ache at the thought that he is really gone. I have to remind myself that he is not here and I can't just call him to have one of our late night conversations. It is a bittersweet feeling to know that he is gone but has also impacted many people's lives and continues to do so.

My brother and I shared a love for music. We loved any type of music including old rock in roll, 60s, 70s, 80s, bluegrass, heavy metal; we never settled on just one type. We discussed music almost always in every conversation. The last conversation we had he said, "Sis, you have to listen to the song See You When I See You by Jason Aldean. Of course it was fitting that that was what I said to him the last time I saw him; I didn't say good-bye. To this day music brings back so many memories of Jake. I also recall singing Blame It on the Rain by Milli Vanilli at the top of our lungs on multiple occasions.

After losing Jake it has put my life in the perspective of living every day to the fullest because at any moment it can be your last. I know it sounds corny but it is the only way to look at life. I have begun to never let anyone in my life go without telling them I love them and care for them.

My heart and mind still cannot wrap around the idea that he is really gone. Sometimes the thought takes my breath away and my heart literally aches. It hurts to think that when I finally meet the love of my life and get married, or have my own child, as well as watch my sister do these things, there will always be someone missing. And I also know that I will not be watching him grow up and do the things in life that we all can't wait to experience. I can't watch him marry the love of his life and finally settle down or hold his first child. He may have already missed milestones for me and the other people he cared about but I feel it in my heart and in my faith that there is no doubt that he is up there in heaven cheering me on!

It seems like time has not healed the wounds of losing him, but I have learned how to cope. I do believe that losing Jake has made me a stronger person. I have taken on the role of taking care of whatever my mother and sister need. We depend on each other more.

(BIO:) Hannah Lucas is a 2014 graduate of the UPIKE College of Arts and Sciences. She is a Prevention Specialist at Kentucky River Community Care where she provides people in the community with needed resources, including food, clothing, and housing. She has even used her own money to help others in need during this pandemic. Her motto is, "If I am blessed to have it, then I can bless someone else."

CHAPTER 13:

BE KIND
EMMA SUE JONES

This isn't political or even particularly interesting but just something I need to say.

I don't think people really know me. My background. Where I come from or who I am. And that's okay most of the time, but I think assumptions can be dangerous, so I am writing a quick synopsis of my life.

My parents were poor. They both got GEDs and both got some college later in life. My Dad was an insulin dependent diabetic and only got healthcare when his health completely broke down and was admitted to the VA hospitals. My mom was dyslexic and didn't know it. She could read to herself and did so voraciously but not aloud. She could also barely spell. Very intelligent but she sold herself short her entire life because of it.

My brothers and I grew up poor. Tiny apartments and Salvation Army Christmas's. We moved from place to place, state to state every few months. Our parents loved us but were always restless and I've eaten at too many soup kitchens and lived in too many cars to count.

When I was 13 our situation was very bad. Our living conditions were cold and cramped and Dad's illness was affecting him. That year was the first time I began to fantasize about suicide. And even made a very feeble attempt. People were cruel at school and I didn't see life changing.

I made it to Maysville and we settled down a bit. We were still very poor. Living in a house where we drew water at a well and heated it over a stove to wash. And sometimes walked the railroad tracks near our house looking for coal that had fallen off the trains. I'm not saying this to elicit pity. I certainly know this was the norm for many people. I'm just explaining my experience.

Dad lost his job and my parents commenced wandering again. I went to Centre College where I made a series of seriously bad mistakes. I flunked out of school and ended up pregnant and scared. Luckily I landed on my feet. My boyfriend and I got married and I ended up in Pikeville, KY. I worked in the production department of the newspaper and my husband's family gave us land to build a house.

I worked for the public assistance office where I tried to be good to the people I served. I tried to remember my own family's hard times. I then got the blessed opportunity to work as the Long Term Care Ombudsman for this District. The best job in the world.

However, the depression that began when I was a teenager had never really gone away and I began to seriously contemplate suicide again. My husband and I had different dreams. Different goals and values. We divorced. I got therapy and medication.

I went to law school. Married again. Had my youngest son and became a Public Defender. I've traveled to Europe and South America and given my grandchildren my dreams.

The depression is still there. I still take medication. I still occasionally need therapy. I was a single Mom on welfare. I was a child in homeless shelters. I sometimes only had Christmas because of the Salvation Army. I lost my parents to cancer and Parkinson's.

Why am I telling this too long a story? Because I am just one person. I've had all these experiences. People are complicated. You never know what the person next to you has done. What road they've been on. Before passing judgement on anyone please remember this. No one really knows the sum of anyone else's experience. Be kind.

(Compiler's Note.) A couple of years ago, Emma's husband John Howie was diagnosed with lung cancer stage 3b, and she has been very involved in his care. The following summation is from updates she posted on her FB page. Any quotes from her are marked as such.

"The surgeon removed his tumor and chemo treatment was started."

(4/12/2019) Since diagnosis John has gone through his chemo treatment with a few lingering side effects but overall we've been really pleased. He hasn't lost weight and he got to keep his beautiful hair. His main problem has been fatigue. Anyone who knows John knows his incredible energy so that has been very hard for him.

(6/7/2019) Update on John. He's finished with his radiation treatment and we're waiting for his radiation levels to go down so his scans will be accurate. His energy levels are still pretty low, but getting better. His mood continues to be cheerful and full of sometimes dark humor.

God bless the chickens who caused the fall which led to the discovery of the tumor in the first place!

(March 2021) So way past time for an update on John. We've made it through this year. Sad times for John's family with the loss of his mother but new additions as his brother and sister join the grandparents club. A trip to Ecuador. Time with family. All while keeping Covid safe.

This winter John's cancer began growing again. Swiftly and frighteningly. Our team at Pikeville Medical convinced John to do another set of chemo. It's been hard. He's lost his glorious hair this time. Sicker than before. Retinal surgery. But today we found that the chemo has worked. There are a few issues that the doctors have to keep an eye on but we've gotten another year.

They've started him on an immunotherapy regime. I went downstairs to get a chai tea for myself and was texting friends and family. Crying and talking to the phone. "He's got another year!" And a woman on the elevator was so kind and trying to offer me support. She thought I was upset and had gotten the news he would probably die within the year. I tried to explain that this extra year is a gift! Once lung cancer spreads to the bones the prognosis is measured in months. We've had one extra year and now we've been granted another. I pray we get yet another, but our focus is enjoying our lives and our loves.

Thank you all for your support. Love, love, love to everyone! We've had our vaccinations too!

(BIO) Emma Sue Jones lives in Pikeville, KY.

CHAPTER 14:

WHAT GOD HAS JOINED TOGETHER
KELLY AND SHAWNE WELLS

You may have heard the expression joined at the hip. Although this is not literally the case for them, Kelly and Shawne Wells have a rather unique understanding of its implications.

Kelly Wells was playing college basketball his junior year at Morehead State University (KY) when a routine physical for the whole team showed that he was having some sort of problem with his kidneys. A biopsy confirmed he had a rare kidney disease, IGA Nephropathy (Berger's Disease), and he was told that in a matter of a few years he would need to have a kidney transplant. Because he was so young, Kelly was in disbelief and sought a 2nd opinion, which turned out to be the same as the first. He was also told he could not play basketball his senior year unless he had a medical override. He sought and received one, but in his 2nd week of the season, his knee went out and he had to sit out the rest of the year anyway. In retrospect, Kelly feels like maybe God was sending him a message.

Kelly's goal had been to play basketball all four years of college, hopefully go pro, and then go as far as he could in the coaching realm. Those dreams seemed to shatter with the kidney failure diagnosis, but due to the way he had been raised by his parents, Mickey and Doris Wells, he still feels like he was blessed by God; it was just that he was not yet ready to start a career that did not include playing basketball. However, Kelly said that, for him personally, one of the biggest obstacles he had to face dealt with concerns like living wills, etc. It really bothered him as he had just never thought of those kinds of issues before, and all of a sudden he was being forced to.

After his diagnosis, Kelly met and started dating Shawne Marcum who was playing women's basketball at Morehead. He said their common interest in basketball was what got them to noticing the other, but then they got to know each other better, started dating, and in 1997, got married. Eventually he taught full time and coached high school basketball for the Mason County High School Royals. He was starting to feel effects of the Berger's disease, but still experienced success in 2003, guiding his team to the Kentucky State Sweet Sixteen Basketball Championship. One of the members of that team was the future University of Tennessee All-American, Chris Lofton. In a USA Today article on February 25, 2004, Chris Lofton was quoted saying, "his (Coach Well's) show of strength characterizes the attitude of his whole team."

In the same article, his Principal at Mason County High said that Kelly was "not only a coach, but carried a full-time teaching load, and, although he had missed some time from being sick because his immunization system was weakening, he fulfilled all his duties." Kelly had managed his medications according to doctor's instructions, but, nonetheless, in 2004, after seven years of coaching, his kidneys were functioning less and less, and doctors told him it was time for a transplant. Of course, the most important step in the process was finding a donor that matched.

From family and friends that had volunteered to be tested, there were four people that were matches. Shawne, his wife was one of them. Shawne had told her husband that she prayed about it, and, if it turned out she was a match, then she wanted to be the donor.

For Kelly, having Shawne as the donor was mentally excruciating. He realized the truth about it being easier to go through something yourself than to watch a loved one go through it. Even though she was not the one with the kidney failure, still, putting herself at some risk for him was difficult to deal with. But Shawne was sure in her prayers, and firm in her desire to give him a kidney. Kelly said that Shawne showed him the purest form of love.

So at the age of thirty-three, 8 ½ years after the initial diagnosis, Kelly underwent the transplant procedure, receiving a kidney from his best friend and partner, Shawne. The procedure went well for both and they were able to soon resume their normal lives, bonded in a way they had not been before.

Back in 2003, along the pathway to the State Championship with his high school team, Kelly learned many valuable lessons about coaching that would pay off further down the road at the University of Pikeville where he was hired in 2006 as head coach of the men's basketball team. But as rewarding as the 2003 State Championship was, and the lessons learned along the way, Kelly feels like his kidney failure has taught him even bigger lessons.

"It keeps me grounded," he said. "It gives me a strong sense of what is most important in my life. And, with both coaching and in my life, I have learned I must stay focused on the positive. I can't focus on the negative."

Things that have served as restoring/coping devices for him are his family – being a husband and father to daughter Kaylee and son Mason; his church – being involved in service to others; and, athletics – being involved with basketball and other sports. Kelly said his disability has opened doors of opportunity for him to reach others he might not have been able to otherwise, sharing with them the good news that they can bear heavy loads with the help of God, and, God working through others.

He is involved in organizations like KODA (Kentucky Organ Donor Affiliates) that make others more aware of the importance of organ donations.

He referred to Mike McCarthy, who talked about the paychecks we receive along life's pathway which have nothing to do with money. Kelly said he receives some of those via calls from players who want him to know how they are doing, about the birth of a child, or, sometimes, former players telling him about incorporating some of the things they learned from Coach Kelly into their own coaching practices.

In 2011, the University of Pikeville men's basketball team had a pretty good regular season, enough to get them an at-large, non-seeded bid to the NAIA national tournament. Under Kelly Well's leadership, they became the first team in NAIA history to knock off only seeded teams (five of the top nine – including the top seed, the defending national champions and runner-up, and third seed in the title game) on their way to what initially seemed an unlikely NAIA Division I National Championship season He was also named the NAIA Division I Men's Basketball Coach of the Year. Kelly will tell you that he senses the presence of God with him daily. He is also aware of another friend as an on-going part of everything taking place, not only watching from the stands, but in the court-side huddles, locker-room, wherever; after all, "what God has joined together …"

(Compiler's Note.) In 2012 Kelly was with the University of Pikeville basketball team for an exhibition game against the University of Louisville. Before the game, Kelly began passing blood, so after the game he checked into a hospital where he remained for eight days. It was confirmed that his Berger's disease had returned. By December 2013 Kelly accepted the fact he needed another kidney transplant. Kelly's older sister Shelly was married to Brock Walter, who had been tested for compatibility when Kelly needed a kidney years earlier, and was also a match, so Brock volunteered to donate this time. A kentucky.com story (July 11, 2014) stated that if there was an award for Brother-in-Law of the Year that Brock should be the leader in the clubhouse.

Kelly Wells. Seven years later (2020) Who am I now?

What will I do now is an ever revolving question that runs in my mind considering the life changing events that are in my life can/will continue to be something I will have to address. Now that I am in my second kidney transplant and doing well, I have to fight the thoughts of going through this process again (maybe more). I am thankful I serve a loving God and have the most supportive family and friends a person could ask for. I always answer the question of what will I do now with "whatever I have to!" It is amazing what you can/will do when you have no other choice. I don't feel sorry for my circumstance or question it most times, but I try to be humble and appreciative for the grace shown to me by my spouse and brother in law and their gifts of life they have provided me.

Regarding who I am since this incident occurred, I don't think the who I am has changed in my circumstance, but the how I am has changed. With my disease and side effects I have had to have a hip replacement, colon resection, kidney nephrectomy and several biopsies of my kidney. My lifestyle has changed with medications and doctor's visits, but who I am will not change. I still work full-time as a head college basketball coach and director of athletics (really two full-time jobs). Being able to partner with 600 plus student-athletes and 40 plus coaches is very rewarding and keeps me "normal."

Specific activities that have helped me continue to heal are basketball, family, and working with organ donation groups. It has always been important for me to surround myself with the things in life that I prioritize; God, family, basketball, and service. Being in my role as coach, director, leader, husband, father, son, and Christian all give me great opportunities to serve and lead. I am a person of challenge and the opportunity to grow and stretch who I am has always driven me. In all my days I want to keep pursuing to find the best version of myself in all walks of life.

Had I not had the life changing event, then being an advocate for organ and tissue donation probably wouldn't have been in my plans, but with my transplants and seeing how it changes lives makes it very real to me and I feel like I am a living trophy to share my story. Having information and an example is power in all things, but especially in the medical realm. It has always been important to me to live a life of true value and purpose. While there are times I fail miserably and have regrets, I try to get better and do better despite my imperfections and short comings. With God all things are possible!

(BIO:) Since Kelly added to his story, he stepped down from his position as men's basketball coach in order to devote his full attention to his position as the University of Pikeville's Director of Athletics.

Chapter 15:

Let your talents take you around the world
Haakim Johnson

When I was younger my dad bought a drum for me, and other musical instruments for my brothers, and made us practice our little ensemble a lot. He used to tell us, "Let your talents take you around the world." Well, I have played in 14 different countries (15, counting the US), not with a drum, but with a basketball. When I was around five or six I started playing basketball with my older brother and decided I really liked it. Early on I thought that it would be fun to play professional basketball, and eventually did, although some obstacles in my life almost kept me from my goal.

I was raised in New Jersey my early years, and then moved to Orlando, Florida about the time I was to enter junior high. I fell into the wrong environment there and almost got sidetracked. To this day I realize the importance of choices; many of my friends from that time are in jail, some of them for murder, and some have died themselves.

But I still loved, and played, basketball. I started Junior College, and my coach there knew Kelly Wells, Head Basketball Coach at the University of Pikeville (KY), and recommended me to him. This started a transition into a new world for me. One thing Coach Wells would say was, "Never let a situation define your future." Coming to the University of Pikeville showed me a whole different outlook on life. Coach Wells and the assistant coaches, especially Coach Riley, helped me unlearn and relearn a lot of things. That doesn't mean I stayed totally trouble-free, but I made progress.

Coach Riley, whom I just mentioned, was a huge factor in one of my life changers. I was on academic probation the end of 2008-2009 academic years, and I took a couple summer courses to raise my GPA.

I needed at least a "B" in both classes to get off probation. One course I enrolled in was Persuasive Strategies in the Media offered by Basil Clark. I was doing well in both courses, but in the media one, miscalculated. The final exam was comprehensive and worth 50% of the grade, however, I was anxious to get back home, and figured I was okay in the course as I had gotten some papers back with an "A" or "B", so I flew through the test; in other words, blew it off, and left for Florida. I got a "D" in the media class.

(Compiler's Note.) Enter Coach Riley. I received a call from Coach Riley asking if he could talk with me. When he came to my office, he told me that he had talked to Haakim and asked him about his grades, and Haakim told him what he wrote above; anxious to get home, figured he was okay in the course, rushed the exam. Coach Riley said he normally wouldn't even consider asking a professor if there was anything that could be done (btw, this was the only time I had interactions with him regarding a student's grade), and then proceeded to explain why he was there. Coach shared a little of the environment Haakim was going back to and he was afraid that with college out of the picture that Haakim could wind up in trouble with the law, or worse. Coach Riley asked if there was any way Haakim could retake the final. I thought for a moment and told Coach that Haakim could not retake the final, but I did have something he could do. I explained my thoughts to Coach Riley and he called Haakim and told him to get back up to Pikeville. A couple days later I said words to the effect of the following to Haakim. "Haakim, Coach Riley explained to me what happened and although you may not retake the final, there is a way you can raise your grade. There is a book called The Five People You Meet in Heaven *by Mitch Albom. I will let you use my copy; you are to read the book and then turn back in a report on it which will include not only the premise of the book, but also you are to think about the five people you will meet in heaven, explain why, and you need to include Coach Riley as one of those people."*

(Back to Haakim.) Coach Riley intervened and, I guess you could say almost miraculously, I was given the opportunity to return to the University of Pikeville and play basketball. I almost blew it again when

I got into some trouble with the law, and then returned back to Florida. But my basketball dream was still alive, so I enrolled in some training camps, and in time I felt confident enough in my basketball skills that I decided to try out for the Premier Basketball League, tryouts being held at Georgetown University in Washington, DC. My agent sent some game films, and I was accepted. I was ecstatic; my hard work was beginning to pay off, and I was now going to be able to care for my family doing what I loved.

Contracts for teams in the PBL averaged 4-8 months, and then you were free to contract with another one. Due to this, I have been privileged to live my dream in Mexico, Syria, Australia, Lebanon, Dubai, Qatar, Saudi Arabia, Japan, China, Korea, Puerto Rico, the Dominican Republic, Germany, and the Czech Republic. I liked playing in all these places, but my absolute favorite was in Toyama, Japan, a city on the coast of the Sea of Japan on the island of Honshu.

(BIO:) So who am I now? Well, presently I am sitting out a year recovering from a sprained Achilles injury, but, I see myself as a basketball player living out his dream, and a father and provider for my three daughters, Sahia, Giselle, and Paidyn, and my teenage son, Malachi. I've had some people who knew me earlier in my life tell me they can't believe what I have been able to do. I am living proof of what Coach Wells would say, "Never let a situation define your future."

There have been many life changing events in my life, but a major one definitely was when Coach Riley intervened on my behalf, and I'll always be grateful to my dad who instilled the dream in me of, "Let your talents take you around the world."

CHAPTER 16:

WHAT TO DO TO FIX IT
DR. MARK REED

I have to admit, it looked good, the online page with the banner *U.S. News & World Report*; Dr. Mark Reed, Family Medicine Doctor in Pikeville, KY.

Of course, that didn't just happen overnight. I've always had compassion for others, even as a child. My grandpa shared stories of himself giving aid as an Army medic in WWII. My own personal physician, Charles Nichols, MD, was an inspiration in my life. Experiencing healthcare first hand and some mentoring from Dr. Nichols solidified my desire to pursue the study of medicine. Becoming a physician is one of those things I've always wanted to do.

So after graduating in 1994 from Betsy Layne High School, I studied at the University of Pikeville (KY) where I graduated in 1998. Then it was another four years of study at the University of Kentucky where I received my medical degree in 2002, three more years as a Resident Physician at the University of Kentucky, and then back to Eastern Kentucky where I became established with Reed Family Medicine PSC.

On December 18, 2000, I had married the love of my life, Danielle, and we have been blessed since then to have two wonderful sons. So things seemed to be going well, and then in April 2019, at age 43, I was diagnosed with colon cancer, 4 out of 39 nodes positive for metastatic disease, which put me at Stage 3b.

As a doctor I knew that in the U.S. alone there are more than 150,000 cases of colon cancer annually, and now I was a part of those statistics. I was also aware that more than 50,000 people die each year from it.

Now I have no family history of colon cancer. I had recently increased my exercise regimen with some friends as we were aspiring to do our first marathon, so I was running 20 – 25 miles per week. I lost about 25 pounds, but that was intentional, I thought. I began having some right lower quadrant abdominal pain with running. At first I thought maybe I had pushed too hard. A buddy said jokingly that I needed to push through the pain. But the pain worsened over the next couple weeks and I couldn't push through it. I actually called my wife to come pick me up in the middle of a run. The pain resolved overnight and I resumed life as normal. That Friday, I ate a large dinner with dessert, but later that evening developed severe abdominal pain that lasted all weekend. I did stat labs on myself Monday morning and the labs were completely normal. Then I went to have a CT scan of my abdomen which showed my entire small intestine was dilated and inflamed, and both the radiologist and I were concerned. Now Crohn's Disease is in my family history, so I decided that must be what I had. I called a gastroenterologist friend and had a colonoscopy in the next few days to officially diagnose my Crohn's with a biopsy.

When I awoke from anesthesia the doctor told me, "It's not Crohn's. You have a large mass obstructing your ascending colon; you have cancer!" That led to the whirlwind of more scans and surgical consultations which ultimately led to a right hemicolectomy and chemotherapy.

Immediately I was in a "what to do to fix it" state of mind, and also my feelings became more focused on "what would my family do" in the worst case scenario. I have two sons and I always thought it was my honor and duty to make them respectful, dependable young men. What would happen if I wasn't here? After several days of processing the devastating news, I wept with my wife as we held each other. From there we turned to prayer and faith.

I've always been a man of faith; accepting Christ at a young age. I've always been successful and could complete any task at a high level of perfection, so I believe that because of this I took God for granted. I didn't thank him every morning that I awoke for another day to be alive, and I didn't thank him daily for the life I have been blessed with. I definitely do so now!

Faith is what helped me and my family the most. I am used to making the decision about someone else's healthcare; this time I was on the receiving end of decisions. Praying and trusting that God's will be done was the only way for me to cope. And my life verse became Isaiah 41:10: "So fear not, for I am with you; be not dismayed, for I am your God; I will strengthen you, I will help you, I will uphold you with my righteous right hand."

However, a question that lingered for me was, "Can I tolerate the treatment?" Being in the medical field, I have seen numerous people have varying outcomes from the diagnosis and treatment. What was going to be my outcome?

But I knew it could be so much worse! This was still curable, and we also believed that anything is curable according to God's will. In a Facebook post I included, "So I've got this; I'll continue to improve! Keep me and my family in your prayers. We got this. God's got this!"

The end of May 2019 I posted a meme to Facebook; a skull next to a ribbon that said Colon Cancer, and the following: "The Devil whispered in my ear, 'You're not strong enough to withstand the storm.' Today I whispered in the Devil's ear, 'I am the storm'."

I continued to work at my practice, Reed Family Medicine, but there were precautions to be taken. My Oncologist said it was absolute highest priority that I not be exposed to acute illnesses, or anyone with symptoms of being sick (flu-like symptoms, fever, cough, chills, sore throat, skin infections, etc.) He said that if there was an interruption in my treatment it could affect the intended outcome. I notified all patients to notify staff if any of the preceding applied so we could change their appointment to my Nurse Practitioner; that it was potentially a life or death situation if I became ill during chemo. I also informed them that it was recommended that I not shake hands or hug anyone until my chemo was finished. (As you can see, the Doc was taken right out of doctor, but I also knew this was a temporary necessity.)

I became aware of how important family was to me, and that I couldn't have made it without my work family. My crew just kept everything going, and they were all very protective of me.

I don't think I had ever before experienced the fatigue that accompanied certain phases of chemotherapy, and fatigue was not something that I had been used to experiencing. In July there were some days where I would do what I could in the mornings, and then sleep in the afternoon. I've always been active, and now there were periods where I couldn't exercise. I really missed bike riding, and it was a real treat when I was able to mow the lawn again. (Thanks went out to my dad who filled in for me for a while.) But I felt blessed to be alive, and thankful for everyone's prayers.

On October 15, 2019, again I took to Facebook with the following, "I have to take a second from busy work day to post this. I just received news my CT scans and PET scan from yesterday are all completely normal. No evidence of cancer! Thank God! Keep me in your prayers. I follow up with oncology Friday. I still have two rounds of oral chemo to complete."

Now my kids knew their dad was sick, and they also knew enough to associate death with cancer, so they were a little distraught even though I tried to pretend that I was perfectly fine. In retrospect, I'm sure it affected their lives more than I realize. On the day I found out my CT/PET scans were normal, my oldest son hugged me and cried.

On November 24th I posted, "I have so much to be thankful for: God, family, friends, life ... Danielle and I will be married for 19 years next month. She has stood strong and been amazing during this crazy year we've had ... I took my last dose of chemo last night. I am beyond blessed and thankful for the many prayers. I can't put into words how thankful I am. Only God knows the future. Right now I have no evidence of cancer and trust in Him as the future unfolds. Thank you!" #Isaiah41:10.

I do not specifically question who I am now, but I do understand more clearly how to help others with a similar diagnosis. I always had sympathy and compassion toward others struggling with devastating news, but being a cancer survivor has broken the ice for conversations that I wouldn't have had prior to this event. Now I have empathy.

Also, as a cancer survivor, others with a cancer diagnosis have had conversations with me that I could not have done previously. I was also very open about my faith throughout my treatment. This has also opened doors for me to share about my faith, and have an intimate prayer with others in similar situations.

And regarding the title of this chapter, "What To Do To Fix It," I discovered that the fixing wasn't up to me; I had to place my faith in God, and the Oncologist Doctors and their knowledge of treatments.

(BIO:) Today I am a blessed man who continues my practice at Reed Family Medicine, enjoys and appreciates time with my family more, and has again been able to do long bicycle rides.

CHAPTER 17:

NEVER ALONE: A STORY OF ADDICTION AND A BRUSH WITH DEATH
DR. DAVID B. ROBY

I opened my eyes on the morning of December 26, 2004. The first thing I saw was the face of my older brother, Robert, looking down at me. He was saying my name over and over trying to get my attention. I had no idea where I was, how I got there, or why my brother was there. Was I dead? Was I in Heaven? Maybe it was just a dream. I was living in Austin, Texas at the time working on my doctoral degree in Hispanic linguistics and teaching Spanish, and my brother was living in Boston, Massachusetts. I was completely disoriented, but at least I did not think I was in hell. Then, as my eyes began to focus somewhat better, my brother started talking to me.

"You're in the intensive care unit. You had a seizure in your bathroom. The cops found you in your apartment, and you were rushed to the hospital. Mom called me and told me, so I got on a plane and flew down here as fast as I could."

Then, it all came back to me. I remembered being horrified at the sight of myself in my bathroom mirror. I was seizing, and several of my front teeth were broken. One tooth had been knocked out, and blood was gushing out of my mouth and splattering everywhere. I also remembered standing in my bathtub with the water running. There was blood and water mixed together swirling down the drain. My seizing intensified. I had absolutely no control over my body. It was Christmas Eve. I was 32 years old, living alone. None of my friends or coworkers were even in town, let alone within an earshot of me, and everyone else in my apartment building had left for the holidays. No one could save me, and no one was there to hear my screams. I genuinely thought I was about to die. At that point, I had one last resort. I began repeatedly screaming at the top of my lungs,

"Jesus, help me!!!"

Suddenly, my seizing stopped, and I collapsed in a heap in my bathtub with the water still running. My ankle was twisted against the side of the bathtub. I could no longer move, and then everything went black.

An entire day passed. My mom, who was expecting me to travel home to West Virginia for Christmas, was panicked, because I was not answering my phone. The next day, she decided to call the Austin Police Department for help, and the dispatcher agreed to send a couple of officers over to my apartment to check to see if I was there. The police found me in my bathroom still alive, but barely. I was rushed to the hospital in an ambulance and was immediately placed in intensive care. According to the doctors, had I been discovered an hour later, I would have been sent to the morgue on Christmas Day instead.

As my brother was talking to me, I realized that I could not move at all, and I could not talk, because I was hooked up to a ventilator. Not surprisingly, I was in excruciating pain. My head hurt in several places from my having hit it multiple times. But the worst pain came from my right ankle that lay in a twisted position against the side of my bathtub from the time I passed out until the time the paramedics removed me from my apartment. I had a large IV needle in my arm, some electronic sensors attached to me that were connected to another machine, and a catheter inserted in me, which was by far the most unpleasant circumstance of them all. I was still scared.

"Why am I still alive? Why did this have to happen? Am I still going to die? If I recover from this, will I be able to have a life worth living? "Is my life worth having been spared in the first place? Do I even want to live?"

In the days, weeks, and months leading up to my near-fatal seizure, I had been struggling with severe depression and insomnia, and I was using mood-changing and mind-altering drugs attempting, unsuccessfully, to manage both. I had completed all the coursework and passed the comprehensive exams required to earn my doctoral degree. All I had left to do was write my doctoral dissertation, which is essentially a research essay the length of a book. After having spent almost my entire life enrolled in classes and studying together with my peers, I found myself completely alone with no one to talk to but myself. I quickly began to fall into a pit of abject despair, and I eventually cracked. My life did not turn out the way I expected. I was lonely and frustrated, and I felt like a total failure. While most of my friends in my age group had careers, were financially stable, and were married and having kids, I was still in school, racking up massive amounts of student loan debt that I could never pay back, unsure whether I could find a good job after graduating, and I was completely alone. I was regretting having ever begun my pursuit of a doctoral degree in the first place. Instead of being a nerd and spending so much time studying and conducting theoretical linguistic research, I should have been working on finding a job, making money, meeting a good woman, and getting married. However, it was too late to turn back, and I was already financially ruined anyway before my career had even begun. My life was in shambles, and I had abandoned all hope. So, there I was, in my dank apartment, a grown man, hopelessly in debt, alone. Frankly, I did not even want to go home to see my family, because I felt like I had let them down. I did not want to live anymore, but I was neither trying to end my own life nor was I trying to preserve it. The best way to describe my mindset at the time is that I was passively willing myself to death. I cannot pinpoint exactly when my overall health began to quickly, exponentially deteriorate, but I believe it was when that fall semester ended, and I was no longer on a set teaching schedule. My depression and insomnia became so severe, day and night blurred into each other, and time began to pass so quickly that I had forgotten to eat or even try to sleep for days, and I stopped caring. Severely sleep-deprived and malnourished, I literally began to die.

A group of friends and a pastor from a local church I used to attend came to visit me at the hospital. My mom was able to contact the pastor and inform him of my condition. The pastor anointed my forehead with oil and led the group in prayer. When he was finished, a peace came over me. Though I was not looking forward to what might happen in the future, I had decided that I wanted to live, and I knew that I was going to live. Perhaps, it was not so much a desire to live as it was a fear of dying. If my life had gotten so bad that it led me to that dreadful state, what reason did I have for believing that death would be any better? Shortly afterwards, the nurses removed me from the ventilator. I would spend a total of 3 weeks in the hospital, and when I got out, I was still weak and emaciated. My teeth were badly broken, and I had to temporarily use a cane to walk because of severe nerve damage in my lower right ankle. I was beaten and shattered, but I would live.

Often, we hear stories about people who have a near-death experience, and they come away from that experience with their perspective changed, cherishing their lives, having more faith in their Higher Power and feeling more grateful and positive than ever before. For many years, I was not one of those people; my perspective had not changed at all. As I was physically recovering from my event, I still viewed my life as the same rotten, miserable, lonely, seemingly meaningless existence it was before, and I could not envision it improving in the foreseeable future. Nothing had changed. I had taken a severe mental, physical, and spiritual beating for no apparent reason. What was the point of that entire experience? Did I do something to deserve it? Why did God save my life? Was it simply because I asked Him to save my life? If that was the case, then I regretted having asked for His help in the first place, because my life was not improving at all. Was I just incredibly stupid? A lot of people I knew were atheists, and they did not have such problems. Were my troubles somehow made worse by my belief in a power greater than myself? Countless times, as I sat alone in my apartment, I expressed anger toward God for saving my life and begged Him to finish the job. It felt like because I was not fully committed to dying, I failed at it, and as a result, I found myself failing at being alive all over again. Life would continue, but years would pass before I could ever truly smile and laugh again. Nothing made sense. I was healing on the outside, but I was still very sick on the inside.

My feelings of inadequacy and loneliness did not manifest themselves in graduate school. From an early age, I always felt like I was somehow different. Though I had some close friends and played sports,

I never truly felt like I fit in well with others, and I spent a lot of time alone. Starting in my early teens, I had always relied on getting drunk or high to feel good or to at least feel normal. I made a conscious decision to experiment with alcohol and other drugs, but I did not choose to be an addict. Most people can drink alcohol or use drugs recreationally on occasion without becoming addicted to them. They can stop at one fix, one pill, or one drink and would have no difficulty abstaining from such mood-changing or mind-altering substances indefinitely thereafter if they so choose. I am an addict, and thus, I am different from most people. Once I get high, I have an uncontrollable urge to stay high, get as high as possible, get high as frequently as possible, and search tirelessly for ways and means to obtain more drugs. That urge is a mental, physical, and spiritual force whose strength far exceeds that of any willpower that I can muster to resist it. I alone am no match for that urge; I am powerless over drugs. As the years passed, the use of mood-changing and mind-altering drugs had steadily made my life more and more unmanageable. I could not live with or without the use of drugs. When I was not using drugs, I was unhappy, because I could not mask my pain and disconnect myself from reality. On the other hand, the use of drugs contributed, in large part, to the uncontrollability of my life and was one of the main causes of reality being so unbearable for me. I was trapped in a deadly cycle of misery and insanity, and I hated myself. Six months after my near-death experience, I began using drugs again. Somehow, I would go on to complete my doctoral degree, but that did not alleviate my problems. Three years after my near-death experience, after what would be my fourth and final drug-related stay in the hospital, I finally sought help for my drug addiction in the rooms of 12-step recovery. If I was not willing to kill myself and was to continue living at all, I was going to have to find a new way to live.

When I began attending meetings with other addicts and hearing them talk about their struggles with addiction, I was timid, and I did not know what to expect. However, after listening to the other addicts discuss their struggles and share their experience with the group,

I soon realized that I was neither so unique nor so alone after all. We were all practically identically afflicted; their stories were simply different versions of my story. I hated myself and what I had become, but the men and women in that fellowship loved me unconditionally and were willing to love me until I learned how to love myself. It soon became obvious that I could not save myself and that they were my only earthly hope. After attending meetings for a few weeks, I found a sponsor. A sponsor is like a mentor who guides you through the process of working the 12 steps, and the 12 steps are the solution to recovery from addiction. To clarify, recovery from addiction is not a cure. Recovery is the process of practicing complete abstinence from all mood-changing and mind-altering drugs while taking steps to heal mentally, spiritually, and socially. A cure would suggest one's attainment of the previously nonexistent ability to drink or use drugs responsibly and stop whenever one wanted with no discomfort or withdrawal symptoms. Many people believe otherwise, but addiction is a disease, and it is diagnosed as such by the professional medical community. There is no known cure, but the disease can be treated and arrested, thus making recovery possible. After spending a few months in the program working the first five steps, the physical cravings for drugs had miraculously disappeared. Working steps with a sponsor taught me to become more willing to trust my Higher Power, gave me the opportunity to find the root mental and spiritual causes of my uncontrollable urge to use drugs at any cost, and truly begin the healing process. Ironically, by accepting that I was powerless over the disease of addiction and that I needed to surrender to it, I was able to string together more and more days clean and begin to heal inside. Being in a fellowship with other addicts taught me to be humble and understand how little control I really had over my life. I can have dreams and make plans, but outside circumstances will not bend to my own self-will. Therefore, I must live life on life's terms. I learned how to be more honest, open-minded, and willing to do whatever it took to stay clean. That said, my work had merely just begun, and I was still very sick and very scared. There were times when recovery seemed so painful and futile, and I believed that I would have been better off had I just died in my bathtub years earlier.

Instead of being financially stable with a good career, a wife and kids, and a car that at least starts every time I turn the key in the ignition, there I was, just doing all I could to make it from one day to the next without falling apart. As the drugs had then become the least of my worries, I was going to have to learn how to do something I had never done before: lead a quality life without drugs and do it for the rest of my life. At least I knew, for the first time in my life, that I was not alone.

For the next couple of years, I would continue to teach college students and attend 12-step meetings. I was over 150,000 dollars in debt with growing interest, and because I was a teacher, I was barely able to live paycheck to paycheck, let alone make student loan payments. At that point, I had all but written off ever getting married or having children, because financially, I could not even take care of myself. I left Texas and moved to Pennsylvania. My new job there was so abysmal; I would ask God to kill me in my sleep at night so I would not have to go to work the next day. I was trapped again, but instead of being trapped in the cycle of addiction, I was trapped in my own undesirable existence, which I could no longer block out with drugs. Was that "as good as it gets?" When I spoke during 12-step meetings, I mostly ranted about how bad my life was. The other members thought I was crazy, and they were right. What helped me to survive those times were the unconditional love and acceptance from the other addicts in those meetings, my willingness to listen to them, and knowing that I was not alone. Moreover, those friends reinforced in me the principal of gratitude and to not lose sight of how much progress I had made in my recovery. Though I was still generally unhappy, I knew that I was at least better off at that time than I was when I was using drugs. When I heard other addicts express their gratitude, it inspired me to not give up. With two and a half years clean, I moved to Pikeville, Kentucky, where I would have to start over again with a new job and a new, much smaller 12-step fellowship. My life was the same; I just moved it to a different location, wallowing in the same cycle of discontent and feeling trapped. Everything looked bleak, and I was increasingly angry at my Higher Power, but I kept coming back to the meetings, because they were all I had.

Just as I was contemplating giving up on the fellowship, with three years clean, a miracle began to take place. New members began showing up at our meetings. Just as I was when I first started attending 12-step meetings, they were desperate and confused, and they needed help getting clean and staying clean from drugs. They asked me for help and advice, they called me, and we would drink coffee and eat dinner together just to talk more. They needed my help to stay alive, and without my realizing it, for the first time in my life, my primary focus was on helping others instead of whether my own life was improving. Furthermore, the more time I spent helping new members who needed me, the more I realized that I needed them just as much. In our recovery community, we were always there for each other, on the best of days and the worst of days, to help each other stay clean no matter what, and to help the next newcomer that walked through the door needing our help. My life was still not where I wanted it to be, but because I was still alive, I found myself in a position to help others, and I embraced that opportunity more and more each day. It was not until one day as I was sharing my recovery story to a room full of addicts in an addiction treatment center in Corbin, Kentucky that I truly began to understand that my life truly had a purpose. Toward the end of my speech, I looked at the crowd and said,

"It is miracle that I am still alive. I should be dead. I don't know why God spared my life that day, but if it was for no other reason than to deliver this message of recovery to you today, then that is a good enough reason for me."

More than any academic achievement, that very moment in time gave me a true sense of purpose in this world. All the suffering I had endured, along with my near-death experience had given me the tools to help countless other people who I otherwise never would have been able to help. My perspective changed, I began to change, and I would slowly grow to trust God more. I would go on to work the 12 steps multiple times and become a sponsor myself to several other recovering addicts. While I lived in Kentucky, I performed a lot of service work for the recovery community involving public relations work and web design. Through helping others, I became less self-centered and more altruistic. My relationships improved too. Over the course of time, I became slower to anger and to get frustrated when faced with adversity and more willing to listen to others. The day for me to leave Kentucky would eventually arrive. I was still single and still had massive amounts of debt, but I was not alone. I had been given a new lease on life. It took me years to understand it and sign it, so to speak, and I was looking to the next stage of my life with anticipation rather than dread and desperation. It had always been a dream of mine to live in a foreign country for a long time and learn a completely new language and culture. I had already mastered the Spanish language and carried a Ph.D. in it, but I wanted to do something extremely challenging and adventurous, even crazy. Thus, I decided to move to China and teach at a high school. Lost dreams were awakening, and new possibilities were arising.

Today, I still live in China, and I still teach high school students. Life is not always easy, but every day is an adventure. Even as a linguist, I find Mandarin Chinese extraordinarily difficult to master, and at times, the culture can be even more difficult to understand. Being a high school teacher in China, just as it is anywhere else, is hard work, but my students are a lot of fun, and I am living the dream. Simply moving to the other side of the planet did not fix me or cure my addiction; thus, I still must maintain my recovery to ensure that I stay clean, and part of that process is helping the addict who still suffers. Because God spared my life 15 years ago, I have been given the opportunity, not only to help recovering addicts in the United States, but to help them in Mainland China and Hong Kong and to reach out to those in other Asian countries during my travels. I delight in having been able to teach the hundreds of college students I taught in the United States and the hundreds of high school students I have taught in China, all because I did not die in my bathroom in Austin. I acknowledge that I have not always been a perfect educator, but if I have had at least some positive influence on those students, then my life has more meaning than I could have ever anticipated since that day I woke up in the intensive care unit long ago. At the present time, I have paid off 75% of my student loan debt thanks to my job as a foreign teacher with a Ph.D. in China. I still have debt, I own no stocks or property, and I have no retirement funds to speak of, but I am much richer than I could have ever imagined. Still, I am not married, and I am not getting any younger, but I have a good social life and I date often. That is more than I can say than for those days when I was wasted out of my mind or just moping around with my head hanging. To be honest, I am grateful that I never got married when I was younger, because I would have only contaminated another person's life with my debt and dysfunction and perhaps passed it on to offspring. Today, I get high every day, and I do not take a single drink or do a single drug. I wake up every morning clean and fully experience all that life has to offer, and that includes all the joy and happiness and all the pain and agony too. I cannot claim to know exactly why I did not die on Christmas Day in 2004 or why the conditions or events leading up to my near death happened to me in the first place. Perhaps, I will never know. Once, while I was at a 12-step meeting in Kentucky, a fellow addict got tired of hearing me complaining about how bad my life was. So, after the meeting, he walked up to me, put his hand on my shoulder and said with a thick eastern Kentucky accent,

"Dave, God didn't wash you up on the beach just so He could beat your ass!"

As hilarious as that statement was, I took it to heart, and it has always stuck with me. Why would my life be spared in such dramatic fashion only for me to stay miserable forever? The more I pondered those words, the more I realized that I needed to embrace gratitude and trust in Divine Providence. Please do not mistake this story for a religious tract. Religion never helped me to stop using drugs and to have a better life, but I strongly believe that a Higher Power greater than myself did. I have sat in 12-step recovery meetings with people of all races, all walks of life, and all faiths, including agnostics and atheists. We all share a common story, and that story is one of addiction and recovery. My story is no better or no more important than any of theirs. We cannot recover and make it through this life alone, nor should we. We all need each other, for an addict alone is in bad company.

(BIO): *Still in China, here I am, 15 years later, and I am still recovering from that experience in Austin, TX. I do not have everything I want, but I have everything I need, and I have my health. I am still a work in progress, and I am still writing my story. If I find myself lying on my death bed tomorrow looking back at my life, I will not exactly be looking at a masterpiece, but I can be at peace knowing that I tried to use my second chance at life as best I could to help others. Today, I am not alone. In fact, I do not believe that I was ever alone, not even when I almost perished in my bathtub in Texas. If you are reading this story right now and are suffering from addiction, know that help is available. You are not alone, you are loved, and you are worthy of recovery. There is hope. Help is available, and recovery is possible if you pursue it. Your life matters, it is worth living, and it has a purpose. I am infinitely grateful that I lived to tell my story here. If the reading of it can save just one person's life, then it was worth living through and surviving every part of it. Thanks for letting me share.*

CHAPTER 18:

CHRONIC OBSTRUCTIVE PULMONARY DISORDER, AND MORE – LEWY BODY DEMENTIA
CORA'S STORY

The first question I always get asked is, "Are you still smoking?" or, "When did you quit smoking?" Sorry (not really), I never started. I did grow up in rural Graham County, NC; all our heat came from a wood stove, and I was around second-hand smoke all my life. According to some doctors, those factors, and maybe a touch of genetics, are probable contributors.

An older commercial for COPD that started with the elephant sitting on the chest were right on target. And another way they portrayed the reality of COPD was when the woman walked down the street and the elephant, although no longer on her chest, was right there with her. I love the little 'brush away' move she made with her hand against his trunk, but the truth is, that is all one can do, push it to the side for a while, he's still right there with you.

For example, a few years ago, in the Red River Gorge in eastern Kentucky, Basil and I walked the trail from a parking lot to Chimney Rock. Not a difficult trail at all, but the elephant kept his place, close by, but behaving himself. However, after we were down at the overlook, 'Mr. Pachyderm' decided to make himself a little more known, and it turned into a terrible walk for me back to the car. It took me some time to get over the subsequent pneumonia.

Fortunately, medicine has come a long way since I was a kid. I know others may have felt I shirked on my chores when I was younger, especially ones outside, maybe even faking, but I didn't; sometimes I just felt like I was smothering. I guess it affected other areas of my body too. One of my ears drained a lot, and it seemed like I had a persistent infection until I was twelve years old. Those infections led to severe hearing loss. I was never allowed to go swimming as a child either because of my "constant cold."

I moved to Maryland when I was eighteen. I knew I had these breathing problems, and was regularly under a doctor's care, but it was never mentioned that asthma might be a part of the picture. When I was in my mid-20s, I took my son to his pediatrician for a normal follow-up visit, and the doctor, because of my wheezing, asked how long I had had asthma. I said I didn't know I had it, and he told me I needed to get it taken care of. I wonder sometimes how much better my system might be now if I had been diagnosed and treated for asthma at an earlier age, anything to help that being smothered feeling.

Even with all the treatments available now, I still feel like I am smothering sometimes, and I'm constantly wheezing or coughing. The coughing embarrasses me, although it shouldn't; that's how I get the junk out of my lungs. I guess you could say, I'm just not allowed to suffer in silence. Changes in temperature, and dampness, bother me a lot, shut down my system. In March of 2009 Basil and I went to the University of Minnesota, Crookston, where they were performing his play about a troubled Vietnam Veteran, *Starkle, Starkle Little Twink*. We arrived in a major snowstorm and freezing temperatures. There was a good turnout for the play, but in retrospect, it probably wouldn't have hurt to have had one less person in the audience. That trip nearly did me in. When we got back home I had a lung infection for a long time.

Something that bothers me is that the bacteria in my lungs build up resistance to the antibiotics; once I'm given one, the doctor has to wait ninety days before she can re-prescribe that particular one again. And I'm being told that each time I use them they are becoming less and less effective.

I would like to go outside on hot days and enjoy a really long walk in the woods, or a swim, or even perhaps a picnic in the woods, but I really shouldn't. I'd better stick to books. It used to be a bit depressing, almost embarrassing, trying to figure out a way to avoid explaining why I didn't want to take a long walk, or go outside on a hot day, or go to a concert. I guess I could have just come out and said "I have COPD," but I have always been a rather private person and I just didn't always feel like I wanted to share that information.

So, who am I now? Well, the older I get, of course, the worse it gets. I know it has got to be an aggravation to others when I have to change plans because of what's going on with me at the time. I know and accept that. But I still want to do as much as I can; I can't just give up; I just have to respect my limitations. Some of my limitations I put on myself based on how my lungs are behaving; some come from listening to my doctor; things like avoiding large crowds and making sure I always take my prescriptions and get my flu shots.

Concerning advice to others, all I can say is, if times are tough, keep going; you can't quit. You may have some limitations, but you can still enjoy life. And follow your doctor's advice. Realize that there may be things going on with someone that you can't see that may be contributing to why that person seems detached, or maybe even a bit anti-social.

Along with faithfully taking my prescribed medicines, the best thing for me to do sometimes is to relax, read. But the panic can about overwhelm when it feels like the elephant is starting to sit on my chest again. Perhaps the most accurate statement in the world is, "when you can't breathe, nothing else matters."

(Compiler's note) She really is a private person, but I convinced her that her COPD story would help others understand what this inner, subjective wounding is like.

Now, to the "and More" addition to the story. About three years ago, as I was walking across the room in my pulmonologist's office, he said to me he noticed something about my gait that raised concerns for him. He told me to check with my primary doctor who arranged for some tests that he said showed the possibility of Parkinson's disease and Lewy Body Dementia, and referred me to a Neurologist. I took the news of these possibilities rather hard, as I was already concerned over my memory at times, and also was having occasional hallucinations. Since then, my diagnosis is considered closer to Lewy Body Dementia than Parkinson's.

It didn't take too long for my attitude to become more positive as I have tried to be optimistic throughout my life, but it was also difficult fighting increasing fatigue and a decrease in mobility. A side effect of one of the medicines for Parkinson's is hallucinations, and I started to have an increase in them, so I requested my doctor to take me off it. The next medicine he put me on caused a lot of nausea, and I was sleeping more than usual, so I asked him what the medicines were designed for. Would they reverse the disease? He told me that they would not reverse, but rather slow down progression. My thoughts were, *why take this medicine to slow it down if I'm going to feel this bad all the time*, so I told the doctor I wanted to discontinue taking them. I found, and find, it much easier to face this difficult time in my life when I'm not burdened with grogginess and nausea.

I wanted to move back to North Carolina to be closer to family in Robbinsville, so Basil and I started spending quite a bit of time on Zillow looking for houses in Graham, Cherokee, Macon, and Clay counties. We made some trips in 2020 to just look over the areas and addresses, masked of course, as we saw COVID-19 raising its ugly head. On a visit in late August a realtor showed us a place we thought we might like, at the end of a road halfway up a mountain. Upon examination, we had some doubts about the place, and then Sherry told us that there was another place she'd like to show us that had just come on the market that morning. We looked at it and immediately decided to put earnest money down before someone else did. Things went through okay and in September 2020 we moved to where we have a beautiful view of Lake Chatuge out of our sunroom.

Basil had to do most of the preparation for the move, and settling in afterwards, and to this day he does the cooking, housekeeping, and assists me in areas where I need help with mobility, etc. Sometimes I have a little confusion about where things are located in the house and need to be reminded. It's challenging for me to realize that from being an independent, self-sufficient woman for most of my life, I now have to depend on assistance to do some of the most basic tasks of living.

For example, Basil has to put my socks, etc. on for me. I can no longer drive, and I used to love driving. (Of course, the up side of this is there will be no more speeding tickets.) But there is a certain dignity that one loses when you have to depend on others to do things for you that you used to be able to easily accomplish. However, Basil and I spend at least an hour or two every morning drinking coffee, talking, and enjoying our cats and the view of Lake Chatuge.

Of course with COVID-19 a concern, visiting with family in a nearby county was on hold for a while. Basil cooked a full 2020 Thanksgiving dinner (and with just us two, and a thirteen pound turkey, etc. we were able to enjoy leftovers for the next few days.) And the most difficult thing recently is I lost my younger sister (who for years I had called daily) and due to COVID and my health we felt we could not go to the funeral and graveside services.

We also try to find and enjoy humor where and when we can. One story we both have told to some family and friends (and my doctor) is about the morning not too long ago when I woke Basil up around 7 a.m. and told him I needed his help. In either a dream or hallucination, I don't know which, my younger sister who recently died was there and said that Basil was missing. So I awakened him and told him that he needed to help us find him. He responded that he was right there in the bed, and I told him, "I know, and you need to get up and help me and Midd find you."

Something else that is somewhat amusing (maybe.) Little Bit sleeps cuddled up in Basil's arm nightly. But does she get there from the foot of the bed, or his side? Of course not! She comes to my side of the bed, climbs up and over me, sometimes even over my head, and then settles down with him. As Rodney Dangerfield once said, "I don't get no respect." But on the other hand, Scooter sometimes comes up behind me and puts his paws on my shoulders and peers over.

I guess the most difficult thing (which I alluded to earlier) is the lack of dignity one feels with this illness. Sometimes I feel just so tired, and it really bothers me that I can't help more around the house. And sometimes I feel like a little kid having to have someone else put on shirts and pants and tuck in a napkin before I eat. And I'm also tired of asking what day it is, and starting a sentence and forgetting halfway through where I was going with it.

A good note. In early 2021 my new family physician in Hayesville wanted to start me on a new medication. I have been taking it for several months now and it helps. She also prescribed physical therapy, and we have been fortunate in that regards also. The VA prescribed physical therapy for Basil's back, shoulder, and knee issues and ran it through the community services, and the facility has worked with us in scheduling our visits concurrently, which is nice, considering it is a 50 mile round trip twice a week.

More recently, since a trip to the ER for a possible TIA, Home Health Services has been approved by Medicare for some short-term in home treatment and physical/occupational therapy which has also been a stress reliever.

So who am I now? I am more aware of the fragility of life. I'm appreciative of my husband and our babies (Scooter and Little Bit), and I know that no matter what, I have a beautiful view which makes it easier to enjoy each day. We are blessed in so many ways.

(BIO:) I am Cora Larson Clark, and retired from mortgage banking after 40 years in the DC area in order to move to the Chattanooga, Tennessee area (Ooltewah) to be closer to my son and his family who reside in northern GA. Basil and I first connected in late 2008 through eHarmony and met in person early 2009. We married in 2011 and enjoy retirement life together.

Basil's note: A backstory. Cora and I connected through eHarmony (more on that in Chapter 45: "A Truly Life-Changing Climb") and before we met in person, during one of our phone conversations Cora was telling me about when her husband Darwin died, and the pain and loneliness and helplessness she experienced afterwards, and I had the strongest feeling sweep over me that I never wanted her to feel that again, that I wanted to be there for her, no matter what. My biggest fear is to fall short in meeting Cora's needs. There are times when it is difficult being on call 24/7, and even some nights having flashbacks to the sense of being on constant watchful guard in Vietnam, but I have never felt more in my life that I'm where I'm supposed to be, doing what I'm supposed to do.

CHAPTER 19:

TNBC – I WOULD FIGHT AND WIN
DAWN IRIZARRY

Over two years ago I fell and soon after got a lump in my breast. Then it got bigger and bigger until it hurt and I finally went to the Emergency Room because I was in a lot of pain. Upon examination there, I was referred to a primary care physician who further referred me to a surgeon who did biopsies.

So, anyway, I was fifty-five when I was hit with news that I was diagnosed with breast cancer. There are different types, HR+ being the most common, accounting for more than 70% of breast cancer cases. This type can usually be treated with hormone therapies. HER2+ is a more advanced cancer where the tumors are more aggressive. This is generally treated in multiple ways, including chemotherapy, but it does not respond to hormonal therapy.

And then, there is Triple Negative Breast Cancer, known as TNBC. These tumors can be very aggressive, and are usually treated with a combination of surgery, radiation, and chemotherapy. TNBC also does not respond to hormonal therapy. The doctor who did the biopsy confirmed it was TNBC and I was sent to the oncologist.

Initially I was in shock; after all, this is life changing news, but then I told my doctor I wanted an immediate plan of action. Of course I was told that TNBC is very aggressive and that the drugs used to treat it are super strong. However, I just felt secure in my faith in God, and felt a deep sense, with no doubt in my mind, that I would fight and win.

That doesn't take away from the fact that after initial shock I was angry. There was a normal anger over the fact that I had cancer, but it is important to point out that there is a chemo anger triggered by the chemicals. So I was doubly angry and pretty much growled at everyone. There was also anxiety, which I discovered was two-fold; part was due to my situation, but again, part of it was also a side effect of chemo. I guess this could be labeled chemo anxiety.

Up until my diagnosis I had been a massage therapist. I had to stop working because the constant repetitive motion of massaging was aggravating it and causing even more pain. My radiation oncologist also told me to stop working. As it turned out, the chemotherapy was so debilitating that I couldn't have worked anyway. I was very weak and used a walker 2 weeks a month after each chemo treatment. I was treated every 21 days with carboplatin and taxotere.

In spite of my various reactions, I did not wonder, "Who am I now?" I know who I am. That has not changed. My firm foundation is the Lord. Along with my faith and sense of knowing I would beat this, other things that have helped me are plenty of rest, crying, and belonging to a TNBC Support group. I also received encouragement to go back to doing normal everyday things. I found that as I was in a more normal routine, life seemed more normal. This also included lots of praying for peace, but this was a part of my daily routine even before the diagnosis and treatment.

Other than having to stop working as a massage therapist, I really don't think other aspects of me changed. I was very transparent about my journey and others have told me that it helped them with their perspective of things in their lives.

All that being said, during the process, you realize that there is truth to the idea that you've got to walk the lonesome valley by yourself. I had times of feeling loneliness, even abandonment, realizing now that it is very hard to identify with someone going through something you have no experience with. And I have also come to the realization that feeling anger, and even resentment, over this is misdirected, and not at all beneficial.

(BIO:) Dawn Irizarry. I was born in Bronx, NY, in 1963, am of Irish and Puerto Rican descent, and have an adult son. I have worked since age twelve at babysitting, a summer youth program, a Hallmark store, pharmacy, grocery, and then a secretary for many years until I moved to Georgia and went back to school to become a massage therapist. I am not working now.

Since my bout with cancer I have concluded that I NEVER want to do that again!

CHAPTER 20:

EXPERIENCING THE POWER OF PRAYER
DANIEL CLARK

Panama was great! In March 2017 my wife Marsha and I flew to Atlanta and then on down to Panama City to arrive a day early so we could relax before the tour started. Among the things we got to enjoy were visiting Panama Viejo (Old Panama), visiting the Canal Museum, and just enjoying views of the Pacific Ocean. Further Panama Cruise Itinerary included crossing the isthmus to Colon, a boat ride on Gatun Lake, viewing the Atlantic Ocean, strolling down rainforest pathways and through butterfly gardens, engaging in some dancing, fine dining, and shopping for handicrafts. We visited the Embera Tribal Village to see their culture; the Gamboa Rainforest Resort just north of the Continental Divide, and the Playa Bonita Resort located on the Pacific Ocean was spectacular.

We met a woman from Omaha who was visiting family; she mentioned that her husband was on oxygen, so she had told him that he should not come along because if anything happened to him she was concerned about the Panama medical facilities. At the time, we did not realize how much we would reflect on her statement later on.

So on March 22nd, just five days after arriving back home in Sterling, Colorado, at the ripe old age of 62, sometime between 7 to 8 a.m., I was lying in bed listening to the sounds of Marsha getting ready to go to the Logan County Visitor Info Center where she volunteered when I felt like there was an explosion in my chest and then severe pain ran down my right side. I instantly knew I had to get to the hospital, so I called out to Marsha, and after she came in she immediately called 911. The gurney was too wide for the hall to the bedroom, so they had to walk me out to where it was, in the living room. By the time I was taken the six blocks to the Sterling Regional MedCenter Emergency Room I no longer had any feeling in my lower right leg. I didn't find out until later it was an Inner Aorta Tear, with a 30 % survival rate. I don't remember a lot at emergency room. I do remember heading out to the Flight For Life helicopter and someone came out and said, "You can't take him to Northern Colorado in Greeley; they just had an emergency come in! By the time they got me back into the hospital they found that UCHealth in Aurora CO could take me. I remember taking off in the helicopter and then the next thing I can recall is the next morning lying in ICU, with Marsha by my bedside. While I was out of it, the following occurred: I arrived at UCHealth, and underwent 7 and 1/2 hours of surgery which included two grafts, one stint and a new heart valve.

My pastor and his wife drove down from Sterling; he drove his vehicle, and his wife drove Marsha's car so that Marsha would have transportation at the hospital. Also, my sister Paula spent a lot of time with Marsha during that time period. Paula told me later that Marsha first texted her about the aorta tear and that I was being flown to Greeley. She (Paula) was supposed to be taking care of two of her grandchildren, but told her daughter-in-law she needed to get to Greeley (from Littleton where she lived.) Paula said my brother-in-law Keith was driving in the far left northbound on I-25 when Marsha called her and said not to go to Greeley as they were sending me to Denver instead. At that time they were right at the exit they needed to use to go to the hospital so Keith just cut across all lanes of traffic to get off. I wouldn't be surprised if he motivated a few people to spout some choice words, but I am glad it worked out all right. Paula told me that as it turned out, they were at the hospital before the helicopter even left Sterling.

Paula and I have always been real close, and she told me that while she was waiting she had this oxymoronic thought, "Dan, if you die, I'm going to kill you!" What can I say, she's my sister. She also said she remained terrified until she knew I was in surgery, and then calmness took over as she believed and trusted that the doctors were doing everything they could to save me.

Over a 6 to 8 month period of follow up visits with Dr. Reece, the surgeon who operated on me, I heard more than once, "I can't believe you're the same person I operated on; you are doing so well!"

I know at least once I responded, "Well, I had a great surgeon and there were a lot of people praying for me." And he said that I also had a surgeon praying for me. In that same 6 to 8 month period he told me some things that I wouldn't have known otherwise. When the folks at the emergency room in Sterling called up to see if UCHealth could handle my case they were told "yes". However, by the time I arrived, UCHealth had three other emergencies come in and that is how I ended up with the surgeon I did as he was 4th down the list on call that morning. They also had a patient coming in with a similar condition, and had a room prepared in case surgery was needed. When I came in, the doctors thought my situation was a higher priority and used the already-prepared room, which saved on prep time.

For the first four days my thinking process was real slow, it just took a while for things to register. However, the day after the surgery when it became clear that I was doing well and would live to tell the tale, Paula and Marsha started to tease me about a variety of things. I was on a liquid diet, and on Thursdays some volunteers brought cookies and tea to all the rooms. My lovely wife and sister made it a point to vocally enjoy the treats that I was not allowed to have. There was laughter all around, which was good, except physically, sometimes it also caused pain when I laughed too hard. On a serious note, I think we might have mentioned the fact we were glad that the inner aorta tear did not occur while we were on the Panama vacation.

On another grateful note, at the time of this event, my dad was 95 (he's 99 now), and lived a block from Marsha and I. Of course I was at his house daily, and we took him shopping or wherever he needed to go. Paula visited every couple weeks, but wanted to be with me at the hospital, so our youngest brother, Joe, came in from Missouri to stay with Dad until we got back home and Marsha was able to settle into a dual-caregiver role.

About my 4th day in the hospital I was given a pacemaker as my heart was starting the beat but it wasn't completing functions to the lower chamber, and on March 30th, eight days after entering UCHealth, I was released home where after approximately a month I started extended rehabilitation. Further checkups have revealed that I have a dissection which is common after this type of surgery. At some point, if it gets worse, they will have to go back in and take care of this problem.

Also, Dr. Reece talked with me about family history, and asked, "Have your siblings been checked?" Until then, I didn't realize that this was genetic. As it turned out, my sister Paula had not ever been tested for this, she discovered that she does have some issues, and is now being examined every year. Since she wouldn't have known of her problem if my situation hadn't happened, she tells me I took one for the team.

One of my brothers-in-law had serious medical issues some twenty years or more ago and he has told me that he often thinks, well, I'm enjoying time I didn't think I'd have. I guess, in those regards, my being in the 30% of people who survive inner aorta tear means 70% don't make it. I have always felt spiritually that I'm ready to depart this life whenever God calls for me, so I presume there are still some things left for me to do here.

Marsha and I have always enjoyed time with our nephews and nieces, attending ball games and other activities of the ones nearby, as we can. We also have many in other locations we don't get to see so much. We found out later that when people were notified of my situation they prayed. I am so glad that they still have me around as living proof of the power of their prayers. And I believe I appreciate even more the times we spend with everyone now.

I am thankful that my sister Paula now knows of her heart problems and hopefully will not have to experience everything I did because of the early discovery. And I am especially grateful for the opportunity God has given me to spend more time with my spouse. We realize more than ever before just how quickly things can change.

(BIO:) Dan lives in Sterling, Colorado and is retired from Accounting/Bookkeeping positions in Logan County, Colorado. He and Marsha enjoy visiting nephews and nieces, playing games with them, and watching their school and community sports activities.

They also enjoy occasional dog sitting for a couple of their friends and family.

Dan also lives three houses away from his (our) dad (age 99, January 2021), checks in on him frequently, assists where needed, and takes him shopping and to his (fortunately, not so frequent) doctor appointments.

(Compiler's Note) During the time period I was working on final proofing of this anthology manuscript, our dad, Ralph Clark, had a stroke and passed away.

CHAPTER 21:

A PINNACLE MOMENT
DAVID CYRULIK

So when I first arrived at my unit in Vietnam there was a conversation that went something like this: Mike Mitchell, also known as Stache because of his large mustache, asked "So, what's your name?" I said "David Cyrulik". He said it sounds "Psychedelic", and that became my nickname. Later on, it was shortened to Psycho. That was not a pinnacle moment, but does explain my Viet Nam nickname of Psycho.

I was assigned to Delta Company, 1/12th Cavalry, 1st Air Cavalry Division in July 1968 to the Third Platoon, second squad and was given the option to walk point or carry the M79 (grenade launcher). I chose the latter. After a few months, I became the squad's RTO (radio telephone operator) where I carried roughly 75-80 lbs. of equipment in addition to 23 more lbs. of radio (PRC-25).

In December 1968, the Third Platoons lieutenant asked me to be his RTO because he did not trust anyone else. He was afraid of being fragged so I accepted the "position". In February or March 1969, I became the Company Commander's RTO. This was a promotion to E-5 which meant I was in charge of all company radios and communication with all platoons in the company. During my last 2 1/2 months in Nam, I went back to the 3rd Platoon until my departure home in July, 1969.

During my first six months Delta Company had experienced many enemy engagements. We were up in I Corps, and then sometime in October moved down to II corps for the upcoming Tet Offensive. We experienced losses; both killed in action (KIA) and wounded (WIA). Even though I had some close calls, these did not seem personal to me until January 1st, 1969 which changed everything, what I guess you could call my rude awakening.

Supposedly there was a New Year's Day Truce in effect, something I guess higher-ups in our government declare in order to make war to seem a bit more civilized. For American forces that meant that we were not to fire upon or engage in of hostile action unless it was initiated by the enemy forces first. I'm not sure how the truce was interpreted by the other side.

The night of December 31st personnel from around the company perimeter, especially the 3rd platoon sector, reported hearing throughout the night what sounded like people climbing trees. The Listening Post personnel set out earlier in the evening were whispering into the radio that it sounded like they were surrounded with these sounds.

As I said, we were supposedly in a truce period and I believe that is what entered into the Commanding Officer's (CO) decision not to have a Mad Minute. Under "normal" circumstances, with the sounds of movement like the ones occurring, at daybreak the Listening Posts would be called in and then everyone around the perimeter would take position in their foxholes and open fire into the area in front of them with whatever weapon they were assigned. But, again, we were in a truce, under orders from the highest command levels to not fire first.

When daylight finally came, the nighttime listening post personnel were replaced by the daytime observation posts who would keep watch as everyone else fixed C-Ration breakfasts and prepared to move out through the jungle to our next destination. As this exchange was taking place I was returning from the Company RTO position when all of a sudden all hell broke loose. As the bulk of night movement was reported from the 3rd platoon sector that was also where the brunt of the attack occurred.

From my location in the center of the third platoon's position I immediately saw one man nicknamed Jose take shrapnel in the chest from mines hanging from the trees. Jose and I came into the third platoon as replacements so we were very close.

A moment later, a new guy who had come out to our location by way of helicopter just the night before, came running back in from where he had been out picking up a claymore mine. He threw himself toward a foxhole but overshot his trajectory and landed at least a couple feet behind it. He was injured and later medevac'd, but when he returned to the unit weeks later I found out his name was Ramon Ramoz (Chapter 10.)

Also a medic had arrived in country in December and become a close friend. His name was Kevin, but was affectionately known as Fat Medic. I had been helping him adjust to the platoon, and life in the jungle in Vietnam. Well, I saw him fall to the ground and I rushed to him where I was joined by another medic and a couple other men, including Basil Clark (Anthology compiler.)

Several minutes passed as we were assisting the medic working on Kevin when a machine gun and small arms opened fire on our position. The lieutenant was in the rear with a dental problem, so it was up to me to keep the CO informed of the situation. So along with everyone else I took cover with my radio. I also started to fire back in the direction of the machine gun, although all I could see was machine gun flashes. At one point I could hear the bullets snapping above my head like a cracking whip and saw them hitting the nearby dirt around me.

After I emptied a few magazines I looked towards Kevin and he was reaching out to me as he was gasping for his last breath of air. Even though my main focus was on immediate survival, it was also the moment of that rude awakening; this became very personal, there is someone out there deliberately trying to kill me and my buddies!

Things slowed down after what seemed like forever and looking around I could see that Kevin was slumped slightly different than when I left, and did not appear to be moving. I left my foxhole and rushed to where he was and was again joined by the medic and a couple others who had been working on him before the machine gun bursts in our direction. Kevin was dead; it looked like a bullet through the heart may have been what killed him. A few days later the CO asked me if someone in the Company did not like Kevin because he died from M16 bullets along with shrapnel. But he was to new to make any enemies who would want to harm him.

The following questions started through my mind, and have persisted for years. Why did I go back to my radio and foxhole without first making sure Kevin was protected? Why didn't I insure he was fully out of danger's way, drag him to safety? Why did I think of my own survival? I could have done more. Why didn't I? I didn't do enough.

When I was drafted and went to Vietnam, I went about thinking that it was okay because I would be helping others. Later I felt like nothing good had come of my time there; that it was all a waste of time and man power.

I can't shake the events of January 1st, 1969; they are always in the back of my mind. The triggers are everywhere, be they sights, sounds, some TV show, whatever. I have tinnitus which has been attributed to not only my exposure to loud noise, explosions and the like, but also because of my position as RTO. I had the squelch of the PRC-25 handset next to my ear. Coincidentally, my tinnitus noise is the same as that of the PRC-25.

After the loss of Kevin and Jose, I looked forward to coming in home in six months, and mistakenly believed that once back home there would be no more issues, that Vietnam and everything that accompanied it would become things of the past.

Something that was kind of stupid on my part was that I didn't wear my ID dog tags, as I believed that they were only used for identification purposes if you were killed, and I was trying to be positive in my thinking. That belief was maintained in large part because my girlfriend, her mother and my mother prayed for me every night and said they believed God would not allow me to die over there. That thought kept me going, although after watching Kevin and Jose die, sometimes I had a difficult time believing it.

After I left Vietnam I had six months left in service and spent them at Ft. Lewis, WA, as an Instructor with the Basic Combat Training Group, on both the Infiltration Course and the Infantry Tactical Training Course. I was honorably discharged from the military in January 1970 and returned to work with Niagara Mohawk Power Company in the Engineering Department, where I had been employed prior to my military service.

I mentioned my girlfriend. Kathy and I met in high school. We married in June 1971 in our hometown, Buffalo, NY. Due to job relocation, we moved to Syracuse, NY, where we resided for 35 years before moving to Sunset Beach, North Carolina.

Kathy has been the most positive aspect of my moving on in life. Without her, I really don't know where I would be right now. She helped me to focus on my work, home projects, and hobbies.

I joined the North/South Skirmish Association which really gave me a sense of the camaraderie and brotherhood that I had been looking for since leaving my unit in Vietnam. I am one of the founding members/officers of the VVA (Vietnam Veterans of America) in Syracuse, NY.

I know that over the years a couple other negative aspects of my experiences in Vietnam were that I didn't trust others as much as I think I did before the war, and I found myself sometimes feeling resentment toward some who hadn't served. I lost a sense of that feeling of closeness with others, discovered that you could be in a crowd of over a hundred people and still feel all alone. I guess different people react differently, but I found a certain refuge in self-isolation. I think that for many people currently, COVID-19 creates similar feelings of isolation and loss and lack of camaraderie.

To this day, I continue with counseling services provided by the VA to help me to cope with my struggles.

Having said all that, the war is one of those experiences where I wouldn't trade what I learned about myself, life, and other people, but there is no way I would ever want to do it again.

And most recently, during the storming of the United States Capitol Building, I had flashbacks to the war and all the confusion and chaos that were a part of it.

Overall, aided by my wife, I think I have been able to see things in a bigger picture, and realize that compared to many others, I have had a reasonably healthy life experience. I have met some of the men I served with, and feel just as close to them now as when I left Vietnam over fifty years ago. And yet there are still so many ways that those fifty years ago seem like yesterday.

(BIO:) *David and Kathy Cyrulik are retired and live in Sunset Beach, North Carolina.*

CHAPTER 22:

I AM THANKFUL FOR ... LIFE
JEREMIAH BRYANT

At the age of 52, on January 14, 2016, my heart decided it wanted to quit functioning. About 3:00 that evening my fifteen-year-old son Jeremiah Chase and I were outside cleaning in my woodshop. After a while we went into the house and at 5:00 pm my wife, Lesa, and Chase, began watching a documentary on the "Old West." At the time my chest had no pain, but it felt like a heavy weight was sitting on it. Chase kept asking me if I was all right and I kept telling him I would be okay. From 5:00 to 7:30 pm my chest kept that heavy sensation but it was slowly feeling better. At 7:30 my wife decided to go rest, so I told my son to set up a game and we would play awhile. I remember going into his room and him giving me a remote and then I sat down, and suddenly that heavy feeling in my chest returned. At that moment a sign above our local Hardee's restaurant came to mind, one that read "Signs of a Heart Attack" are not this obvious. I realized then what was happening, so I stood up and told Chase I had to go to the hospital. He asked me, "Do you want me to go with you?" and I remember saying, "You make your own mind up; I have to leave now." I turned, went to our bedroom, told my wife I was having a heart attack, and that I was going to the hospital. That moment, started a whirlwind of adventure for the next several days that still continues in many ways.

During the two and a half hours of my heart attack, I was concerned, but not really afraid. I just kept telling myself that the feeling would go away. It had happened before but not near to this extent. I thought that as long as there was no pain in my chest that I was not in any danger. It was while I was driving to the hospital that I really started getting worried. I had always told my family that if something major happened to take me to Lexington, but on this night when my wife asked where we were going, I asked her where we should go. She suggested calling the local hospital to see if they were busy or not. When she called, they responded that they were not busy.

It was decision time and that was actually scary. It was about that time that I started analyzing how I was feeling and what was really happening. I began to get nervous, I felt my heart begin to race, I started to sweat, but no pain, so even though I still thought I was okay, fear was starting to build inside me. Questions of what may happen next were rolling through my mind. I did not have a will. I had not made arrangements should I die. I was driving at a fast pace and the urgency of getting to the hospital was growing. I guess at a subconscious level my body knew what was happening; I honestly don't know. The drive on Highway 15 South is the one section that I suddenly realized that I couldn't remember a lot about. I recalled the turn onto the highway, the turn at a red light, and then being at the hospital. I still had no pain but the pressure in my chest was smothering me badly.

As I went in the Emergency Room, there was a lady straightening up the chairs in the waiting room. At this point, my mind knew I was in trouble physically. I asked the lady who was in charge, and she responded she was and asked what was wrong. I immediately told her I thought I was having a heart attack. I remember her face vividly changing from questioning to of immediate concern. She about ran past me to the check in window. I began taking all of my stuff out of my pockets, placed them in my hat, and then gave them to Chase who was standing next to me. I sat down and began rocking back and forth. Some man was in the corner watching me. I was scared at this point. I knew, even without the chest pain, that I was in trouble. I could hear Lesa answering questions at the window and then the door to the emergency examining room opened, and a familiar face came through and said "Mr. Bryant, come on back." The next part of my wonderful journey began.

One of my students who had graduated from our nursing program called me back to the emergency room and Lesa went back with me. We were asked some basic questions and then an EKG was done. I remember the female doctor coming in and softly saying that my heart rhythm had come back suspicious and they were going to give me a Nitroglycerin pill and blood thinner. I took the medicine and instantly the world went black. The next part of my adventure lasted about three minutes. I have no recollection, but Lesa told me they asked her if I suffered seizures and she told them no. Then they asked her to leave. From that point on she had no idea of what was going on behind the curtain. Later we found out they were doing CPR and using paddles to restart my heart. Just this year, three years after the life-changing event, we found out they had called the death team for me. At that point God showed mercy and granted me some extra time.

Many people report a near-death experience, some an out of body experience. I cannot say I experienced any of those things. I recall taking the medicine and then waking up feeling people's hands on me begging me to lie down, which I adamantly did not wish to do. I had the dry heaves; I could hear the noise so loud in my ears, but nothing would come up. Voices kept telling me to lie down and breathe, which I did, and stayed focused on that for some time. I did manage to open my eyes once and saw a young blonde nurse over me, her face flushed red, eyes wide open, and a smile on her face as her head bounced up and down as she encouraged me to breathe. I closed my eyes and continued breathing as I had been instructed years earlier in Karate classes.

The memory of dying at the ARH Hospital in Jackson, Kentucky is a constant companion. I am reminded very often of what occurred and the mortality that is us. Even with successful surgery and reassurances from different doctors, I still often get emotional about the situation. There are some TV shows that are far too graphic for me to watch anymore. Any show dealing with heart attacks, open heart surgery, etc., rattles my nerves. I have had to visit the hospital where my surgery occurred for different things. It doesn't bother me too much enroute, but once I get on the hospital grounds a rush of fear and apprehension always attacks me. There is typically a flood of memories from my stay there, but always the day that I was released, Friday January 22, 2016. This day is easy to remember.

After they had me settled down, I was still maintaining the

breathing routine learned from my Karate lesson days. A doctor came to my bedside and explained that I had coded for 2-3 minutes (the official report said 3 minutes.) She said that when performing CPR one of the nurses had to hit me really hard and that I might have some bruising on my chest. She added, quite funny I thought, "Jeremiah, I see you know Karate." She pointed to my former student and said, "It was him who hit you, so when you get to feeling better if you want to hit someone, hit him."

My friend and student looked at me and said, "Mr. Bryant, if you want, you can hit me." But of course I would never do that; they were all doing what they were trained to do to save someone's life, and that night it just happened to be mine.

After I was stabilized in ARH in Jackson they called for an air evacuation helicopter to fly me to St. Joseph Hospital in Lexington, Kentucky, about a 90 mile flight. It seemed like such a long wait for the helicopter to arrive, and then upon their arrival I was told that there needed to be a standard in heart monitoring equipment, so they had to disconnect everything the hospital had attached and then hook me up to their own monitoring system for the flight to Lexington. I have a fear of heights, but it turned out the ride did not bother me too much. I think I had decided that if God had wanted me then he could have had me earlier, so the ride would probably be okay; it turned out to be smooth enough. I was told the ride would be 23 minutes, but it seemed a lot longer. I remember the clear sky night, the thumping of the blades, my breathing through the mask, and the helicopter medical team occasionally asking me how I was doing.

As soon as I arrived at St. Joseph Hospital the medical team there quickly did an evaluation which included inserting a pump to help my heart, and then they did an echocardiogram. Within a matter of minutes I knew what I was facing. I asked a nurse what my condition was and she informed me I was looking at open heart surgery with five bypasses. It was Friday morning by the time I had arrived in Lexington and Friday afternoon I was informed I would have the surgery on Monday. They told me several times that surgery would only be performed over the weekend if it was an emergency; that they were waiting for the blood thinner in my system to clear out for accurate monitoring of the thinner used during surgery for precise control over the thickness of my blood.

Saturday was the longest day! I was unable to move because the heart pump was still inside me and my body hurt from having to lie still, but the nurses did a wonderful job of helping and keeping me as safe as they could. I also had many visitors to offer support to me and my family. I don't remember much about Sunday at all although I was aware there were visitors, but for some reason I can't recall anything specific.

Monday I was prepped for surgery early, and I remember just before being rolled out of my room that I told my family that I loved them. About five hours later Lesa was informed I had come through the operation okay and was doing well. By Friday I was ready to be checked out and go home.

The doctors came into the room and explained that I was being checked out. They said they would see me in one month, gave me one bottle of pain pills and told me not to ask for more. I was confused about that conversation but it wasn't impacting me getting better. A huge snowstorm was camped out over Lexington and dumping a lot of snow. I remember the frantic rush of getting checked out, getting me to the vehicle with the snow blowing, and the slow drive to my niece's house in Lexington. A lot happened that week, I feel very thankful to the doctors, the nurses, and all of the staff at the hospital. My family in Lexington let me stay with them and did what they could to help. My body was still in shock. If I touched a finger in water I would go into uncontrollable shakes. That was, and still is, scary. Now, anytime my chest feels different or I have spell of dizziness, I think it is my heart failing or at least getting weaker. I honestly try not to think too much about the incident because it still brings out many fears. However, it also reminds me of my mortality, and the memories give me reason to appreciate life more and more. I know who holds my life in their hands. I also am more thankful now for all of my family and friends.

What I would do, initially, was really not a question that stayed in my mind. I was more concerned with my family; my wife, Lesa, my son Chase, and my 17 year old daughter, Tara LaNene. You see, my dad died of a heart attack at the age of 59 when I was 14; it was like Deja vu, and I didn't want this to happen to my children. But the irony is, at some point prior to the heart attack, I had already resigned myself to death. I felt like the situation I was in seemed really dire. Before my heart attack, I had been feeling depressed to the point where I doubted the love of my family. So now, as people came in to visit me, I told them goodbye because I didn't think I was going to make it out alive. Then a wonderful thing happened. My wife told my nurse what I was saying to everyone. My nurse came in and gave me a military chewing out. I remember her sitting down beside me, telling me that I was not going to die on her watch, that I wanted to live to see my daughter get married, to see my grandkids, and to hold them on my knees. She gave me a really good virtual slap in the face. My attitude immediately changed to wanting to live, just to live and see my family; I didn't want to die and leave them alone. So then question of, "What will I do", was answered. I was going to try to stay alive. That was the focus. I am very thankful to God for my nurse and her military background. A different nurse without her background may not have been able to give me the chewing out that I needed and to place some desire to live back in my heart. I am so very much thankful to God for her.

Before my heart attack, there was a period of time I felt useless. I had a good job, good wife and fine children. However, there was something missing. I still felt very much alone and that no one loved me anymore. I knew it wasn't true; however, my thoughts outweighed the logic my mind drew upon. I just felt my life was over. Maybe it was my body telling my something was wrong with my heart, I don't know. But during my stay at the hospital, so many people came to see me. They came from different counties to check on me. My wife got so many messages, at one point she gave her phone to her niece and asked her to respond to the questions. My family, friends, came to my aid as best they could. They showed me and my family they cared, and that I needed desperately. I hope I can always be grateful to them in return.

There have been some specific things that have helped me heal and discover who I am now. I am very much aware of my mortality and how quickly life can end and eternity can begin. Before January 14, 2016, I had started a hobby of wood turning. When I got home from the hospital I wanted to start working on my lathe again. However, I wasn't able to go out to the wood shop and my wife wouldn't let me bring a lathe in the house; she said it would be too dusty. After my first follow-up appointment with my heart doctor, I gave him something I had made. When he asked if I had made it, I told him I had and that I wanted to start doing it again. I remember, he lifted his coffee cup, said "Get back to it" and then looked out the window. A great load lifted off of my shoulders, mind and soul and I felt free in a special way that I cannot explain.

Since then, I have done some wood work, but it is not as important to me as it once was. I no longer enjoy being in the wood shop for hours alone. I much prefer company than doing anything by myself. Part of that is fear of what may happen if I am by myself, but another part reminds me that time is precious and to use it wisely. Time is given to use to enjoy our friends and families. But more importantly, time is given to use to inspire others to be better than they think can be. Time is a gift for us to set a higher standard, to get people to look up from their own worlds and see the greater world and the importance of our role in it. I am different than what I was before my heart gave out, family times means more to me; I try harder to listen to others as they tell me what is important to them. Time is a gift, and as one of my favorite authors wrote, "Live each day with as few regrets as possible." (Salvatore, R. A.) I try hard for that goal, to live each day better and be a better person and a greater inspiration to others.

I think I have gained new perspective since my experience. Life is a gift. We partially realize our mortality with the knowledge that death will eventually come for us in its own way. But for those that meet death and survive, we are blessed as Hezekiah with additional time. We understand that mortality becomes more prominent in our minds, at least for me, that is the case. When I tell others my adventure, that is what I call it, I remind them that none of us are promised another year, month, day, and hour, minute or second. I often tell people, "I know it is in him that we live and move and have our being". Yes, I definitely know that now. I still take life for granted sometimes, but, I have a constant reminder that I am not promised any time to make things right with my fellow man or God. We should all truly live each of our lives in respect, in hope, in recognition of our Father that holds the universe in his hands, and our soul.

I would like to add that I look forward to enjoying more life and the precious things in this world. I will soon meet my first grandchild. I wish for him a greater and more wonderful walk with the Creator. I hope he does not have to face death to realize how important and precious life truly is. I wish for him a better world and a joyous life, as I do for all of us.

I am very thankful for my wife Lesa, my daughter Tara, son in law Cody, and Chase. I am thankful to all of my family, friends and so many that did not know me but heard and wished blessings on me.

I am thankful for the doctors, nurses, hospital staff, chopper pilot and emergency crew who volunteered to be a part of this journey, and to the hospital chaplain who ran up beside me, gave a quick prayer and told me he would let my family know I was there. And I am especially grateful to the head nurse, who gave me a military chewing out as I was telling everyone goodbye and for telling me I was not going to die on her watch.

Last, I know that when death does come back for me, my soul will be in the hands of a just God. I am thankful to my God who gave me extra time to be with everyone and to continue to be a positive influence to those I meet. I hope, each day, that I can be worthy of these precious extra moments that he has granted me with. I am thankful for the opportunity to share my story. This is the short version. There is so much more to my story than what I have written but this is enough. I hope this may bring some kind of hope, peace and inspiration to anyone who reads it.

Since the first initial writing this, I have had another heart attack. The first one was in January 14, 2016 and the second one was in May

27, 2020. This recent heart failure has again reminded me of how short life is and how important it is for us to spend our time wisely. This last heart attack was very painful, much different than the first. Both of these events have forced me to change many areas of my life. In this document, I focus on the first heart attack and how it impacted not just my life, but many lives. I am thankful for extra time I have been given

(BIO): My dad was a coal miner and my mom was a housewife. My dad passed away in 1978 due to a heart attack and other issues. My mother continued to be with me until 2008 when she passed away. The hills of Eastern Kentucky have been my home for most of my life and I plan on continuing to live here as long as God allows. From 1978 until 1981, I attended Oakdale Christian High School in Jackson, Kentucky. There I met a host of wonderful people and learned so many things. I attribute my love of traveling to my years at Oakdale. Currently I teach computer, fiber optic and drone classes at the local community college. It is a wonderful job and I get to be a positive influence to so many people. I hope my story gives many people courage to continue living after a life altering event. God bless all and my thanks to Basil Clark for the opportunity to share my story.

CHAPTER 23:
A LIFE NOT LIVED FOR OTHERS IS A LIFE WASTED
GARY DeRIGNE

Basil Clark and I served together as infantrymen in Vietnam in 1969, and experienced some things that few people who are civilians will ever really know or understand.

One prime example is the bloody, horrible death of our close friend, Rodney Evans, on July 18, 1969, the day after his 21st birthday. Rod was killed in an ambush that we almost knew for certain was going to happen, but had no way of avoiding, since we were following orders from higher-ups who cared little for our welfare, and were willing to sacrifice our lives for the sake of "body count." (Our option would have been to disobey the direct order to "reconnoiter" the area of the ambush, and face court martial and possible imprisonment or dishonorable discharge from the military.)

Rod died a hero's death, and was later awarded the Medal of Honor for his sacrifice. On July 18, 2019, Basil and I were honored to speak at a memorial service in Rod's home town of Florala, Alabama, on the 50th anniversary of his death, for the benefit of his surviving family and friends from the area.

Rod's final act, smothering an enemy mine with his body, saved me from being killed or severely wounded, and I have carried the survivor's guilt of that ever since. I still wake up with nightmares about it, something I'm assured will happen for the rest of my life. But that example, Rod's willing sacrifice of his own life to save mine, and those of others in our squad, has been a very formative one in my life.

Another incident that Basil and I experienced together occurred on the night of September 18, 1969, exactly two months after Rod's death. Our infantry company, which was only at about 60% strength, was surrounded by a far larger force of North Vietnamese Army infantry, who we later learned were intent on overrunning our position and wiping us out. The firefight started just as the sun was setting, and lasted until early the next morning. I was the platoon sergeant at that point, and was wounded in the first few seconds of the fight by mortar shrapnel, as was our platoon leader. While we were being patched up, Basil took over the platoon leadership, and singlehandedly rescued our listening post from almost certain annihilation by the NVA, acts for which he was later awarded the Silver Star for heroism.

Again, these are only a couple of examples from among many experiences that Basil and I shared in Vietnam, that have indelibly changed our lives.

I entered the Army National Guard when I was eighteen, and spent my nineteenth birthday in Army Basic Training at Ft. Polk, Louisiana, under the control of drill instructors who were tasked with turning teenage boys into "fighting men," and were none too gentle about it. After Basic and Advanced Individual Training I was released from the Army back to my National Guard Unit, to serve the remainder of my six year commitment going to bi-monthly evening drills and two-week summer camps. That plan came to an abrupt end in April of 1968 when Reverend Martin Luther King, Jr. was murdered, and our unit was activated to help keep the peace in Kansas City, after nationwide civil disturbance and rioting had begun. Upon being released from that mission, we learned that our unit had been re-activated for up to two years federal service, so our men could serve as replacements for the hundreds of American casualties being suffered each month in the war in Vietnam.

I had been married for two years by then, had a good job, and expected to serve out my time in the National Guard without being further affected by the war. So the notification of our federal activation came as quite a shock. I would be leaving my young wife, who, because my Army pay would be so much less than my civilian pay, would have to move back home with her parents. We would be separated for up to two years, and there was the fear that I would likely be sent to Vietnam, with significant chance of being killed or maimed there. We were both afraid.

Long story (you can read about it in either of my novels, One Young Soldier or Angie's War) but I wound up volunteering to serve in Vietnam after I had been overlooked in the "levy" that had sent most of my National Guard friends there ahead of me. I've analyzed that decision many times in the years since I made it, because the war had such deep and lasting consequences for my family and me. The bottom line is, I did it because I felt I owed it to … someone. My country? My family? Myself? I don't know.

I do know that shortly after I arrived in Vietnam and was assigned to my infantry company and sent into combat, I realized that we were fighting an unwinnable war in an unwinnable way (President Nixon had already announced that we were no longer trying to win… just holding ground until the South Vietnamese could take over their own defense and we could be withdrawn) and I thought that I had made a tragic mistake by volunteering. But by then there was no way out of it, so I had to accept that I might well have sacrificed my life and caused my sweet young wife unimaginable anguish, for no good purpose at all.

I did find a purpose there, though, beyond just trying to stay alive. It was to help keep the men with whom I served alive and unharmed so they could return home to their families. Obviously those of us who took that mission upon ourselves were only partially successful, since we had many casualties. But it helped keep me going in an extremely difficult time, and it helped shape me into someone who has tried to help other people, in many ways, ever since.

Looking back now after fifty years, three marriages (and two divorces), raising two fine sons, a long and successful business career, two published novels and scores of lectures given about the war, and many, many other experiences, I have grown to believe that God sent me to Vietnam so that I could have the experience of it, and live to be shaped by it into someone who does what he can to help other people, and to help communicate to as broad an audience as possible the evil, and ultimate futility, of war.

I have to say here that I'm not a religious man, and don't go to church, synagogue, or mosque to worship. But I do believe to the core of my being in an all-seeing and all-powerful God, who created our universe and has a plan for each of us in it. And I believe this was his (or her) plan for me.

I have thought many times about what my life would have been like if I hadn't chosen to volunteer for Vietnam. And I just can't imagine it. I might have been like so many other people I see, who seem to live very shallow, materialistic existences, worried about getting the newest and greatest car, flat screen TV, iPhone, Nikes, makeup, etc. and apparently unconcerned for the welfare of those around them. Willing to shave a corner here and there, bend a rule, compromise their ethics, to get what they want.

I don't believe everyone is that way. Clearly there are many, many good, selfless people in the world who do everything they can to help others, and to help make the world a better place. But without the experience of Vietnam, I'm not sure I would have turned out to be one of them.

There I got to witness first-hand the total horror that occurs when people set out to kill each other in order to further some political cause. I got to experience self-serving leaders who would willingly sacrifice my life and the lives of all around me to achieve their "goals." (P.S. There were many, many fine leaders in the American Army in Vietnam. But there were many, many others who were definitely not fine leaders, either because of their ineptitude, or because they simply didn't care about the people for whom they were responsible). And seeing and experiencing that first hand convinced me that I never wanted to be one of those people. It helped me develop my own personal code of ethics that I believe in to the core of my being.

I was fortunate, in my fifties, to receive an MBA from a Jesuit university here in Kansas City. It was the result of two years of hard work on my part, and I learned a lot. But out of it all, one short expression has stuck foremost in my mind, and I think captures the essence of what I have come to believe, my life philosophy if you will, because of the horrible experience of war.

"A life not lived for others, is a life wasted."

So ultimately, as much as the war has affected my physical and mental health (I have several permanent medical conditions because of the Agent Orange we were exposed to and the unimaginably loud environment of combat, as well as measurably severe Post Traumatic Stress Disorder), I have come to believe that God sent me there in order to strengthen and evolve my spirit, and make me someone who cares for and helps other people, animals, and the world we live in.

I guess you could say that at least on some level, I have come to terms with my own "life changing event," and because of it, have a much better understanding of "who I am now."

(BIO): Gary DeRigne is retired and a writer and Veterans' Advocate. He is married to Karin Tiemeier, and they reside in Overland Park, Kansas. He is a Storyteller and has two published novels (Angie's War, One Young Soldier.) He is also a frequent speaker to all kinds of groups about the human cost of war and the issues facing American veterans.

He was Sr. Vice President of Information Systems and Engineering Services at Butler Manufacturing Company, Executive VP and Chief Operating Officer at Affinity Internet Services, and most recently before retirement, President and COO at the Yarco Companies.

CHAPTER 24:
THE TIP OF THE SPEAR
SFC JACOB GOBLE

(As told to Compiler) "'The tip of the spear', that's what they called us," said retired SFC Jacob Goble. He was referring to his job while on duty in Afghanistan. He had been in Bosnia in 2000, Kosovo in 2002 (peace-keeping missions); in 2006 he helped establish the ROTC program at the University of Pikeville, and then in 2008 went to Afghanistan. His unit traveled all over the country, from Kabul to Kandahar, as they engaged in route clearing operations.

"My wife is a teacher,' he said, "and she used to have her computer homepage set to MSNBC News, but she changed it. The reason; one day she opened it to a headline which read, 'The most dangerous job in the most dangerous place in the world'. She did not know exactly where I was at the time, but she knew that I was with the unit the article was about."

The reason SFC Goble's unit had the above description, and why it was called the tip of the spear, was because they were the ones leading the way in troop movements. Their vehicles were like armored tractors with panels in the front that were mine rollers searching for IEDs (improvised explosive devices).The danger level was high as, sometimes there were almost daily "blow-ups." When the Army first tested the new Ground Penetrating Radar System (GPRS), his unit was the first to use them.

"One thing I'll say," he said, "my unit was given the best equipment available for the job. Our job was to save lives, and they equipped us to try and do that. Our platoon saw a lot of men wounded, but due to advances in medicine, most of them received treatment, and came back to us."

They also led the way to firebases under siege. A day in particular that stands out to SFC Goble is August 10, 2008. His unit was engaged in an intense firefight for over an hour and a half, completely surrounded. When he became aware that some of his men were pinned down, SFC Goble went out and brought them back into safety. For his heroic actions he was awarded the Bronze Star with "V" device (for Valor under fire).

SFC Goble retired from the military in February 2012, with Traumatic Brain Injury (TBI). He also deals with tinnitus, the continual ringing in the ears. Both the TBI and tinnitus came about over time due to his repeated exposure to combat which included around 100 IEDs and 40 – 50 firefights. During one 33-day period, they had almost 30 IEDs blow up, and, the longest firefight he was in was against some 300 – 400 Taliban; a time when, even beforehand, he thought he might die. SFC Goble said he was able to visit with his wife by phone shortly before his unit went out on the mission. Although he did not tell her, he thought it might be the last time he talked with her.

When I asked him how he felt heading out on the mission, he answered, "There was a peace; I was okay."

However, after the firefight, figuring that he couldn't encounter anything worse than what he had just been through, he "stopped caring". When I asked if they used the same term we did in Vietnam, "don't mean nothing", he laughed. "Yeah," he answered, "'don't mean nothing', and we also used 'embrace the suck'."

SFC Goble got really serious again. "I mean, when you pull one of your guys out of a vehicle after an IED, and he's lost both legs, it's hard. These guys were like your family over there. If you lost any, or saw them hurt, you want to get the guys that got them. And, I've had to deal with guilt in this area. On the one hand, our mission was to sweep a path through the area so that those coming behind us would be safe. If we left IEDs undiscovered, it would kill those men. On the other hand, I had to order my men into situations that put their lives in jeopardy in order to accomplish the mission. But I also began to want to come upon Taliban in order to destroy them; I wanted them dead. When I left Afghanistan I planned on going back, but my being diagnosed with TBI prevented it."

I asked SFC Goble about the TBI. "Well," he started, "I knew something was wrong. I had trouble coping. I kept losing things, forgetting things. I can only speak for myself, but I wondered, how could I let this happen? I'm losing a part of who I am. Of course, now, part of who I am is who I was in Afghanistan, too. And I feel guilt over the larger role my wife has had to take on. When I was gone she had to keep the family running and together, and now, again she's had to take on more, even though I'm back. She has completely taken over finances; I can't keep my memory organized enough to do that."

SFC Goble and I talked some about the role that military spouses take on when the other is on deployment. They are left to handle everything, functioning as a single parent, working to keep their children focused on doing well in school, and not worrying about the absent parent. "For the person being deployed, you're assigned to new territory, jobs that call for a lot of focus; in order to stay alive; you have to concentrate on the mission. You really don't have too much time to think about other things, at least at the beginning."

I asked what the hardest part was for him when deployed, a total of three times, about a year each time. "My family; my kids now are seventeen, fifteen, and eleven (2013.) But being away from my wife, and them, was hard. You miss a lot of their growing up; you miss them. He said that his kids wouldn't watch the news so as not to worry."

"It's different than past wars in some respects," he added. "During WW II the whole nation was involved; some of that with Korea. There was a lot of national attention during Vietnam, but much of it was negative. In Iraq and Afghanistan, it seems that much of the nation goes its own way. Except for family or friends, when you're deployed, you're pretty much out of mind. And these wars have had repeat deployments; the average being 2 to 3, but some have gone as many as 4 to 6 times."

SFC Goble said he had some questions that still remain. "We were involved in a major firefight one time because we were trying to retrieve a five-ton truck that didn't even run. Maybe they didn't want the Taliban to try and duplicate it, I don't know. But I do know I have the question, why? Guys almost died, some were injured, some scarred for life; the question still remains, was that mission worth it?"

"And there was a situation where we had some EOD technicians from the Air Force pinned down, and we had to get them. We killed some Taliban, but I really remember this particular battle because there were some people we were getting ready to shoot up, and then we realized they were just kids. We came so close to killing them; I still have to deal with those memories."

"I feel like I functioned well in what I call 'controlled chaos'; I was able to stay calm in the middle of everything going on, and, to a certain extent, enjoyed it. Some may condemn me for that, but I realize that trait is also part of who I am. I could go for 14, 15 days in chaos without things making me sick. But after we were all safe, I got sick."

We talked about General Ulysses S. Grant who was criticized because, in his words, he "had a stomach for violence." General Grant realized that that was part of what made him a good soldier, being able to function in the midst of turmoil and circumstances of war. The simple fact is there are those who can, and those who can't. SFC Goble and I talked a little about how we tell ourselves sometimes, *I hope I never have to be in combat with the person who can't.* (Those who have been there will relate to this).

SFC Goble said that in reference to those who served in the war theater, but spent their whole deployment in the more secure areas, he had no trouble with that. "Some guys seeing frequent action called them 'Fobbits' and kind of looked down on them. I didn't. I figured they had their job to do, and they did it. Someone has to make sure that those out in the field get their mail, their money, their food. That was the role they were in. I can't hold that against them."

SFC Goble said that the places where he finds the most inner peace is when he is exercising, or running. I asked him what advice he would give to others trying to cope with traumatic situations, military, or otherwise.

"Find what you enjoy doing, and do it. Talking may, or may not, help. It's probably different with each person. For me, I like to run."

Typing this, I am aware that his advice sounds similar to what I have heard at times regarding healing; get occupied with something you enjoy doing, and do it.

(BIO:) (Jacob) I retired from the army and really after that I've just been trying to find a new purpose in life. After I retired I was lost for many years after because I felt like I no longer had a purpose; in the army I felt like I had that. After I separated from service I lost a lot of sense of who I was. I'm not really sure I'll ever get that sense of self dignity back.

CHAPTER 25:
WAKE UP, SAM; DAD'S DEAF
SAM WADDELL

I was sound asleep in my bedroom with the door closed, and I never heard a thing. Then my younger sister awakened me saying, "Wake up, Sam. Dad's deaf!" When I asked her what she was saying, she repeated herself, "Dad's deaf!"

I got out of bed and followed her into my parent's bedroom, and my mother was sitting on the bed, cradling my father. At the angle she was holding him, I didn't see anything gruesome on him, but I could see blood spatters and hair on the wall. Then I understood that my father was dead. I was in 6th or 7th grade thirteen years old I'm forty-four now (2013), and that is really the main image that has stayed with me from that time.

I was named after him Sam Waddell. He had been a good dad. We used to go camping and he'd take me out on a boat, fishing together; we did that quite a bit. I don't know if you remember the old yellow Pinto he had, but he took me over to the University of Kentucky Commonwealth Stadium parking lot and taught me how to drive there.

And as a good typical parent, he had certain boundaries, or restrictions, for us. But shortly before his death, it was like he lifted them. If my sister or I said we wanted to do something, my father would say, "Okay, let's go do it."

I have never been angry at him over killing himself. He had been acting a bit strange, and I realized that he didn't really know what he was doing. The next few days afterwards seemed dark, and I was numb, but I didn't blame him.

He was in Vietnam, but he didn't talk much about it. He had a picture album, but most of them were of when he met up with my mother for R&R in, I think, Hawaii. He said he inspected cafeterias, and that you couldn't trust people. He said you couldn't even trust the little children in the area. With his other pictures, he did have a picture of a helicopter riddled with bullet holes. There was blood on it, and he said the pilot was the only one who survived. But he didn't say anything more than that.

After my father's death, my grandfather came to Lexington and picked us up and took us back to eastern Kentucky where we lived, and the next couple days the family was getting ready for the funeral. I had an uncle, Danny VanHoose, who was fun to be around, and he was there, and it was good to be with him. It helped me cope, I guess.

My grandfather, his name was Estill, immediately stepped into the role of father figure for me. He knew my dad and I fished together, so he took me fishing at some pay lakes. At first he took me with some friends and dropped us off, but then he started joining us; he loved fishing too.

My grandfather was in WWII, and he said in France that he was with a unit that would go through towns to make sure they were clear after an advance unit had fought and secured them. He didn't talk a whole lot about the war, but the thing I remember the most was he would talk about the waste how things in the houses were just destroyed, pictures, furniture. He said he was struck by the waste.

My freshman year of high school, my grandfather passed, and that was really hard for me, harder even than when my father died. I remember it was the most pain I have ever felt in my life. When my dad died, my uncle and grandfather helped me cope, but by the time my grandfather died, I did have a faith in God, and that helped me cope with his death. Besides, he had a massive heart attack while fishing. He was actually reeling in a big fish when he died; he died doing what he loved. I was twenty-three when my grandmother passed, but I saw her death as merciful. She didn't have to suffer anymore.

Still, after my grandfather died, I think my personality changed. I started keeping my distance from everybody. I became guarded, didn't really trust anyone. Maybe if people had been more like my grandfather I would have let them in. But I also guess I was afraid if I got too close, they would leave me too.

And I guess I have continued to keep my distance, except when I got married. I have let down my guard with my wife, Tonya, and now our two daughters. They're six and ten (ages at time of the initial interview, 2013.)

Something that came out of all this that might not have happened had I not had the life changing event, the traumatic death of my father, is my current career. I started college at Prestonsburg Community College because my mom wanted me to. That's the only reason I went, and I didn't do well my first year. I was more interested in hanging out with friends and having a couple beers than I was in studying. Of course, at the end of the first year my grades reflected my lack of interest. I think I had a 1.9 GPA or something like that. Then I saw one of these posters on the wall of the college asking if you wanted to be a Pharmacist. I thought that's what I would do, become a Pharmacist. My grades substantially improved. I was doing it for myself, for something I wanted.

During my rotations there was a time when I was observing an operation on a man in his 40's at the Appalachian Regional Hospital in Hazard (KY), and I remember thinking that I was really learning a lot from the experience, and I was feeling pretty good about that. Then I walked out into the hallway and there were several of the man's family members standing around waiting, and it really hit me hard emotionally, I guess similar to a flashback.

I remember a lighter time too. There was a man who had asthma so bad he could barely breathe, and they were working to clear out his lungs. He was unconscious, and then they finally got him cleared enough that he started breathing. He opened his eyes, looked at the doctor and said, "Oh, thank you; you just saved my life." The way he looked, and sounded as he said it, just struck me as funny.

I do think that my experiences have helped me relate to others suffering. I have comforted some friends going through a loss, and encouraged them to turn to God for strength. I feel a strong sense of spirituality. I know I have a personal relationship with God, but, I guess I'm not a real religious person. I don't much go to church. My advice to anyone experiencing a life changing trauma like I did is to be aware that the clock keeps ticking. Time doesn't stop just because we're going through a difficult time. We have to go on; we have to find a coping mechanism and go on. Fishing and spending time with my grandfather, and then later pursuing what I wanted to do in school, and finding God, these all brought me to where I am today. Things started out rough, but I really feel blessed now.

Earlier, when I said my personality changed, that included my, I guess you would call it, my emotional level. I'm moderate. I don't get real excited, but I also don't get too sad. I really only remember getting real excited a couple times. The first time was when I received notification I had passed the Pharmacy board. I was opening the large envelope, sure that I was getting word I had failed the exam, and my license fell out of the envelope onto the floor. And, when my first daughter was born, she was six weeks premature, and the doctor wasn't sure if her lungs were developed enough. We were told, "If you hear her cry, it's a good thing." When she cried, I was excited.

I was having minor surgery on an ingrown toenail once, and was watching the doctor, and I felt real detached, like I was watching him work on someone else's toe. I think about that feeling sometimes. I think that now as an adult, if I were to observe me as a child, I would feel sorry for that little boy.

(BIO:) So, now in 2020, about seven years after the initial interview, there really isn't a whole lot that has changed regarding how I see myself, but my career has had a trajectory change. I sold my Pharmacy and now I do on-line consulting from home. I like working at home and really enjoy the new direction in my professional life.

So, in summation, being suddenly awakened in the middle of the night and told by my younger sister "Dad's deaf," is a memory that will always remain. And there will always remain the question and deep mystery about whatever troubled my dad enough to end it all. He was becoming increasingly troubled and I'll always wonder if the picture of the bullet-ridden helicopter entered into the equation?

Who am I in regards to the prior paragraph? There are some things in life we have to submit to God, let them go, and then, go on.

(Compiler's note) (from his initial story in War Wounded: Let the Healing Begin*): My family and I lived next to Sam and his family while I was taking graduate courses at the University of Kentucky. My sons Ralph and Rocky played with Sam and his younger sister. I had an early morning paper route, and the morning of the day his father died, when I went past their apartment, his dad was standing at the window, arms stretched upward, praying. The image sticks with me because it was unusual. I had waved at him, but he stood transfixed with his eyes upward. At his funeral his pastor read a letter Sam's father had written a couple days before he shot himself. It was a somewhat rambling note filled with imagery and talk of the loss of innocence in the world.*

One of the hardest things I think I have ever had to do, while a grad student at the University of Kentucky, was pick up Ralph and Rocky from Glendover Elementary the next day, walk home with them, and on the way tell them that the father of their two friends had died the night before. It was more difficult because I also had to try and explain how he had died, of self-inflicted gunshot wounds, and then try and answer the questions that naturally followed.

*In a conversation with Sam's wife a few months after he committed suicide, she said she had been re-reading letters he had sent from his time in Vietnam and was realizing there were some things bothering him, much more than she had been aware of.

Contacting Sam: I was conducting an interview in 2013 with SFC Goble (Chapter 24: "The Tip of the Spear") for his initial story, and he was looking at a large watercolor I had painted, which was on the wall behind my desk in my office, titled "In Memory." He saw the name Sam Waddell - Suicide, and asked me about him. After I told him, Jacob said that Sam Waddell's son was married to his sister, was his brother-in-law. Jacob put me in touch with Sam. We exchanged a couple of emails, and set up a time to catch up with each other, and, also do the interview. It was good to see him in his own place of business and doing well. And now later, visiting via phone, I am glad he is enjoying the new direction he took with his career.

CHAPTER 26:

THE LONG ROAD HOME
RONNIE HYLTON

I first met him in October 2010. I had a booth set up at "Winterfest" in the Expo Center in Pikeville, Kentucky, advertising my character monologues, and selling copies of my book, Poetic Healing; A Vietnam Veteran's Journey from a Communication Perspective. A young woman, Kim, stopped to look at the books, and then bought one, saying that her boyfriend was an Iraq veteran and was having trouble dealing with some things from the war. Later, she came back by with Ronnie, and we chatted a few minutes. Along with connecting on the veteran level, he was also a student at Pikeville College (later the University of Pikeville) where I taught (I subsequently had Ronnie as a student in several classes).

Backpedal to March, 2007. Ronnie Hylton had been looking forward to the fishing trip for some time. He had been stationed in Iraq for almost half a year and was flying back to the States for the long-anticipated R&R (rest and recuperation) leave. Two weeks of fishing; he and his dad could pick back up with something they loved to do together, and talk, maybe even a chance to sort out some of the feelings that went along with being in war.

As he stepped off the plane, his father wasn't there to meet him, but others were, and immediately Ronnie found out that his father had just died; Ronnie said his memories are vague of that period because something snapped. In the midst of a hazy fog he helped with the funeral arrangements. The initial R&R period was two weeks, but he was given a one week extension for bereavement leave. Then, three weeks after arriving back in Iraq, his unit received notification they were facing a three month extension of duty. Although that was later changed, at the time it just added to the confusion Ronnie was already experiencing. Along with his job routines, bombs and mortars fell almost daily on the airstrip where he was located in northern Iraq.

(As told to Compiler) "My father was my best friend," Ronnie said, "I grew up 'riding shotgun' in his coal truck; his death overshadowed everything, and my attitude changed to one of 'don't give a damn'."

Ronnie was a wheeled-vehicle mechanic and served in Iraq from September 2006 until September 2007, his tour overlapping the Surge. His shop was part of an artillery battery with the 1st of the 14th Field Artillery. As mentioned, the airstrip was bombed and mortared regularly, and the ones that fell short landed on or near the maintenance shop. He laughed as he said, "I twisted my ankle once running from the shop to a nearby bunker."

They also had to deal with improvised explosive devices (IEDs). After discharge from the military, Ronnie received a disability rating for post-traumatic stress disorder (PTSD), and continues to receive annual scans that test for traumatic brain injury (TBI).

Three weeks after Ronnie finished his tour in Iraq, in October 2007, his grandfather died, so, obviously, as he got out of the service, he was going through a rough time. Ronnie said, "I am aware that what I went through was not as bad as what some did, but, still, everything that happened did bother me a lot, and dragged me down. I did some fishing, but also drank to try and kill the pain. I started down a destructive path, but some things happened over time that helped me realize I need to turn around. My girlfriend came into my life in 2010 and she has been a very positive influence for me. I've never known anyone as gentle and kind as her. But, one thing that really concerned me was, when drinking with friends, sometimes I would have outbursts of anger, and the next morning I would feel horrible about it, just horrible."

Ronnie and I talked a couple minutes about Abraham Lincoln describing his religious statement of faith; "when I do good, I feel good; when I do bad, I feel bad; and that is my religion." It appeared that Abraham Lincoln's religion was also starting to convert Ronnie; he was getting tired of the feeling bad.

Ronnie said he decided to start spending more time alone, especially fishing and hunting, where he could reflect, and try to get some thoughts in order. He cut back on drinking, and started to go to bed earlier, and get up earlier (fishing's good earlier, he added). He didn't want to be all medicated up and his early morning fishing and his walks in the woods were putting him smack into the middle of the process of "the long walk home", so he declined some of the medicines doctors suggested for PTSD.

Ronnie and I also discussed those times when anger wells up and one might not really understand why. I told him of a time a few years after Vietnam when at a ball game, during the national anthem I was suddenly engulfed with anger when the lyrics were sung, "and the rocket's red glare; the bombs bursting in air". I just didn't want to listen to it. Ronnie said that he had once experienced a similar reaction. We also found commonality in talking about reactions to fireworks; they make you jumpy. He told how in September of 2012, his vehicle was T-boned by a car in a parking lot. The driver, high on pills swerved off the road into the lot, and hit the passenger's side where Kim was sitting. Ronnie said feelings and memories of the war immediately surfaced as he angrily jumped out of the vehicle and headed toward the other driver, but then he realized where he was.

We then talked for a few moments about all those things that can bother you which may sometimes be triggered quite easily, and, it seems, always unexpectedly.

Ronnie started classes a while after his return from Iraq at Big Sandy Community and Technical College, and a year later transferred to the University of Pikeville. He said that writing became another factor in his healing process, especially after his enrollment in Dr. James Riley's creative writing course. He wrote about fishing, and PTSD, and some poetry about war, and engaged in other journaling.

Some of his advice to others is, "In your darkest hours, don't quit, realize that it's a long walk. Get involved in something; school, work, whatever, and keep going. During my roughest times, when I was drinking more, and at my angriest, I still went to my classes, and did my assignments. Show up and be responsible toward your duties; I guess the Army ingrained that into me. I was in a dark stretch, early on the long road home, when I started college, but I still graduated with a 4.0."

He continued, "Spend time with, and appreciate your loved ones. Find the things you love to do and do them as often as possible. Realize that money can't buy happiness. It's nice to have, but it can't bring contentment. I see people chasing after money and the things it can buy, and I have decided I don't want to work 70 to 80 hours a week for stuff. Once you lose everything, you find out what's important; you can get jaded if you think it's all about money. I'm happy with a small house and an old truck, as long as I can find a good spot to fish and a place to go walking with my dog in the woods. You can't put a price on those things."

Ronnie added, "Something else that bothered me while in Iraq; I just don't trust politics much. There was a time when we needed Humvees, and the funding was delayed by Congress because of other non-war related projects that politicians wanted to tack onto the bill. I just hate the way wars are fought. We used to say that if we could sit down with the farmers over there, we could probably agree to put away our guns and each head on back to our homes."

I laughed at this point and told Ronnie that in Vietnam we said similar things; "Just let us sit down with 'Charlie' and I think we will decide we can both go back to our families and call this whole thing off."

Ronnie talked about a Sargent he worked with who had served four year-long war tours of duty in Afghanistan and Iraq. "He taught me a lot of lessons about life; especially respect. He had high expectations. I learned from him that some people demand respect, but then there are others who deserve respect. I want to try and live in such a way that I can be someone who deserves it."

Ronnie wrapped up our interview with a couple more thoughts on how the war in Iraq was handled. "Particularly in the job areas of security and drivers," he said, "there were civilian contractors. They received much larger salaries and were able to ride big buses, and their living areas had Taco Bells, Pizza Huts, and the like. But the people who cleaned the latrines and performed laundry services were from 3rd world countries, and were paid less than minimum wage, and just treated differently. If they were on a supply convoy, they didn't get the same level of protection as contractors; as far as I'm concerned, these people were some of our unsung heroes of the war. One time something really bothered me. They were not allowed access to the Post Exchange (PX), and, of course, this was where you could buy phone cards, so it affected what they would have to pay if they wanted to call their loved ones back in their home country; they'd have to pay higher reverse charge rates."

He continued, "One time I was going into the PX and one of these guys held out a $20 bill and asked me if I would buy a phone card for him so he could call his wife. I took the money and said I would, and when I got inside I decided to buy the best card there was; I think it was for 60 or 70 dollars. When I got back outside I gave him his card, plus his twenty back, and told him to enjoy his calls to his wife. He started crying, and hugged me. I'm not bragging, just telling you what happened. I don't know; but I think if we could all do a little more of this, and treat others better, the world would be improved, a better place to live; it might even help us all on the long roads we sometimes travel."

Ronnie Hylton. Six years later (2019) Who am I now?

The question, "What will I do now?" is probably one related to most in the events surrounding my father's untimely death due to his drug use. Unfortunately, he died of opioid abuse at the age of forty-nine. This occurred during my deployment to Iraq. It just so happened he passed while I was flying home for two weeks R&R, and I wasn't able to be notified until I landed back in the States. While I was still in the terminal, I was informed by my former step-father, a Marine Vietnam veteran that my father had died. So then, the question "what will I do now?" hit me like a freight train. I had just spent six months on a combat deployment, and now, as the only child of a father who wasn't married, I was thrown into funeral preparations. I have always said that I felt something snap inside me, and I have never been the same person since.

Fortunately, the army had instilled a since of purpose and drive in me, so after an evening of mourning, I immediately went into a mode where I viewed the funeral as another mission. I knew what I had to do, and in the words of my First Sergeant "I just did the damn thing". I was emotional at times, but probably not as much as I should have been. I was hardened and calloused by my deployment and to much of my family's surprise, I was able to take care of all the business surrounding a death in a short amount of time. To be honest, I really just wanted to get it over with and go back and finish my deployment. I felt at the time, my real family was overseas and I needed to get back to them. Even though I struggled with depression on my return to Iraq, I felt that that was where I had to be.

I don't know if the "what will I do now question?" really stayed with me for long. It may sound cheesy, but the army really ingrained the "drive on" mentality in me to a point where I didn't even know how to mourn like I probably should have.

I really don't remember specifically wondering, "Who am I without this person since this incident occurred?" Pertaining to my father's death, I don't think the thought ever crossed my mind. Now if the Army were a person, I have asked myself numerous times since returning to civilian life "who am I?" without the military. There's a sense of being a part of something bigger than yourself. You always had people on your left and your right that would be there no matter what. If one person stumbled, the others were there to help, and this just didn't pertain to combat. It was a lifestyle that most civilians will never understand. Especially in today's world, it seems like many people are mostly concerned about themselves and what will benefit them. Sometimes it seems like it's a me-first and a gimme-gimme society. It wasn't that way during my time in service. You may have had to go through rough and god-awful experiences, but so did everybody else around you.

But once I returned to the civilian world, it felt like I was alone. I almost felt like a ghost walking among the living, like there was really no one I could relate too, who could understand the things I had done. I believe that this feeling of isolation is probably the number one reason veterans have difficulties returning to civilian life. I guess I decided to embrace that feeling and that's how I've handled my life since; I enjoy solitude.

In terms of continuing to heal and discover who I have become now, time just has a way of easing up the pain I guess. I still think about my father every day, probably more so now than the first few years after he passed. I take some comfort knowing that at least he isn't suffering now. I guess I've grown and accomplished a lot, and now I have a family, and I find myself wishing I could see him more now. I guess I'd just like him to know I'm doing alright, and I miss his company. But I have also come to realize that my father's death was a huge part of all I have been through, in some ways, kind of a cruel joke life can play on you.

I guess a combination of fishing and hiking has helped me to heal and deal with the pain from the war and the loss of my father. Fishing and hiking are so peaceful. You can just leave today's fast-paced world of greediness, consumption, and electronics and get out and see how the world really is. The mountains and trees and rivers don't have politics, they don't care about the latest I-phone or what kind of clothes you're wearing. They don't care if you're rich or poor or black or white. You just get out in the middle of nowhere and you can see through all the crap we're supposed to worry about. Almost all the stuff that stresses us out every day, whether at work or whatever, doesn't mean a rat's ass out in the mountains. The natural world operates off a set of universal rules that we cannot change; you have to adapt to how the natural world operates. It never gets in a rush, but somehow everything gets done.

It seems like every time I go out on the river or up in the mountains, I'll see something incredible, whether it be battling a big smallmouth in a favorite hole on the river, watching a bear cross the river and scurry up a cliff, seeing the sun put on a light show through the clouds as it rises in the morning, witnessing an osprey dive on a fish, or seeing a bald eagle soar overhead. If you're out there, and you're quiet and being are part of the environment instead being some fool out there hollering and yelling, you'll see the most incredible things that most people never see. These incredible events in nature happen every single day, but most people are too busy looking down at their phone or rushing to their next meeting or event or whatever to even notice it. No matter what, the sun still rises and sets every day, and if you spend enough time out there, you realize you don't have to live by all the rules that society sets.

Regarding any aspects of who I am now that probably would not have occurred if I had not had this life changing event, I believe that just about every aspect of me now has been shaped by the loss of my father and my deployment to Iraq. As years pass, I realize the events that have made up my life make me see the world through a different set of eye balls than probably 95% of other people. I realize it's important to work and to be damn good at whatever you choose to do, but it shouldn't take up your whole life. We're only here for that short dash between the year you're born and the year you die, so you'd better make the best of it, because nobody knows what's on the other side. Time with family and time you spend doing things you want to do are extremely important. The biggest way I have changed is that I constantly strive to slow the pace of life down, which is really hard to do nowadays. The whole world seems to be moving faster than ever, and if you get caught up in it, life just ends up being that you're constantly trying to get from one thing to another without ever taking a look around and enjoying just being alive. Now a person has responsibilities, and you have to make a living, but it's real easy to chase that carrot and miss out of some of the best things in life. The older I get and the more I learn, my goals are not to get more and more, but to enjoy the most out of what I have right in front of me. I fought hard to get back home, and now that I'm here, I want to enjoy every minute of it that I can before I take on the full-time job of pushing up daisies.

I have witnessed quite a bit in the short time I've been alive. Especially in the times we live in now, I wish people would respect and take care of one another better. It seems that although we have more access to information than ever before, as a society in some ways we're becoming stupider and lazier because we can have everything at the push of a button or tell Alexa or Siri to do it for us. Many in our time seem not to give much thought or craft to the way they're living right now. Personally, I don't wish to live my life looking at a screen or rushing to the next meeting. Maybe the secret isn't getting and doing more, more, more, ... but learning to get by on what you already have.

(BIO:) For me, getting to return to my home in eastern Kentucky in the mountains has been the biggest reward I could ever ask for. It might be a little slower paced and the economy is in the tank right now, but I feel I am blessed to experience more true freedom than what someone does if they live in an urban area. Because I'm willing to get up a little earlier or walk a little farther than most, I get to experience some of the most incredible things that many people never get to see. There's a whole other world out there, one without highways, buildings, or screens. It requires effort and work to experience it, but man is it awesome. The only rules up in the mountains are the ones God made. And they are shaping who I am now.

CHAPTER 27:

THE LOSSES WE BEAR: THE GLUE IS GONE
ELISHA TAYLOR

I think that initially, the most traumatic part for me was realizing that the glue that held our family together was gone. For a couple years afterward, a disbelieving part of me hoped, every time I heard a car in the drive, or the front door opening, that he was coming back to "fix things."

I was fifteen when it happened, a sophomore in high school. School was over for the day and I was waiting for my dad to pick me up as usual, so I was real surprised when my brother came for me instead. When I got in the car he just said we were going to Mamaw's house.

Most of the family on my dad's side, and a lot of his friends, were at Mamaw's (my dad's mother) house. Dad had been in an accident. My best friend had heard and she came over, and, soon after, the police arrived with more information. There had been a head-on collision, and both my dad and the driver of the other car were killed. As details came out, it turned out the driver of the other vehicle was someone that I knew and had gone to school with. That didn't matter anymore, now he was the teenage driver on drugs, running from the police, who had killed my dad.

As I mentioned, I really was in disbelief for some time, shock, then that hopeful disbelief. Although I never dwelt on anger, I touched it for a while. I'm not a person who normally holds grudges, but, reflecting back, I was angry at the driver of the car that hit my dad, and the circumstances, a high-speed chase. Like I said, I knew the boy driving, and I always felt that his involvement with drugs came from peer pressure from some of the friends he chose to hang with, so I was angry at them too. I guess for a while I was just angry at everyone over what had happened to us. The question of "why us?" Mamaw was real distressed, and my mom was real troubled by it, and there was no one there to fix it.

When I was eighteen, my best friend and I became roommates, living in the family house (without my mom). Others had moved out, but I guess I was consumed with the weight of the house; I felt that by living there I was somehow still keeping my dad alive. I kept that role until I was twenty-one.

About a year ago, a turning point for me, I guess you could say a significant point in the healing process, was when circumstances dictated that it made sense to move. At first I was against it, but then my roommate and I did move. That was when I started to let some things go, especially realizing that it was not on me to keep my dad alive. I mean, I'll never fully be over it. You don't ever fully get over things like this, but you don't have to be consumed by it; you can move on.

Of course, things are different, better or worse, I don't know, just different. I've achieved some things I might not have otherwise because I had to struggle, and grow up rather early. If my dad was still alive I would probably be a twenty-two-year-old still living at home, but I was forced to become independent.

And, another thing, back to thinking about any anger that I felt. I guess I used it as a motivator, to keep the fire going, so to speak, to help me focus on where I wanted to go, and to survive.

Something else that has been a major factor in my healing is my dogs. I have four; one from when my dad was alive, one I got the Christmas after he died, and then two more since. They have helped me a lot, just being there. The support a pet can offer is irreplaceable.

Another thing, one month after my eighteenth birthday, I got a tattoo of a cross with my dad's initials. He probably wouldn't have liked it, just because he wasn't the biggest advocate of putting permanent things on your body. However, whenever I get too overwhelmed, or miss him, or catch myself wishing I could change everything, I touch that tattoo, and know he's with me wherever I go. He's infinite now; never changing, never moving forward, or going back.

I'm trying to be closer to my family now; more appreciative of who is still here, and of what I have.

If I have any advice for others it has to be, grieve on your own schedule; don't let others try and determine where you should be in the process. It's different for each person. It is okay to hold on to the grief for as long as you need to. Don't let it cripple you, but realize the world won't stop its day to day demands.

If after some time you feel you are not where you think you should be, then you might want to reassess where you wanted to be in the first place.

You can reach out to others who are grieving, but if you can't be comforting, then just don't say anything. At the funeral someone told my brother that "it would always be there." He felt like they were throwing a hot iron at him at that moment. Sometimes it is better to just be quiet; give a hug.

I've found that talking about it when I can, helps. It makes me stronger. It is also a way I can try to reach out to others. You need to realize, that although it may feel like it, you aren't alone; you're not the only one who has gone, or is going, through this. Yes, the circumstances may be different, but the pain and loss are universal.

Social work terminology includes the word resiliency. When studying it, I found it most interesting that some people have it; some don't. So sometimes I wonder what someone else might have done in my situation, or, even, what I might have done, had I not determinedly pushed through day to day.

Nonetheless, wondering aside, I am where I am. I'll never know if I am better off, or worse off. I do know that from that day forward, things were, and always will be, different.

(Compiler's note) I have known Elisha for some time. She is a survivor, caring, reliable, and someone who affects others in a positive way. Elisha is an example of dignity in the face of extreme difficulty, and of holding close to her heart the precious moments and memories she still has.

Elisha Taylor - 6 years later (after initial story written.)

Thinking back, in the aftermath of my aforementioned life changing event, there were many times I asked, "What will I do now?"

After my dad passed, I was thrown into a tailspin My family was starting to break apart, and I was feeling lost and adrift from everyone. I was only 15 and had always had him to depend on, and here I was feeling utterly and completely alone. I now realize that I had support and that I was far luckier than some in similar situations. However, in that moment all I could think was, "What now? How do I keep going? Who's going to love me now?" It was difficult; it still is. Sometimes the grief is still crushing but most days I push it to the back of my mind and still keep going.

But then, and still to this day, the question still arises, "Who am I, and who will I be without the guidance and support of my dad?" I feel like I lost my mom shortly after I lost my dad, although she didn't die. She just stopped being there, and it felt like she stopped caring about anything but herself. Even now, 15 years after his death, I still feel separated from my estranged family when we get together for special holidays. How can I belong there when my connection to them has been severed?

There are some specific things that have helped me continue to heal and discover who I am now. My dad was always so proud of my school grades and test scores, so I know that if he could see me now he would be very happy with how far I've gone and what I've done.

Regarding any aspect of who I am now, that probably would not have occurred had I not had this life changing event. I think I'm more independent now, and more resilient. I was always a Daddy's girl, and depended on him to see me through difficult situations. At 15, when he died, I remember being so lost and confused about what was to come next. I felt insecure. I struggle with change to this day, some 15 years after that loss. The changes that come naturally with life can leave me unmoored and lost and throw me back to the days of insecurity and loss. But surviving something traumatic means you become stronger. You know that now, in in the future, no matter what happens, you will survive it. I doubt I would have this understanding of myself if my dad were still here.

Finally, if I may pass on any words of wisdom that hopefully can help someone else – Remember, we all face trauma and the unknown differently. I believe the first and most important step is to keep moving ahead. Getting lost in "what could've been" means you will never see that good of "what is." That, in itself, is a tragedy.

(BIO:) I recently completed a Master of Science in Communication, and am now working on the certification process for becoming a Certified Archivist. I'm following my dreams and trying to be the best me that I can.

I also spend as much time as I can with my pets and my partner. They make me very happy and also keep me grounded in the present. Sometimes I need help in getting out of my own head, so to speak. I'll get too caught up in everything else and forget to take time to appreciate how far I've come. This is when I need their presence, and they never fail in making me live in the present.

I am 30 years old and work as the University Archivist at the University of Pikeville. I have a Masters in Communication from Purdue University and am working on a second Masters in Library Science from the University of Kentucky.

I'm in a long-term relationship and have a multitude of pets that help me stay sane in an otherwise crazy world. I couldn't ask for a better job and a better work family.

(Additional note) I recently married my partner and best friend, Lori Elswick-Taylor.

CHAPTER 28:

FINDING A WAY; TURNING FEAR INTO FAITH
DR. DAVID A. SMITH

I was five, and one of my sisters was four, and when we went to school we realized that the other kids had more than one pair of shoes. So we decided to start changing shoes, actually brown boots, with each other every day so it would look like we had more than just one pair.

(Cmpiler's Note)The thing that was reinforced to me as I listened to Dr. Smith tell this was just how young we can be when we start to notice something is different about ourselves, and how creative we can become in trying to hide those differences from those around us, especially our peers. Of course, what we frequently find out, sometimes later on down the road, is that some of the things we did were seen through; we really weren't fooling anyone.

Dr. David A. Smith is Associate Professor of Business and MBA Program Director at the University of Pikeville. He is an internationally recognized speaker on corporate behavior and the impact upon capitalism. The road he traveled to get to where he is started out with doubt, unbelief, and fear, but he learned in life to turn these attributes into confidence, belief, and faith. This is an insight into his journey.

I was born in Harrodsburg, Kentucky, one of ten children. My mother passed thirteen years ago. She was married to my father for fifty-five years and was an amazing little woman. She accepted standards based on her Biblical beliefs, so when my father wanted to leave, she accepted that. But she would not grant a divorce because she believed marriage was for life. So he left to go into business in Cincinnati, and she stayed to raise ten children on her own. We were poor.

When you're four or five years old, you don't think things are irregular, when your family doesn't have a car, therefore you never travel; your neighborhood is your globe, your world. Everyone around me was African-American, and all were poor, so I believed that was the way it was with the whole world. I thought all drinking glasses started out as jelly jars, and as I got a little older and visited some white friends I was surprised because their glasses didn't have the little rings around the top. I also wondered why their whole houses were carpeted instead of having tile, or cement, or, as in the case of our bathroom, just ground. I noticed another area where things were different; my mother was always working.

Like I said, my father lived in Cincinnati. He only came around about once a year, and I vividly recall the first time I saw him: tall, 6'3", a giant in my eyes, and very black. To this day, he is one of the blackest African-Americans I have ever seen. He never really talked to me, was there for a short while, and then left. I asked my mother why he didn't live with us, and she replied, "He does what he wants to do."

I found out he was worth about a million dollars, and back in the 1970's, that was quite wealthy. He lived in a nice, new house and drove a new Lincoln, always had women around him, and was in business with white people. My skin was black. I began to compare. All the poor people I know have the same color skin as me, and the people who aren't poor have white skin ... I began to conclude that black was bad and white was good. I got to thinking, *My mother reads the Bible faithfully, even though she works a lot. She goes to church regularly, and she talks to the "Lowud."* I knew the "Lowud" wasn't Santa Claus, but from the pictures I had seen, I knew he was white, and he did nothing for black people.

I heard all the time that, just like cleanliness, being poor was next to godliness, because Jesus was poor. Some things didn't make sense to me. God owned everything, so he was rich, but he sent his son down to this earth and his son was poor. If this was the case, then, I decided, this "Lowud" I've been hearing about must be a "no-good daddy," just like mine.

On my first day of first grade I also noticed that all the white children were there with two adults, and I was there with just my mother. I also observed that this was true of a lot of the other black children. I told myself that either their daddies were at work, or they were "no-good" like mine. This reinforced to me the idea that black must be bad.

I compared clothes too. I cried to my mother because other kids were teasing me about what I was wearing, and she said, "Don't worry, Honey, the Lowud will provide." I got angry, and, I kept it to myself, but I was saying, *Stop talking about this Lowud! When he does provide he doesn't get his clothes from very good stores! Someday I am going to have all the things I need, and when I get there, I will share my situation with others like me so that I can help them get out of their circumstances.*

I hated giving speeches in high school. I would rather take a zero than give a speech or book report. I had headaches, sweating, and my hands would shake. Some of my friends would skip another class just to come and watch me, and my teacher would allow them in. But they were there just to laugh at and ridicule me. The teacher even let other teachers know when I was presenting, and some of them would come to watch, too. It was terrible. I figured no one wanted to hear what I had to say – after all, I was black. I had no confidence, didn't think what I had to say was important, although I did know I was just as smart as my peers.

So, after high school I enrolled at the University of Kentucky, which at that time was known as the "white university." Most of my African-American friends had gone to "black universities." I had to take public speaking my freshman year, and the instructor would make us get up in front of the class every day. I don't know if it was because he was more mature, or a man, but I started to view him as a male role model. With his encouragement, I started to realize, the other people in the class didn't know me, so I had nothing to lose. Some of the students had parents who were paying their way, and some, like me, were on grants. But none of us had a lot of money left over, and I realized that as students we were all equal. I started to feel at home.

Of course, I have since come to realize that God's name wasn't "Lowud," it is Lord, and his son is rich. My mother interpreted her

Bible wrong in this area. A lot of poor people do this, and they over-looked scriptures that say things like, "Above all, I want you to prosper and be in good health." Faith comes by hearing the word of God, and acting on it. I came to realize the Bible is a living document. My situation was not something God did to me because I was black. Actually, Jesus was more like me in color than those pictures I saw when I was a kid. He was darker skinned; he was sent for everyone, and he loved me. When I arrived at that knowledge it fundamentally changed my life.

Back to public speaking. With practice, I started to gain more confidence, and I realized that, for me, it was "sink-or-swim" time. I had these little voices of doubt that were talking in one ear, telling me I was black, no one wanted to listen to me, and so forth. These doubts were the ones I had had for years, which only led to unbelief and fear. But there was another voice in the other ear telling me, "The demon on your other shoulder is not as tough as he claims to be; if God owns the cattle on a thousand hills, why listen to your demon?" And so I started to turn my doubts into confidence, which led to belief and faith.

Being black, I cannot place blame on whites. That's an excuse. People need to take advantage of opportunities. The enemy isn't white; it is ignorance and bigotry, and that is found in all colors and races. This knowledge freed me when I realized that in the Lord's eyes I was on an equal basis with everyone. They were, are, all my brothers and sisters. If someone didn't love me, it didn't matter; I could love them back. I decided to integrate more, see what else was out there. As a teen I did a lot of reasoning, and discovered there were a lot of things and people God put into my life for a reason, even those I might, at the time, have considered an enemy. That person was there for a reason.

As I read the Word more, my confidence grew. I came to realize that God loves me as much as he loves his son, Jesus. I have found he meets all my needs and has filled my life with many blessings. I'm not perfect, but I do believe I am here in this life, and in this particular place right now, to be a blessing to others, and help them through some of their hard times.

I'm chuckling because I just had that image flash in front of me again, my younger sister and I trading brown boots. They had white fur inside. Can you imagine what we looked like in gym class with brown boots?

(Dr. David Smith, 6 years later. Who am I Now?)

Many global traditions embedded within various cultures include a belief system related to a brief period of suffering before receiving the just reward as the final achievement of final goals (Northouse, 2015.) Just like Christ suffered before his crucifixion, death and ascension to heaven, I suffered embarrassing moments of poverty before my ascension to eventually earn a doctorate degree decades later. Sharing the same shoes as my sister when I was a child allowed me the opportunity to know that life is unfair to all (white, black, Latino, Asian, etc.), so I had to stop feeling sorry for myself and engage in educational adventures to escape poverty. If it was not for the early suffering in my life, I would not have achieved many professional, educational, and personal goals that I am using to bless thousands of other individuals.

Achievement and success are attributes that most human beings strive to attain. The bedrock of any nation depends upon the strength, intellect, and quality of her residents (Locklear & Kienzler, 2014.) Whenever I have a problem in life, I always think of those shoes I shared with my sister when I was a child, and I think of the strength that it took to overcome those obstacles at the age of seven. I transpose those attributes to the present-day issues that always lead to successful outcomes. If it had not been for the Almighty God giving me the opportunity to experience poverty at an early age, along with the tools to overcome them, I would not be helping the poor right now in my profession. Empathy resides with one who has experienced pain. I thank God Daily for choosing me to be His selected vessel to spread His Word.

(BIO:) I possess a Doctor of Business Administration Degree, and I have expertise in creating, implementing, and evaluating accredited Master of Business Administration Programs and Master of Science in Healthcare Management Programs. I also have robust experiences in university teaching in undergraduate/graduate programs of business,

medical sales consulting, and consumer products management. I bring a wealth of knowledge, experience, and professionalism to organizations that desire maximizing efficiency and profitability.

For more than 29 years, I have earned a reputation for providing skilled and practical guidance as a business consultant, sales manager, and entrepreneur, which adds substantive value to productivity with proven results. I have taught American Psychological Association (APA) Writing Workshops to undergraduate and graduate students for over 10 years called The Art of Research, Writing, and Public Speaking: Turning Fear into Faith. *I am a bilingual professional, as I read, speak, and comprehend Spanish at the Intermediate level from living in Colombia, South America, and also the Dominican Republic for two years. "*

CHAPTER 29:
GOOD KID; MAD CITY
BRANDEN TEASLEY

I grew up in Compton, California. There was a time, due to gang violence; it was called one of the most dangerous cities in the United States. It's gotten better; there are still some problems, but there are some things that have been improving. My mother was pregnant with me when she was fifteen; my father was twenty. My father was murdered when I was three; he ran out of gas in the wrong neighborhood and a local gang member targeted him. He ran and tried to hop a fence and was shot eight times in the back. So my mom and I were left to find a place to stay with family and friends. My dad's family hardly knew us, but they reached out and took us in. My grandmother and my mom raised me, and looking back, I can see the odds were against me. I was being raised by a black single mother in a ghetto, not a real bad one, but, still, it had a reputation for gang violence. I was fortunate; I didn't get into the gang lifestyle too much, for a couple reasons.

First, my mom had to work and so she wasn't there a lot of the time, but I saw a lot of things, and learned from the gangbangers, the homeless, and people on drugs. I was almost paranoid when living there that something was going to happen to me. What I learned was that I wanted my life to be in the opposite direction. I guess you could say that the gangbangers taught me the difference between right and wrong.

Now, my grandfather didn't live in the ghetto area where my mom and I did, but I visited him a lot. He had some guns, and one time, when I was thirteen, I was playing 'gang-wars' with a cousin, and we got ahold of a 9 mm Glock and were taking turns putting the gun to the other's head and clicking the trigger. I didn't know my cousin had a bullet in the chamber, and so I clicked the trigger, accidently shot him in the face, and he almost died from the wound.

For the first time, life got real for me. I had almost killed my cousin, and I would have thrown my own life away in the process. I could have gone to jail and my cousin dead. That really got my attention. My mom and the rest of the family were real upset with me; I moved to live with my grandfather. This was when the second main factor kicked in that got me away from the gang lifestyle. My grandfather, who was a veteran, became the main influence in my life; he raised me kind of old-school, less emphasis on rules, and more emphasis on values, morals, respect, and responsibility.

I had a lot of respect for him, and, the things he said to me. This was a man who saw signs that said "Whites only" when he was growing up. He truly knew what it was to be held down, but had a lot of ambition, and was goal-driven.

Once I came out of the ghetto, I took 100% advantage of the opportunity. I started getting better grades in high school, and then after I graduated I started junior college. When I was a sophomore I met a girl on Facebook, we got together, and before long, she got pregnant. When I realized I was going to be a father, I knew I needed to be responsible. My daughter, Lyric Teasley, was born when I was a freshman at the University of Pikeville (KY) where I had decided to go in order to play football.

About a year ago I was at a club in Williamson, West Virginia, and I was dancing with a girl, and I'm not sure why what happened next, happened. One thing I was told was the girl's brother – he's the one who stabbed me – didn't like me dancing with her. The other thing I was told was that since the guy had gotten into an argument with some guys on our football team, he thought he might get beat up and so he struck first. Anyway, I was out on the floor dancing with this girl and her brother came up behind me and sliced me with a knife across the back. I've got about a nine-inch scar running from my vertebra over to my right side.

I didn't know what happened, but I was losing my balance and my vision was getting blurry. I stumbled over to some friends and told them to call 9-1-1; that I had been stabbed, and they thought I was joking. I knew to keep my composure and tried to get away from the crowd, but then I collapsed. Luckily, there was a nurse there who took my shirt and slowed the flow of blood. I got my cell and called a friend from junior college who called my daughter's mom, and she called my mom and put us on three-way. I was sure I was dying and I told them to tell my daughter that I loved her. Things kept shrinking and getting littler and littler, and I started going into some kind of hole. The nurse said later I stopped breathing and she was able to revive me. When I came back out of the hole, my mom was on the phone crying, there was a brawl going on in the back of the club, and police were there with Tasers.

Someone had called 9-1-1 and they transported me to a hospital. I was told if the wound had been 1 cm either direction I would have bled to death, or been paralyzed. They told me I stopped breathing again at the hospital but they, also, were able to bring me back. I got eighty-six stitches inside the slice and fifteen staples on the outside. They told me at the hospital they didn't know how I had survived because I was in such bad shape when I got there. That really frightened me, and got me thinking even more seriously about my life.

My mom begged me to come back to live with her as she said it was too dangerous here for me. I told her, 'No; I'm not going to let these people scare me out of my future'. The doctor said it would be a couple months before I would be able to walk, but I did it in two weeks. When I got back to the University, a good friend, Jocelyn McCown, helped me a lot. She nursed me, cleaned and changed my bandages. If I remember right, she e-mailed you and then you called me while I was still in the hospital. She was there for me which is a nice feeling when you are so far from home. Also, for a while I got depressed some; actually got paranoid every day for some time, but I kept pushing on through the darkness. My good friend, BJ Iverson, he helped me a lot with my attitude and gave me a lot of encouragement.

I figured if I went back home I would just become part of the crowd, with no education to help me. My GPA had been a 2.3, but I bounced back the next semester and got a 3.5, and this last semester I got a 4.0. I'm getting a degree in social work, and I started to get more involved on and off-campus. I got involved with Black History Month, and I also went to some middle schools in the area to talk to kids about not bullying, and take their education seriously. I did a practicum with the WestCare Homeless Shelter. I want to do anything to show people you can overcome when odds seem against you.

For a while I was angry a lot because I didn't really know why I was stabbed. I was sad because people were telling me Williamson was a dangerous place to go, and I thought that it was crazy, because I had come from a real ghetto, to be stabbed here. I was also angry because the guy couldn't come up to me man to man and face me if he had a problem. I mean, I was 5'9" and weighed 200 pounds, and he was 6'4" and weighed about 250 pounds. I mean, why did he have to stab me in the back? But like I said, BJ and Jocelyn encouraged me and helped me through these times.

When I was growing up, as far as religion goes, I guess I only had my mom's faith, but now I've found my own; it's more of a spiritual thing. I want to tell people to take advantage of every day. You never know, you could be gone in an instant. Be responsible and get an education. Don't let procrastination keep you from achieving your goals; learn to make smart choices. I'd rather have my mind full of 'what ifs,' like what if I had stayed in the hood and gotten into a gang, than regrets over actions I didn't take.

I have something I want to say to the black population. Quit limiting yourself; don't feel like if you are goal-oriented, or getting an education that you are becoming white, or betraying your race. People fought and died for us to be able to take advantage of opportunities. There are a lot of things you can do now that you couldn't sixty or seventy years ago. Do them. Use your God-given abilities for good.

That's why I went into social work; to help others and be a role model. It is so easy in today's society to be influenced by the negative. I'm going into the Air Force this summer, and I want to get my Masters Degree and use my time promoting change for the better.

(Compiler's note) I met Branden's mother when he graduated from the University of Pikeville in May 2013. She exuded so much pride over her son's accomplishments.

(Branden Teasley 6 years later)

I have spent the past six years of my life using the social work profession as a vehicle to promote social change and cognition awareness. After graduating from Upike in June of 2013, I proudly joined the U.S Army reserves as an E4 68R in October of 2013. Though I never deployed, I learned structure and met people I will know for the rest of my life. Also in October of 2013 before being shipped off for basic training, I landed a full time position as a Service Coordinator with the responsibilities of a social worker and case manager. There I worked with children and adults with developmental and intellectual disabilities, serving as a resource to assure their equality, where I maintained a 77+ case load, numbers varying according to assignments.

Over my six years as a Service Coordinator I had the opportunity to see systems, system development, and how the developed systems affect the population they are designed to serve. This at times led to lack of sleep and sometimes a fear of little hope for change. After proudly serving the intellectual and developmentally challenged population for six years, I resigned in May of 2019 to transition into the technology field. I attribute this transition to the desire to do more in less time. My new goal is to acquire an AA degree in cyber security then a BA in Computer Engineering and lastly a PhD in Anthropology which I will use to be a professor at my selected HBC; and in the meantime inspire everything I come into contact with.

My best advice is to seek what I call the "Silence." Many professional athletes and professional personalities refer to it as the Zone, and many spiritual personalities define it as the Aether or quintessence; to that I say, to each his own. The realization of the Silence is the realization of self, removed from perceived reality. I go further to describe the Silence as the God Frequency. Just as humans have a frequency of communication at which typical human speech ranges between 50 Hz and 300 Hz, there is a higher frequency contributed to the human imagination. To quote the late great American Serbian immigrant, Nikola Tesla, "If you want to find the secrets of the universe, think in terms of energy, frequency and vibration." For once you can see, nothing can hide, not even you from yourself.

I dedicate my chapter to my fellow Light-Worker Ermias "Nipsey Hussle" Asghedom, American rapper, Poet, entrepreneur, community activist and Father. Stay in search of new light. The Marathon continues.

(BIO:) *When asked, who I am, my first thought is I am a child of God, mainly because I do not put much thought into the question. More so, I put thought or focus on who I am becoming and why. But for the sake of answering the question, who am I? I answer, I am an American-Native Black American, a descendent of slaves and freemen lost to history; as so, I am my potential.*

CHAPTER 30:
THAT WILL PROBABLY NEVER HAPPEN TO ME
RICHARD DEMPSEY

College life is something that we hope all of the younger generations will be looking forward to in order to help further their career choices and life paths. We hear about the positive things that come from college such as the friends and experiences, and often times we hear about that dreaded student loan debt, but there is something that is not often talked about when we enter the life of a college student, college rape. When I started as a freshman, I became friends with three young ladies over a period of time, and each of these young women all shared something in common, and that was childhood rape. This was something not in my realm of comprehension, not from my past, or anything that I would have imagined in my future experience. It was also something that I was not ready to handle as a person.

Life was cruel early in my college life experiences. I received voice mail messages from people acting as if they were a local health clinic to report that I had been diagnosed with HIV Aids; the fact is I had never been to this health clinic. Shortly after I received the first message to this effect, I was about to walk into Walmart with my mother and experienced my first ever panic attack. There was a bench in the entryway just inside the front doors, and I sat there for a while, just trying to breathe; trying to somehow fathom the thought of someone wanting to be so cruel. Little did I know this was foreshadowing.

When young college students who have never experienced rape first learn about it, they may often think "Well that will probably never happen to me." This may be because they think that they have lived eighteen or more years without it happening, so it is not going to occur. But some of these people thinking this are wrong, and I was wrong, because I also thought that way. At the age of nineteen I invited someone over to my college dorm to have a casual conversation that led to nonconsensual sex; I was raped, most painfully.

At first, I didn't know what to think, and then I felt like I should just ignore it and move on, and that maybe everything would be okay. It was not. That was the start of something I will have to live with for the rest of my life. The next morning, I woke up to muscle spasms in my back and I was hardly able to move. I had never felt like this before, and so I went to my doctor where I was diagnosed with a herniated disc. I was in a wheelchair for a few weeks and then gradually made it to being able to move around with a cane, but this is not something I could prepare myself for. The worst response came from the perpetrator stating, "I wanted to leave you with something to remember me by."

I battled with myself over do I report this, or do I let it go, an inner conversation I had many nights as I would try to lay down and feel the nerves in my body twitch like they had never before. Most of the left side of my body has remained numb since that day. All I did in the beginning was re-live that night, thinking "What could I have done to avoid this?" These thoughts continued to get worse and eventually led to two suicide attempts. The first attempt was by medication, but I now believe that subconsciously I didn't really want to die and so I didn't take a lethal dose, although at the time I thought it was. But I was still being tormented by thoughts that my life was useless and not worth living, and there was a dark voice taking over my mind and telling me to give up and just kill myself, so I decided to make a more decisive second attempt. I drove to a trail that led to a cliff, parked my car and got ready to make what I thought would be my last walk. But as I headed out, something happened that I now believe was a divine intervention. First I heard a dog began to bark, and next thing I knew a Saint Bernard was blocking my path, and the voice that had been overwhelming my mind immediately stopped. Chills ran through my entire body, and I walked back to my car, got back in, and just sat there for I don't even know how long, and cried. But in that time period I knew I had to turn to faith, to Something or Someone bigger than me.

Once I was aware of what I needed to do in order to continue on in life, I began attending a group at the University of Pikeville called BUG, Blessed Unity of God, where people from all religions and experiences came together to discuss their faith. This was the beginning of very eye-opening experiences where I was able to create new bonds with people dealing with similar situations, and also learn some coping skills from them. There was still one thing I was dealing with that I was unsure of how to handle; telling my family. I started by telling my mother, and then I told my grandparents, but I swore I would never tell my father because of fear of how he might react. So, I decided that I just needed to focus on college and worry about him later.

I thought that overall I managed my depression well. My grades did decline in school, which could have impact on how many courses one could take, but I talked with the Dean of the College about my rape, and expressed my desire of finishing up classes as soon as possible. His response was, "Say no more; you can still take whatever classes you wish". So, for me, he never gave up on me wanting to take more class hours per semester, and I was able to still take twenty-three hours for two semesters in a row and graduated with my Bachelors in three years. Some people wondered why I wanted to get away from college so quickly, but for me it was always a constant reminder of what had happened. My goal was not necessarily to finish in three years, and accomplishing it didn't bring a greater sense of satisfaction; I was just happy to be away from that dorm room where everything happened.

For one of the last classes I took at college, I decided to take a dream psychology course with one of the psychology professors that had previously worked with me on my trauma. During this class, I was aware that I kept having a reoccurring dream of the rape and the rapist, was also having flashbacks, and was informed that most clinical staff would consider this a diagnosis of Post-Traumatic Stress Disorder. While in this class, we began dream journaling and role-played shamanistic rituals to reenter the dreams and try to discover more of their meanings. This is considered a technique by Carl Jung; there are also techniques for dream psychology with Gestalt Therapy that are more confrontational.

My reoccurring dream was of a woman who was in what looked like a psychiatric hospital. She kept screaming she was okay, but you could see in her eyes she was not. The room was very dark and all she wanted to do was escape. Then it flashed to an escape where she busted open the doors and started running down a hill in her hospital gown as if someone was chasing her. I could sense her looking around and feeling scared and then she found a place where she could hide; it appeared to me as a wall that went down to a boat ramp because she stopped and had to grab onto the wall and climb it so as not to fall into the water. As she got to the other side, she began to climb up and all of the sudden there was my father waiting to grab her. He jerked her up and then it flashed to my grandparents' home where the girl then hid in the bathroom and the dream cut to my maternal grandmother yelling at my father asking if he had raped the female. Then it flashed to my father breaking into the bathroom and I woke up.

When I chose to reenter this dream, I had preconceived notions about how to work on my trauma. I had been telling everyone that I was fine, but my dreams were telling me otherwise. The first thing that happened when I reentered my dream was I was sitting at Williamson Memorial Hospital in the night gown. This jarred me into realizing that I was the female in the dream and the hospital was not a psychiatric ward, but rather the place I went to the night after I was raped. Water in dreams usually represent the unconscious mind trying to tell us something, and for me, it was that I had built a wall with my father about the rape; that he would be willing to listen if I told him. I decided to go home that weekend and reveal to my father I had been raped. When I was with him, my hand had curled up as if I was trying to make a fist and he asked "What is wrong?" and I told him, "Oh, it has been like that since the rape." So that was how I told him. It came out with no thought, and the moment that I explained it all to him, my reoccurring dream stopped. Since that day I have not had a flashback or another dream about the rape, and this truly made me a believer in therapeutic techniques to help with trauma.

The reason why that is important to note, is because once I graduated college, I thought I would always want to be a teacher, but

I wanted to gain experience with other real-life jobs and then begin to teach or do something with the field of psychology.

So, who am I now? I was given the opportunity to work for a mental health agency in substance abuse and trauma and worked for over two years in the mental health and substance abuse field. Many of the young people that I would meet who were addicted to drugs had some form of trauma happen to them earlier in their life. I heard stories of someone being used as payment for their parent's drugs as a child, someone selling themselves to be able to afford drugs that helped them avoid withdrawal, or how a tragic vehicle accident led to being overly prescribed opiates that led to a worse addiction than that person ever expected. This is when I realized I was called to this field for a reason.

I recently finished up my Masters of Education in Counseling and Human Development and am working on my licensure to be able to work with more than just Medicaid clients. Licensure allows you to work with all private insurances, and the population that I can serve is much broader.

I now realize that although I thought I could easily overcome my own trauma, I couldn't. I tried to avoid all thoughts of help, but I shouldn't have. If I had had more social support at the time, I do not believe that I would have attempted suicide, perhaps not even thought of it. When I avoided telling my father about the rape, it only caused me to relive the trauma because I was unable to get past something that deep down I felt I needed to do. I am convinced that the therapeutic techniques that helped me are something to consider if dealing with any depression, anxiety, or trauma related symptoms. I challenge you as you read this, that if you are dealing with issues that can cripple in physical, emotional, or mental areas, please seek help with a mental health professional. Keep in mind that although you may have fears about asking for help, sometimes those you are seeking help from have been in your shoes.

(BIO:) "My name is Richard Dempsey. I grew up in southern West Virginia in a small double wide trailer. My brother and I were the first to receive a college education, and I am the first to get a Master's

degree. I didn't let my upbringing or my environment change my path of life, and I chose to overcome any adversity. I currently work in the corrections field with inmates that have faced battles with addiction. I plan to continue to work in the counseling field. "

CHAPTER 31:

THE LOSSES WE BEAR
JEFF AND LYNN WALDROUP

(Compiler's note)I was sitting with Jeff and Lynn at the kitchen table discussing the most difficult time they have ever gone through in their life.

"It was very hard," Jeff said. "You're not supposed to bury your children; it's not right. They're supposed to bury you."

"People have said," Lynn had a pained look on her face as she spoke, "Time heals; it will get better with time. They don't know," she added, "It doesn't get better with time."

In 2000, Jeff and Lynn lost their eleven-year-old daughter, Lindsey, to Cystic Fibrosis. Lindsey's older brother, Lamar was also stricken with the same disease. Jeff said they buried Lindsey on a Wednesday, and had to take Lamar to the hospital that Friday as he had a downturn. Jeff said that, looking back, they didn't have time to focus on Lindsey's death right then because they had to shift attention immediately to the worsening of Lamar. It was another five years of emotional peaks and valleys, and then they had to lay their oldest son to rest. Lamar was twenty.

Their youngest son, Lance, was fourteen, so again, after a second heart-wrenching loss of a child, they immediately re-focused on being parents to the remaining child. Jeff said, "Although you never get over the ones you've lost, you need to appreciate and enjoy the moments with those you have. We hold Lance close."

"But," Lynn added, "you always live with thoughts of the others; they're always there." Jeff also said that as far as any favorite memories; they have all become favorites.

When I asked Jeff if there was anything in particular that helped him get through the times right after losing each of the children, his reply was quick and certain. "Knowing that I'll see them again someday, and fishing."

Soon after Lamar was born the doctors made the diagnosis of CF,. He was in and out of hospitals from there on out, more so than Lindsey. Because of that, everyone thought Lamar would be the first to go, but not so. Three years after his sister's death, and two years before his, Lamar was able to have a lung transplant, and Jeff said that Lamar enjoyed living every day to its fullest. "He loved to fish; we fished together a lot. If I can live my life as full as he did in those two years," Jeff said, "I'd be living a lot. He had received a gift of life with that transplant; most people don't know what it is to get the gift of life. I know I look at life differently now."

As parents, Jeff and Lynn were concerned with the dignity of their children, and so they learned how to give the necessary treatments at home. "They had no privacy in the hospital," Lynn said.

"That's no way to live," Jeff added.

There's something else they have had to live with. Jeff talked about survivor's guilt. "Sometimes you just can't help feeling it," he said. "They're gone, and you're still here."

We talked a little about how common that is. I mentioned that I could relate to that as an Infantryman in Vietnam, knowing that some had died, and here I was, still "bumbling my way" through life.

"And people don't know," Lynn said again. "It just doesn't get easier with time."

"But we do know we'll see them again, someday," Jeff added.

(Compiler's note) Jeff and Lynn really just can't tell you how much it turned everything upside down. It was hard; first, Lindsey, and then Lamar; both from Cystic Fibrosis; just five years apart. And unless you've lost a child, there is no way you can understand the daily pain they still live with. Watching the children suffer through the illness was tough, and then they had to give them up, and lay them to rest. They have some comfort in knowing the children are now pain free, new bodies, and they'll see them again, someday, but, it's still hard.

Organizing, then writing, about Jeff and Lynn was difficult. First, I do not want to bring fresh pain to anyone, but rather reach out in a way that helps all of us in our "woundedness." Secondly, I run everything I write past my main proofer, my wife, Cora. I was reading to her what I had, so far, written in this chapter, and had to stop several times to regain my composure in the midst of weeping. My feelings were so mixed. So far, my loss experiences (including during Infantry time in Vietnam, other friends, and with the loss of my mother) only touch the surface of what Jeff and Lynn, and so many others, have been through.

Yet, I am becoming increasingly aware, that at one time or another, we have all been left hurting, some at much deeper levels than others. My prayer for all of us is that we can see others through the eyes of God, and try to reach out with the heart of God. Sometimes one may feel like there is nothing they can say to bring comfort to someone, especially to those in sorrow over the loss of a child. And yet just the presence of a friend may be what the mourner may need at that moment as they wrestle with loss unbearable, beyond belief. We may ask, "How can they …?" Yet many do, somehow, go on in hope.

Life to the Fullest and It's Shadow World; Jeff mentioned how Lamar lived life to its fullest in the two short years he was given after his lung transplant. Many people have talked (and will continue to) about this concept. The paradox of this is the awakening occurs so often with those who are keenly aware of their limited time in this life, and then, soon, those left behind have to suffer to the fullest.

Jeff and Lynn are examples of dignity in the face of extreme difficulty, and of holding close to their hearts the precious moments and memories they still have. They seem very aware that, as brought out in the play Shadowlands, *and the writings of C.S. Lewis, especially* A Grief Observed, *we live in a world where there is pain, but these are only passing shadows in the world to come.*

I wrote the following the evening of the day I initially talked with Jeff and Lynn, and called it Losses - My Prayer (02/02/2013, Saturday 12:45 a.m.) Lord, help me to write or pray and live every single day with a sense of your eternal vision, and with a sense of your love for others.

And again, reflecting that evening, I also wrote, All I Want is ... All I want is fulfillment of a little request. Pain of the losses to lessen; even leave! Be gone! Scat! Is that asking too much? Why can't you give me a break and move along? Why can't you be nice enough to take my advice? I know life doesn't work this way, so, Lord, help me one day at a time.

(BIO:) Talking with Jeff in late 2019, Jeff said he was not able to fish as much as he used to as his current job kept him really busy all week, and he sleeps a bit more on the weekends, but that he was doing all right. Feelings expressed in the 2013 story are about the same. He said he really like his work and that helps him a lot. He and Lynn seem to be personifications of the words, "One day at a time, dear Lord, one day at a time."

(Compiler's Note) We regret to have to include that Lance, age 30, recently passed away. This has been extremely difficult for Jeff and Lynn.

CHAPTER 32:

A COUNTRY BOY CAN SURVIVE
MARK ROGERS

(As told to Compiler) I may have had it tough in the early years, but that's how I learned to survive. We had it rough; there wasn't any such thing as money. There were times we nearly starved. If we killed something, then we ate meat; and we had a garden. I'm fifty now. When I was growing up in the 60's there weren't a lot of government programs; didn't want help anyhow.

Like I said, it was rough; if we got sick we just had to deal with it; there wasn't money for doctors. But at school, it seemed like anybody I looked at had it better. I didn't understand the differences until I was older. That's just the way it was. When I look back on it, I realize my mother was like a lot of other people in the area; she did the best she could.

(Compiler's Note) Mark sat back on the couch in his camouflage jacket and relaxed a bit. I was visiting a sister-in-law in Graham County, North Carolina, and Mark had come by the house to visit for a while. He and I left the others in the kitchen and went into the living room for this interview.

My dad wasn't around when we were kids; my mother remarried; some of my uncles pretty much raised me. When I was around seventeen my stepdad got killed in an accident while working on the Cherohala Skyway; a packer rolled over on him. But one of my brothers and me, I guess we were maybe eleven and fourteen; we had already left home, and raised ourselves. We learned responsibility; more kids these days need to learn that. We lived together in an old house for some time; I stayed a lot in the mountains and just did what it took to survive; I married when I was thirty-one; that didn't work out so well. I did better this time; I've been married for fifteen years now (2013.)

I never did like school; I would just sit and think about hunting and fishing. I quit going when I was fourteen. They never did come for looking for me, so I just stayed out.

I learned to hunt when I was eight; a couple uncles helped, but I pretty much taught myself. So I knew how to trap, fish, hunt, and stay in the mountains. I'd work construction in the summer, and in the winters I'd go to one of the camps I had in the Santeetlah Mountains, for about eleven weeks. That's where I've always been the happiest, in the mountains.

I asked Mark what was the hardest part of his life in the mountains.

Even though I was happy there, sometimes it was hard when I was all alone. You can get lonely out there with no one.

When I asked if he was able to make any pets of the animals in the mountains, he laughed.

Had to eat; didn't think of making pets of any of them. I shot my first big deer when I was thirteen, that was before I even left home; before then I ate a lot of squirrels and other small game; I love squirrel meat. Since then I've shot a lot of bears and hogs. I have an old wood stove, and I can most of what I shoot. Can the old fashioned way; outside sometimes. I can just about any kind of meat, and taters, any kind of vegetables, trout, and other fish.

I told Mark I had never heard of canning trout before. He laughed and said he liked canned trout even better than salmon. Mark got quiet and thoughtful.

You know, in the mountains is the only place where I really feel normal. In a way, the world ain't changed there; it's the same as when I was a boy. I'm at peace there. I like the old ways.

I asked Mark if he had any days fishing or hunting that stuck out to him as the best. He was quick to reply.

I've had a lot of them; there've been a lot of them good. I guess with fishing, maybe the day I caught a 28" brown trout. That was really good. And hunting, the biggest animal I ever killed was near Wilkesboro; I got me a 530 pound wild hog. The biggest bear I ever got was 438 pounds. That old hog was even bigger. I've killed lots of bears and hogs, canned a lot of the meat. Of course, we got us freezers now, so we save some that way.

I like to garden, too. And make a little shine. My uncle taught me. I've been around stills ever since I was a baby."

I asked Mark what advice he had for others who might find themselves in particularly tough circumstances.

People need to appreciate what they have, their health, the people in their lives. All that can change quickly. Enjoy each day. As far as an answer to what I have learned from my life, or who I am now, I believe we're supposed to be happy, so you need to find what you like to do, and do it. My peace and happiness is in the woods and the mountains. I'm not a real religious person, but I'm spiritual. My communion is with nature. I learn about God in a garden and in the mountains, and survival; a country boy can do that."

Mark and I went back out to the kitchen to join the others. A family friend was there with her young son, Conner. Mark asked her if it was okay to give Connor some candy. He laughed and said, "The youngun's like candy."

(BIO:) Mark Rogers lives in Graham County, NC and has been featured on Moonshiners *(Discovery Channel.) He is one of the few remaining genuine combinations of a woodsman, hunter, and fisherman. If you were lost in the woods, Mark is the best person (probably in the United States) that you could run into. He learned to make moonshine as a boy from some of his uncles.*

CHAPTER 33:

WHY ME, LORD? WHY NOT ME?
MARY BETH ULRICH WEBB

In 1974, Mary Beth Ulrich was fresh out of undergraduate school, and a first year teacher of math and science at a middle school in a Chicago suburb. Things were going well; as a college student, she had to study, of course, but, overall, concepts "came easily." Now, she was finally getting to strike out independently – first apartment, first car, more social life, the usual dreams.

Starting her senior year of college she had dealt with headaches some, but didn't think too much of it. As a teacher she didn't focus on the headaches, but rather "the joy of teaching". But the children in the class noticed that she was bothered some by headaches, because one of the Christmas gifts from students in the class where she was teaching was a pretty silver jewelry box, with aspirin inside.

She still visited regularly with her parents, and her mother noted that she seemed to be sleeping quite a bit. In retrospect, Mary Beth says she believes it was a defense mechanism; when she was sleeping, the headaches didn't bother.

On Friday, February 1st, 1974, Mary Beth was working with two little girls in her class who did not know the answer to, "What is 9 plus 4?" She said, as she tried to explain it to them, she realized, she didn't know the answer either.

She spent that weekend, like she often did, with her parents. That turned out to be providential. One of her aunts had had a stroke, and, on Sunday, February 3rd, her parents went to the hospital to visit. Mary Beth declined going with them, as she had a headache, and wanted to sleep. When her parents returned around 5 p.m., they found her lying on the bathroom floor.

As best the doctors could determine later, she had suffered a stroke around noon. She was seen initially by her family doctor who knew that the University of Iowa Hospital had the facilities equipped to deal with her situation. Mary Beth's father told her later that a very difficult thing for him had been signing a release for an angiogram. The doctors made clear that it could either provide information that would help save her life, or it could kill her. Within the team of doctors working in her, some were saying that an operation could very dangerous, but one of them said, that given the alternative of what her life without the surgery would be, they ought to go for it.

The initial ordeal was successfully dealt with. Mary Beth was kept alive, and was in the hospital in Iowa for exactly a month. But the next phase was waiting in the wings, recovery. This involved going back home to Illinois, and starting the rehabilitation process.

Several things became huge factors in the process for Mary Beth; her family, her friends, and her dreams.

The family factor was first and foremost. After a few days, her father had to return to work, but her mother quit her job to stay with her. As she started to recover, many people sent flowers and cards. Mary Beth was not aware of them at first, but, of course, her mother was, and felt comforted by the outreach of others. As she did improve, Mary Beth not only started to be more aware of gestures of love and support, but also became aware that the ordeal was, by its very nature, putting added stress on her parents and her brother. She now believes that her recovery was in part strengthened and hastened because she wanted to be the best patient she could be, so as not to add to their stress.

Her father later related to her that, after the stroke itself, the hardest thing for him to do was pack up her apartment. He told her it was extremely traumatic for him as he felt like he was violating her personal space, papers, etc. In addition, her mother felt guilt as she wondered if the stroke had its origins in genetics.

However comfort came for both her parents as they celebrated the joys along the recovery path: the first time tying her shoes, walking without a cane, getting in and out of a bathtub. And later, they joined with Mary Beth as she decided to start celebrating February 3rd as her "second birthday."

Friends were also an important part of the recovery process for her. She was overwhelmed when she realized that the cards she had received filled up ¾ of a large, black leaf bag. It was life-affirming to her to realize how many people cared for her. It also was significant, Mary Beth realized, that through visits, and later, walks and other activities, she was receiving the message that, even though she had lost some aspects of her life, the core of who she was, was being recognized and affirmed by her friends. Also, as some friends encountered some difficult questions in their own lives, they sought her out for advice. Those people made her feel important and feel good about the fact that she was able to help someone else, rather than always being on the taking end of things.

Another dynamic element in the recovery process for Mary Beth was her dreams. She didn't dwell on whether she could teach again, but rather, how she could get back that part of her prior life. It wasn't a question of what she couldn't do, but rather what was still possible. At some point in her rehabilitation process, she was asked to be a guest speaker at a Rotary Club meeting. There was a priest who spoke before her, and afterward, she realized that their two messages couldn't have been meshed together any better. The priest's message also reinforced her belief that God had something for her to do because of what she was going through.

A prayer she had was, "God, I can handle the physical limitations that come with this, but, please let me have my mind." At one point, when a thought reared its ugly head that maybe she was done for as far as teaching, Mary Beth asked her doctor if there was any hope in that area. His response was quick and to the point. He told her he wanted her to get back into the classroom as soon as possible. That would become a restoring device for her. So within a year, she started substitute teaching.

One thing different that she felt made her a better teacher when she started back, that from before the stroke was, right after college she taught as a person to whom things had come easily. After the stroke, she saw and approached learning from the struggling side.

After subbing for a while, Mary Beth was offered a position as a Graduate Assistant at Illinois State University. After earning her Doctorate Degree in 1989, she applied for, and was offered a position at Pikeville College (now the University of Pikeville) in Pikeville, Kentucky, where she still serves as an associate professor of math education (*This story given in 2013*).

Mary Beth has become more aware of the fact that helping people understand concepts helps them gain more control over their futures. She recalls the frustration she felt when she had no control. This emotion overwhelmed her once when her mother and an aunt were getting her ready to take her to a rehab session early in her recovery process. Her aunt asked her mother, "What are you going to put on Mary Beth?" Mary Beth realized she wasn't a factor in the procedure of getting dressed at all, and she hated that absence of independence.

A while after she started teaching at Pikeville College, Mary Beth received an e-mail from a girl that she worked with while substitute teaching. The girl had been a senior in high school, and had to pass math in order to graduate. But she just was unable to grasp some of the concepts. The girl wrote to Mary Beth words to the effect of, "You may not remember me, but you were a substitute teacher when I was a senior in high school. There were some math concepts that were difficult for me to comprehend, and, as a result of the time you spent working individually with me, I was able to understand them. I graduated from high school, am happily married with three children. I want to thank you for your help to me. It means a lot."

In one of her classes not too long ago, Mary Beth had a soldier who had returned from Iraq and was facing some obstacles in his life. He told her, "I look at you and tell myself, *If she can do it, I can too.*"

Once when she was in a medical supply store for prosthetics, she was talking to a young boy who had just been fitted with a prosthetic and was trying to get used to it. She was able to encourage him by telling him to celebrate the little victories. She related to him how she had been able to do that – with being able to open her hand for the first time, tie her shoes by herself, and other things. She could tell he was reassured that he could learn to function in life quite well.

After listening to a couple people with spina bifada talk about overcoming obstacles, Mary Beth realized even more just how blessed she was. That even extended to the repair work necessary several weeks after her original surgery. During the first procedure, doctors had to cut a section of bone out of her skull, and then, after they did what they had to do to save her life, they put back a temporary skin cover. Later there was a second surgery to put the cut-out-bone section back into place. Pieces like this were marked and kept frozen during the interim period.

Somehow, Mary Beth's piece got misplaced. One of her doctors said in disbelief to the keeper of the bones (possibly a trembling intern who just knew he was going to lose his position), "Lost? What do you mean lost?"

A thorough search of the freezer storage area turned up an unmarked piece of frozen bone. Tests showed a match for her, and so they were able to proceed. And, she said, the incident not only still brings her a smile, it adds new meaning to the expression, "I once was lost, but now am found."

Mary Beth said she has also been blessed with an attitude of "Why not me? God has decided that I can handle this adversity-blessing as well as anyone, and has allowed it into my life for a reason."

(BIO:) Before her retirement from the University of Pikeville (KY) Mary Beth Webb was recognized by Cambridge Who's Who for showing dedication, leadership, and excellence in higher education.

CHAPTER 34:

EVERY DAY IS A BONUS: DON'T WASTE THE BONUS
DOUG LANGE

(Compiler's Note) This interview took place in 2013. Doug currently re-sides in South Carolina. You can see that even in the original story, the idea of 'Who am I now?" is present.)

As you know, the biggest event in Pikeville (KY) is "Hillbilly Days." Crowded streets; everybody loves to go downtown. I get tensed up; check windows. You had to do that in Khabul and Khandalhar, and you just don't leave that behind. One thing that people need to realize about those who have gone through some form of inner wounding, there are a lot of triggers around.

Doug and I were talking together a couple days after he had started reading some of my earlier writings. He commented on "Starkle, Starkle, Little Twink," the play in Appendix C of my book, War Wounded: Let the Healing Begin, *which he had just finished reading the night before.*

You might not have said it exactly this way, but you nailed it with, "no man is an island; at least not for long." It was when PAM picked up that something was different about DAN when he returned from the war, and he couldn't tell her about everything that was bothering him. When people go through certain experiences, sometimes they can't describe them to someone else who has not been there. They have difficulty communicating about them. And yet, there's a connection that people make with others who have gone through like experiences.

Doug referred back the play again.

After the war, DAN and PAM still connected and communicated at an emotional and intellectual level, but there were some levels they could not relate to each other on because they were in separate lives for a year, and with DAN, the veteran, there were some things at a deeper level he just kept inside. I think I've done that with others at times, kept my distance.

We talked a couple minutes about the idealistic visions people can build up about others when separated by war; the almost fantasy-like vision of "he or she is over there fighting for his country, or, the other is back home, holding everything together."

We can get very idealistic, but we reconnect at the new reality of different experiences for a year, not idealism. However, let me give you an example of when you can communicate with someone at the experience reality level, and you know you should.

From my experience in Afghanistan, I know how it feels to senselessly lose friends, co-workers. So when the shootings took place at Ft. Hood, Texas November 5, 2009, which were senseless killings, I had a nephew I knew I had to call. He had served two tours in Iraq, and returned to an assignment at Ft. Hood, a place where he, and his Army buddies thought would they were safe. When I got him on the phone, he started to spill over with his feelings. I just knew he would need to do that. I was aware because, in a sense, I had been there.

Doug was a Civil Affairs Officer, Deputy Commander, Brigade level, with approximately 230 personnel in his command. His jurisdiction included eight cities and some storm troopers from the 101st and 82nd Airborne Units, also known as Helmets. He spent twenty-seven ½ years with the military, ten ½ of those on active duty. He was with the Reserves when called up, both to Kosovo, and Afghanistan.

I was fortunate to be part of the early units both in Kosovo in 1999 and in Afghanistan in 2002. At that time, a lot of the locals were happy we were there. That changed. But, still, maybe one of the lessons of Vietnam was there are times and places where we can be more effective talking with the locals, than fighting with them. My real job was to coordinate aid and work with a Khabulcentric government as liaison.

But I really enjoyed it more when working directly with the people. I have been told that that 80% of the people are honest and industrious and the other 20% are politicians and crooks. That's the way it was; maybe I should say, was then."

I felt a strong sense of responsibility for those people under my command. The most difficult days for me were those groundhog days; the same thing coming back around again. I hated looking at those metal boxes being loaded onto planes. They were bearing real people who gave their all, heading back to loved ones in mourning. Those are images you don't want in your mind, but they're there. It gives you a different outlook. You find yourself saying, "I didn't expect my life to turn out this way." You face your own mortality.

Those images create a certain pain. My dad was in World War II, and he never talked about his experiences. I was talking with him when he was eighty years old, and asked him a question about the war. His answer caught me off guard. He said, "I can't talk about it; it hurts too much." He lived a very full productive life, and I never knew how he was feeling inside. Now I know. There are images many of us veterans have, whether they originated in Iraq, Afghanistan, Kuwait, Vietnam, Korea, any war. We don't want to see them, but they are there.

Doug paused for a little while, thinking, and then he went on.

I tried to help my people in any way I could, to try and help them stay grounded which also meant using tough love at times. Sometimes it takes that to help people grow and develop into what they can be, and also, to survive. You want to keep them from being in those metal boxes loaded onto planes.

I had something interesting happen one time that hit me at a couple levels. We were in an area where there were a lot of nomadic Afghans. They herded sheep, and basically the way of life had remained unchanged for centuries. They would migrate to the north, and back south with seasonal changes. When we were checking out villages, there were usually a lot of kids standing by the road, and we would give them any leftover MRE's (meals-ready-to-eat) we had. We would take their pictures, and of course then they could see themselves on the camera. They were always in awe. I was talking one time with this boy who was maybe ten to twelve years old, and he asked me what it had been like for me growing up. I told him I had spent a lot of time with relatives on their farm, with the animals, and growing and picking fruit. He said to me, "Oh, you know agriculture; so you're a shepherd." I had never thought of myself as a shepherd.

Then it hit me. In actuality, I was a shepherd, of 230 people. Sometimes I had to go out looking for the lost sheep and bring them back to the fold, and I was always trying to keep them safe. I realized that was, and is, my calling. This is when I feel completed. Often you seek lost sheep one at a time. The journey of life is all about helping others. As people we all want something, and to feel like we have lived a worthwhile life. Your outlook may change because of things that have happened, but, still, we all want to feel like there has been a reason for us being put here on this earth.

I asked Doug what he considered was his best day in Afghanistan. He smiled.

There were a lot what I could call best days. I enjoyed working with people. Throughout my life I have volunteered for things, because I don't want to look back and say, "What if?" But now one of my best days I was able to have due to my position was when I spent an evening with the king in his palace. We had a nice conversation about life, Christmas, and God, dreams and goals, families.

I asked Doug what he has found to be a source of healing in his life after Afghanistan. He was silent for a while, reflecting.

I pray and meditate more. I study my Bible differently and try to internalize goals on how to live my life. Meditation for me is time away from the noise of life, certain memories. Of course, I have mild tinnitus, milder than you do, so there is a certain sense of never getting away from the noise, but we work at it. I read a lot more. I like to walk with my wife.

I think more about the difference between what I do and who I am. They are not the same. I crunch numbers; that's what I do. And I'm a little oxymoronic. There are times when I am a little OCD; and other times when I feel a strong sense of compassion and realize I have a heart to help. I'm here at the University of Pikeville for a reason. What I do is function as Vice President for Finance and Business Affairs (2013, time of original writing.) Who I am called to be is a helper, a shepherd. I believe that what we do for others flows out like the ripples from a rock being thrown into a pond."

I have no right to have survived when others didn't. Every day is a bonus; you don't want to waste the bonus. I want to know at the end of the day that I made a positive difference in someone's life. If I did, it wasn't a wasted day. There are images out of Afghanistan I don't want to see, or live again. But I wouldn't trade the experience. It has helped form who I am. From both the good and the bad, I have learned so much. I don't want to waste my bonus days.

So, in summation, does it really matter what I do over the course of a day? By my way of understanding, yes, it does. I believe we must give our best to helping others, seeking the lost. Little did I know how meaningful that young Afghan boy's words would be to me. He probably never knew the implications of his words, but he gave me new insight into my calling. I can't erase everything that's happened, but I can be a shepherd.

(BIO:) Colonel Douglas J. Lange (Retired) left military service in 2004 and continues to work in Higher Education administration working to make education accessible to all. In 2019 he completed a Doctor of Business Administration degree with emphasis on leadership and ethics. He has begun to teach and conduct seminars to business and industry groups. "Shepherds and teachers don't ever really retire; they change their work environment."

CHAPTER 35:
TO STARE DEATH IN THE FACE
MIKE HAND

I have experienced a sequence of life changing events; in some cases, maybe better called life crushing events. When I look deeply at some of these occurrences I know they have impacted me in ways both good and bad, however, they have also helped me really discover who I am. Nonetheless, I would not want anyone to have to travel the path I have!

I have indeed survived the rough waters of painful and difficult situations; loss of employment, cancer, startup and failure of a company, pulmonary embolisms, cancer (again), and financial destruction. Through all of this, I thank God always for my wife Vicky – my life mate for better and worse.

I was 48 years old when the first of several traumatic life changing events occurred. My position as an elite engineer employed at a very large utility was eliminated. This was the company that had recruited me fresh out of Georgia Tech when I completed my Bachelor's Degree in Engineering.

At the company there was constant change in managers and management structure. I felt like my entire career was being shut down because a Vice President could get recognition for saving the company money while also receiving a very large bonus at the end of the year. To make things worse my particular work group was notified several months ahead of time that two of our six positions were going to eliminated, and that new job descriptions were already being developed for the four positions that would remain. On one hand, you could see this as plenty of advance warning; conversely, you could see it as a time of increased uncertainty, tension, and misgivings because each of us in the work group had very specific areas of expertise.

Two weeks before the decisions were to be made about who would be eliminated, the job descriptions came out, and it was obvious that my skill set was not a good fit for any of the new descriptions. My initial feeling was probably typical (and very human), that some people in my workgroup, including me, were disliked by senior management. So my thoughts ran amok pretty much as follows.

Okay. They got ME; I know that for sure ... the VP involved, well he never did seem to like me even though I've always received grades of excellence in service reviews ... I have twenty-eight years' experience ... some as a technical expert and various positions in management up to General Manager level over 120+ employees as the system operations manager ... I know the work ... I know the people ... I know the processes ... I can show where I have saved this company millions of dollars in operating costs ... I've received approximately $250,000 worth of technical equipment training ... I have significant intellectual property, but that doesn't seem to matter ... for some reason a man I see as having an untrustworthy reputation did not take the time to know me as a person, nor even take into consideration my knowledge, experience, and twenty-eight years of service to this organization ... why, I doubt he even knew that before he became VP over my division that I was given an award of Maintenance Professional, selected out of a pool of over 140 employees.

So let me just summarize my thoughts, I was MAD. I felt like I had no value in a place where I had served diligently for twenty-eight years, most of them being on call 24/7.

Fortunately, I had just reached a retirement milestone that was based on age plus years of service, which gave me a maximum pension multiplier. So, one good thing about the forced retirement was a significant lump sum payment in the severance package that would help me bridge the gap as I began to look for another job. Just a note; historically there were a lot of contractors that hired retirees from the utility to perform engineering design work very similar to what they had been previously doing, so it appeared to me that finding another job would not be that hard to do. I was too young to retire and the opportunity to work full time and also draw some retirement at the same time (aka double dipping) was attractive.

Still I was angry, frustrated, unsure of my destiny, judgmental, scared, and ... as a man, a lot of self-esteem was tied to what I had accomplished and continued to do in the workplace. So overall, losing my job was a very unpleasant experience. In the end, three positions were eliminated from my work group. They had a retirement party for the three of us all at the same time; I went but did not feel appreciated, as a matter of fact, the managers at the party barely gave us any recognition. Actually, it was almost like a regularly scheduled division luncheon, which was all right with me since I did not feel like partying; I sensed a big hole coming into my life.

Going back to when my work group first received notice that some of us would be losing jobs, naturally I began focusing on what I would do if mine was one of them. Should I fight frantically to find another position in the company before the deadline? How could I find a position when there were no jobs being posted and a hiring freeze was in force? I was 48 and the Social Security age for retirement for me as a baby boomer was 66.5 years old. I knew the math! I was 18 years shy of a full Social Security benefit. I would have a retirement pension from the company. In a way, as I questioned the way forward, the only positive thing I could see was that if I found another job, I would have two sources of income. If I found a new job that was equal in pay and personal benefits I would be in a much better financial position.

As I look back on my life since I lost my secure position of twenty-eight years, I see that it looks completely different than I thought it would at the time of the event. And in so many ways, it's a path I would not have wanted or chosen. A bandage was put on the wound of unemployment because two weeks after I packed my desk at my old organization I was sitting at a new desk with a new company with a new job as an engineer. Finding a job quickly was so encouraging. It was in the same sector of engineering and only four blocks away from my previous employer. My new employer was a contract engineering firm, and ironically, the main contract this company had was to provide services for ... my previous employer. That's right – contract work for the company that had just sent me to the house. It restored some of my confidence and a small piece of feeling I knew who I was. To me, it was an answer to my prayers and prayers of others made on my behalf; that God had quickly provided. Although I did not realize it at the time, it was the beginning of a new path for my life that would be a journey through many other extremely difficult and painful life situations and seasons. But the fact that I no longer had a job with guarantees caused me to begin to live life more based on hope, faith, and love.

After about nine months at my new employer their company income was declining (anyone care to guess why) because their number one customer (my previous employer) was making major cutbacks in the building of new supply lines, as well as not maintaining their existing infrastructure. So the company I now worked for had times changing for the worse. Their income was hugely based on steady contract awards that were now in decline, not only for them, but for all the other contract engineering firms in the area as well. There were financial challenges in the utility business as electricity began to be traded as a commodity with a price now much more linked to supply and demand!

So now, again, bang! One Friday afternoon I was called into the Vice President's office and told to clean out my desk and to not report for work on Monday, that I was being furloughed for eight weeks; eight weeks with no income. I had to live off the severance pay I got when I was forced to retire almost a year earlier. At the end of the eight weeks the VP called me and told me he had some work for me, but in a different department, and, that I would have to take a twenty five percent pay cut because the job was in a different group in the company. So I was receiving that strong and dangerous message again – "You are not really worth that much to us."

Naturally I had a lot of questions. But I must mention one thing about myself. I am a man of faith in the creator of the universe, the almighty God. I had studied the Bible a lot and been active in communities of faith long before this event happened. I was and still am a Christian trying to grow stronger and better each day in my faith walk. I knew and still do that God is in control, and says to me, "I made you, and you are priceless." However, I am human, and still experience very human struggles.

So, for me, my worth to the company was declining based on financial situations, but I was learning that my personal worth to God never changed as I learned to trust Him more. I did take the new position with a promise to be restored to my previous pay in a year, however it turned out this promise made by the VP was just plain a lie. It never happened. I worked for a little over a year and got another one of those phone calls to come to the VP's office on a Friday afternoon. "Mike, I am going to have to furlough you for eight weeks, or, just go ahead and lay you off." I was not given much time to choose, but my wife and I talked things over, prayed, and then made the decision. Our thinking was that at least I could get a little unemployment pay for a few months, and I knew then I would never go back again because I could not trust that VP and would most likely get another pay cut with lies about restoration of pay. The leadership was known for cut throat behavior and did not care at all about who I was. So I boldly told that VP that I had no interest in ever coming back based on how I had been treated.

To survive these events, both emotionally and physically, required that I pursue personal healing and growth. I had to do it for myself, my family, and my faith community. Without seeking and reaching to hold on to my faith in who made me who I am, I definitely would not be here to pen these words today. Each time, what appeared to be hopelessness, caused a stronger hope to grow with deeper roots, stronger faith, and more love, which all in all led to greater confidence, and restoration.

So my next step after separating from the Contract Engineering job with only two years of service was, to start our own Engineering Consulting and Design Corporation. Our company was founded in 2010 with just my wife and I and … no work. However, by the end of the first year we had jobs from coast to coast and were growing rapidly. What could possibly go wrong?

Shortly after the first year with my new company startup, I was diagnosed with bladder cancer. I had a very large tumor in my bladder the size of a golf ball. My oncologist/urologist told me as soon as they found it that I was in a very dangerous position, informing me that bladder cancer was one of the most aggressive and hardest to treat. If the cancer was anywhere outside the walls of my bladder, it would be very hard to stop it. He described it as "like a wildfire of deadly growth inside my whole body if it was on the loose." Immediate radical surgery was required. They found the cancer on Friday, I met with the surgeon on the following Monday, and was admitted the next day, Tuesday, at 5:00 a.m. into the local hospital to begin preparation for the removal of my bladder. And this was shocking news to me, that there was to be a nine to ten hour surgery requiring a team of approximately 26 people to perform the operation. It was Saturday before an operating room was available, so my Doctor put together a team to begin the surgery Saturday morning.

In a whirlwind of just days I went from believing I was healthy, to a position of likely little chance of survival. Three days after my surgery while I was still in ICU, I went to the edge of death. My blood pressure was extreme; my heart was not beating correctly, sometimes not at all. My temperature went to 104 degrees and climbing, and my respiration was shallow. There was an entire team of pulmonologists, cardiologists, and trauma doctors trying to keep me alive. While my body was shutting down, I was unconscious, and it was during that time that I had a vision of leaving this world and going to heaven where I caught a glimpse of the real glory and greatness of God!!! Wow!!!

Somehow, in ways the doctors could not understand, my body became normal in the matter of just a few minutes which allowed them to continue on with what they needed to do regarding treatment. To this day I wholeheartedly believe this was not me, but God. For reasons beyond my knowledge, he wanted me to stay alive and tell how great and real and loving he is. This has totally changed my perspective on life. Things here are temporary. I saw a glimpse of where things are forever. I know beyond a shadow of a doubt that tangible possessions we have here cannot leave this world with us when we die, and they have no value or impact on your forever!

Now, some more good news; the surgery went well! I was given outside plumbing, but … drum roll… the cancer was totally contained. I was cancer free at the end of the surgery, no cancer in the lymph nodes, or surrounding organs. I must tell you however, they took out any organ in the area that they could: prostate, appendix, and a bunch of lymph nodes. This surgery left me incapacitated, unable to work for six months. I was left with a large open wound in my abdomen that had to heal from the inside out.

A consequence of all this (me being unable to work) was, our company likewise stalled and ran out of work. We found ourselves locked into a downward financial spiral. We survived by going farther into debt. When I did start back to work, my path crossed (at a gas station) with an old friend.

I don't believe in only coincidence. God had stepped in to provide. I needed help, and he wanted to help, and restoration of my corporation began. Soon, we landed another international contract in the Bahamas designing and installing electrical control systems. It sounded like a great place to work; it was beautiful. However, my customer would wait 120-180 days to pay when they should have paid within 30 days, so again I was faced with financial stress, trying to work out of the country with seriously delayed payments.

Then, after successful completion of the first of five sites, I became deathly ill. I got up on a Monday morning and was having serious trouble breathing. I told my wife to call 911, after which I was transported to the hospital. A quick diagnosis showed I had not one, but two pulmonary embolisms (PEs), one in each lung with blood clots caused by a clot in the leg coming upstream to the heart and then through it to the lungs. Mine were the size of baseballs after they settled in my lungs. One PE is usually a fatality, and I had two.

I was given little hope of living through the night, so you can only imagine how I was dealing with *who I am* when *I may not be*. But I felt God with me … so let me repeat again, imagine what is your *who I am* when *you are not*. Friends from our faith community came to the hospital in the middle of the night, and many prayers went up on my behalf. At one point that night there were over 40 people at the hospital praying that I would live and be restored to perfect health, and because of Christian Community networks, the request literally went around the world to fellow believers. I now have experienced firsthand that prayer changes things and brings hope. Faith makes prayers stronger, and praying for somebody is a tangible demonstration of loving somebody.

An obvious fact made clear by the fact I am now writing this, I did live. The doctors got things under control. They thinned my blood to prevent further damage by any remaining leg clots, and installed a filter inside me to catch another one if it tried to journey to my heart.

Now, let me move this into a spiritual analogy. Friends, this is something we all need, something to catch and stop the emotional and physical damage of hard life events, something to intercept and recover from the damage when something difficult is happening our lives.

I survived the PEs, but two weeks prior to this event, my family doctor had detected a problem with my white blood cell count and had referred me to a hematologist. I'd met with the specialist once, and after some additional tests he wanted to do a bone marrow biopsy. He recommended I stay in the USA, but I had put him off a few weeks because I felt I needed to leave the country to work on our second site in the Bahamas, but then, the pulmonary embolisms. I was still in the hospital receiving treatments for the PEs when the doctors did do the bone marrow biopsy where they discovered I had Acute Leukemia (APL), which was an extremely rare and often fatal diagnosis. I later learned that only one out of four people live 30 days past the day APL leukemia starts in a person's body.

Again, I believe, by no coincidence God had already provided me with a great Hematologist/Oncologist, one who had recently reviewed a case study of APL Leukemia with a panel of other Doctors. I was the first case of APL he had seen though, and he thought I was only the second case in the Tri-State area in the past decade. The next day I received my first dose of aggressive chemotherapy to treat this leukemia. I was in the hospital for 32 more days, taking chemo doses of arsenic trioxide every day. My body could only survive this leukemia by receiving an IV infusion every six hours, but they could not give me chemo every day as it was taking my blood counts way down, and causing enough strain on my heart that it stayed on the edge of stopping. I had an EKG almost every day.

The treatment regimen for the leukemia was brutal, staying at the hospital infusion center every day for six hours, Monday thru Friday, four weeks on and then four weeks off. I was very sick, and the treatments were driving the entire schedule of my life, receiving one hundred doses. In addition, I was administered 1,420 doses of oral chemotherapy, two weeks on, two weeks off, where my heart was pushed to its limits. During that time I had to have an EKG every Friday morning before treatment to make sure my heart could withstand the stress.

My emotional heart had to withstand this stress also. I was unable to work at all, and again I repeat what I said at the very beginning, thank God for Vicky – my life mate for better and worse. My greatest life changing event was when she became my wife in 1979. Vicky, my wife of almost 41 years, has lived out the events I described, always by my side. Her faith in God has always been something I drew strength from. She seems to never waiver in her faith that we are Children of the King. She never stopped loving me, even when I was not lovable. Without her by my side with her unconditional love, I would not have survived these life crushing events. Vicky has been my rock to depend on. She took care of me so many times when I could not take care of myself. I have been so blessed to have her as my life mate. She has been, and continues to be, so patient, loving, kind, and strong.

So let me address a core question – Who am I now?

How large of a piece of whom I am comes from what I am achieving in a workplace career? Let me tell you that my human nature made it a large piece of who I was. Being forced out of a job is a serious emotional event. I think it is in the Top Ten Hall of Fame of major life events, the list including things like death of a spouse or child, marriage, divorce, separation from family, major accidents, and disabling health problems. It is easy to burn up or fall apart from anger caused by bad significant life events. Human nature tried to take me there, but I had a weapon to help me survive on this battlefield, my HOPE driven by FAITH in the creator of the universe, my God! I had Faith, Hope, the love of a life mate, the love of a Christian friend, the love of God. And somehow it all worked.

I thank God for my great friend and coworker Tim, whom I hired after reuniting at a gas station almost a year prior. Again, I believe it was no coincidence. I believe it was a divine meeting set up by a divine power! Tim completed the remaining four site jobs in the Bahamas and took over the company for us. I never did have to worry about anything he was doing, and there was enough income to pay him some and us some. However, when that job was completed there was no more work. Fortunately, I was able to help Tim get a job at an Engineering Consulting Firm that a friend of mine owned, and to this day he is employed there where he enjoys the work and work environment.

I treasured inspirational verses that were written on index cards and sticky notes for me by a women's Bible study group my daughter Jennifer was teaching. I got these the first week I was hospitalized for my first battle with cancer. These cards traveled with me along with my Bible for every chemo treatment. The chemo treatments lasted for nine months, but at the end of the seventh month, they did the third bone marrow biopsy and determined that I was in remission!

The three years of my life journey after I started my own corporation eventually led to financial destruction. I could no longer keep up with my financial obligations. I could not work, and only had a pension income. I had qualified for Social Security disability; however there was a six month waiting period before any payments were received. The medical bills were astronomical, and I was in extreme debt. The cancer didn't kill me, the PEs didn't kill me, but the stress of being bankrupt gave it a good try.

I can testify that being unable to provide for your family really impacts how you feel about who you are. As a husband and father, this is a deep emotional area. I had ten years of secondary education and I had attained a Master of Science degree in Engineering Administration, and yet I was not able to provide for my family. I had to depend on the One who provides all things – our heavenly Father.

Let me also address the question of, if there is some aspect of who I am now (positive or negative) that probably would not have occurred if I had not had the aforementioned life changing events?

I understand Who I Am today better than ever. I use my life experiences to encourage others. I have found that since I am a two-time cancer survivor, I can encourage people who have just learned they have cancer, and those who have been battling it for years. There is a couple with whom Vicky and I are very close, and just within the last month of writing this I sat at the hospital all night with the wife, as her husband had just had a PE and was only given a 50/50 chance of living through the night. By the way, he did survive. The next morning I got to see him and pray with him in ICU. He is back working today and is a now a member of the miracle man club.

Through all these years since I lost my job in 2008, my life challenges have taught me so much about healing and what our priorities really should be. Life is uncertain and can change in a minute. I had three of those life changing minutes with cancer and the PEs.

I am a walking, talking miracle and no one will be able to convince me otherwise. Against the odds given by man, I am alive today and taking my refuge in Christ. It is He in me that makes me who I am now. I can help others. I try to be compassionate. I understand what a potentially fatal illness is. I know what it feels like to stare death in the face. I wondered for months during my chemo treatments if a poison being put into my body was effectively killing a disease that is known as a fast killer. The physical possessions of this world mean nothing when you are dead and gone. What stays here is what you have done for others. The Faith, Hope, Love, and knowledge you have personally offered to other people truly are the earthly remnants of your life. Your legacy, whatever it looks like, stays.

Are there negative aspects of who I am now that probably would not have occurred? Sure. I know this may read like everything was easy, and only affected me positively. However, I must say again what

I said at the beginning. I would not want anyone to have to travel the path I have. It is still easy to get depressed. To put it in real words, my human emotional makeup holds onto some bitterness. Did it have to be so painful? Why me Lord? Obviously, my financial situation would be different. When I compare myself to my peers that I had worked with at my first employer, most are still employed there and making great incomes while I live on a small pension and disability and a small amount of part time income. I believe I would have significantly more physical stamina if the illnesses had not occurred. The chemo affected my hands, feet, and brain. My memory is not so good. I have extreme neuropathy in my feet and lower legs. My feet hurt all the time. I struggle walking sometimes because of the loss of sensitivity on the bottom of my feet. The chemo attacked all the nerve endings in my body. Some people that know me well say I have lived out a life like Job did in the Bible.

I try to let God fight battles for me now as best I can. My faith and trust and love for God grows greater every day. I am reminded of a song I was taught as a child – "Every day with Jesus is sweeter than the day before. Every day with Jesus I love him more and more."

(BIO:)Today (in 2020), some twelve years downstream from the loss of my career job, I am cancer free!!!!! Yeah !!!!! I have been in remission from leukemia for over seven years. I am typing this dialog sitting in the study of a home Vicky and I were able to purchase in 2008. We have 1.5 acres and a small ranch house in the country where it is so peaceful. There are horses in a pasture across the street I can see from the window of the study. Vicky and I try to spend time praying with and for people that are sick or have found themselves in difficult life situations. We are active in the community of Christian believers at our church and in other ministries around the world.

Vicky and I read a devotional book together at some point every day with an entry for each day of the year. The author is Sarah Young and the title is Jesus Today – Experience Hope Through His Presence. *In my mind I know it is no coincidence and is so reassuring that today there was a written message in the devotional book for Vicky and me.*

When I think about the timing of us reading from Sarah's book (which is written as Jesus in the first person) for today's date (January 14, 2020) it contains a message so appropriate and timely. I will quote what the devotion says as I finish penning this document. It was an affirmation to me and a God wink (something we experience that is definitely not a coincidence) supporting all my words in this writing. And I quote Sarah Young:

"Learn to live from a place of resting in Me. Since I – the Prince of Peace – am both with you and within you, you can choose to live from this place of peaceful union with Me. This enables you to stay calm in the midst of stressful situations, by re-centering yourself in Me. We can deal with your problems together – you and I – so there is no need to panic. However, the more difficult your circumstance, the more tempting it is for you to shift into high gear and forget My Peaceful Presence.

"As soon as you realize you have wandered from your Place of Peace, return to Me immediately. Call upon My Name, for this reconnects you with Me and helps you feel safe. Don't be discouraged by how often you wander from Me. You are endeavoring to form a new habit, and this takes time plus persistent effort. The rewards, though, are well worth your efforts. The more you return to Me – to our resting place – the more peaceful and joyful your life will be."

And I, Mike Hand, close with this thought. I know who made me – "The Great I Am."

Chapter 36:
I Want to Live Each Day to the Fullest
Lanny Sparrow

Lanny Sparrow had Cystic Fibrosis (CF.) He attended Oakdale Christian High School, now Oakdale Christian Academy, in Jackson, Kentucky in the late 1970's. I was attending college and working at Oakdale as a part-time cook. I remember sitting at the dinner table with Lanny one evening, and we became engaged in a rather serious conversation which carried on after the meal was over, even after others had left the room.

Lanny told me that both he and an older brother had CF, and that his brother had died from it a few years earlier. Lanny said that when his brother died he overheard his mother and aunt talking about the illness. It turns out his brother was dying right about the age the doctors had predicted he would. Lanny added that he heard his mother say, "And the doctor says Lanny will probably go when he's around fifteen."

That was almost two years ago. I'm going to be a senior next year, and I'm not sure what to do. I love Biology and I'd like to teach. But there's a part of me that says, "Why bother going to college, and doing all that work; you're not going to live much longer, anyway?" But another part says, "Ignore everything and live as though you were going to be here until you're in your eighties."

We talked a while about the unknown factor regarding our life span for all of us; some just are more aware of it than others. Then Lanny expressed concerns about falling in love, marriage, and children. He said,

Although there's no one right now, I dream about the possibility of a normal life with a wife and children. But then I always ask myself if that would be fair to someone. Is it fair to ask someone to marry you, knowing that you probably won't be there for them very long at all, and, what about children? Would it be right to have children knowing that they would most likely lose their father early on?

Lanny decided to go on to college, and later came back to Oakdale to teach Biology. He was accompanied by his wife Bonnie. When he was twenty-six I invited him to be a guest speaker at convocation at Lees College where I was teaching at the time. He talked to the group about living each day to the fullest.

I love life. I want to get the most out of each day that I can. The doctors said I would die at fifteen. I'm twenty-six now, and I'm shooting for forty.

Lanny died a few years after that, but not before he had the chance to have a huge influence on my oldest son, Ralph. As a matter of fact I think that other than me, Lanny has been the most significant male role model in Ralph's life, and I am forever grateful to Lanny for that.

I'll share a rather humorous memory about Ralph and Mr. Sparrow (Lanny.) I was taking Ralph (13, maybe?) on his first real date with a classmate. I was taking him to pick her up at her house, drop them off at the local Pizza Hut for an hour or so, then get them and drop her back off at her house. As we traveled toward the girl's house, Ralph started asking about proper procedures after we picked her up. Do I open the door for her? (Yes) Should we both sit in the back seat? (Yes)Do I let her in first and ask her to slide over? What do I do, Dad? I told him to play it by ear, if she got in and slid right over then he could get in that side next to her. If not, then close the door and walk around the car and get in the other side, and then he could slide toward the middle. When I said that, Ralph excitedly exclaimed, "Oh yeah, that's what Mr. Sparrow said when I asked him! It's all coming back to me now!"

A poignant aside; in September 1992 Bonnie gave to birth to Amanda, Brittany, and Montgomery. Thanksgiving weekend 1993, when the triplets were 14 months old, Lanny passed.

(Compiler's eulogy to Lanny) Lanny, for someone who was quite a bit younger than me, you taught me a lot about living. I marveled at your fascination with the intricate, and the mundane. Because of your

love of Biology the world opened her arms to you every day, invited you to step outside, and live. You did too, to the fullest.

I am forever grateful for the positive effect you had on Ralph's life. He was on a good track already; you just helped keep him there. By the way, after you taught him, he wound up playing the cowbells just as good as you. I sometimes feel like you lived more in less than thirty years than I have in (now) seventy (and counting).

Lanny, I pray I find even more your love for life; find a way to absorb as much from each day as you did. Your favorite pet, of course, was a boa constrictor. Why not? One of God's beautiful creatures, and, I imagine that somewhere (in the place I hope to join you) you are trying to find where it slipped away to (between the walls, maybe?)

Recently I was able to phone visit with Bonnie. Following is her response to some things I asked her.

(Bonnie M. Waters) I don't think I asked God, why, but I did ask, why now? Lanny and I of course discussed his illness when we started dating, and I was drawn to his joy of living in the moment. As a matter of fact, he was a huge advocate of the saying, "Live as though there will be no tomorrow; plan as though you're going to live to be 100." He was a planner; he always had a plan, and then would adjust to reality accordingly. But ironically we never discussed plans about the children and me if (when) he died. We always concentrated on living in the now. The triplets were preemies, born two months ahead of schedule (we didn't plan that), so they were 14 months old when he passed. Had they come on their due date, they would have just turned one.

The last couple years of Lanny's life were an emotional roller coaster journey with many trips to the hospital and each one the doctors giving another guesstimate of Lanny's life expectancy, except the last time. At that one the doctors were saying he was exceeding expectations, looking good, might even beat 40. And then he passed.

I was devastated. We planned so much, and all of a sudden I was in position where at times in frustration, anger, and feeling overwhelmed with the fact that I didn't have a plan for what to do, I definitely asked, "What do I do now?" Then I started revisiting Lanny's and my past conversations and proceeded to use them to assist in my decision-making. One thing that really helped was that Lanny frequently would ask of me, "What do you want to do?" I would have been lost without the children; they definitely kept me busy.

Regarding the question of who am I now, for me for quite a while it was more, "Who am I without the Cystic Fibrosis situation in my life?" I had moments of panic thinking, oh no, I forgot to give Lanny his medicine, and even nightmares wondering who was giving him his medicine now.

I thought I would just stay in Ohio and continue on like before, but within a week I knew that wouldn't be. So I moved back to North Carolina to be near my family, thinking I would stay there just 3 – 5 years. Nope. In three years' time I found myself looking for my own home in the area. I discovered life doesn't stop, that I needed to keep on planning life for me and the children. One thing that was difficult was I did not want the children out of my sight. I was afraid something might happen and I might lose one, or all, of them. It seemed like I was filled with, what ifs? At some level that continued for a long while. I'm not sure if I ever had a night of sound sleep until they were in college.

The triplets are doing well. Brittany is married to a businessman and she is in Seminary working on her Masters in Divinity, working toward becoming ordained as an Episcopal priest. She hopes to graduate Spring Semester 2021. Amanda is married to a nurse and was associate pastor at a church in Nashville. She was just recently ordained and became senior pastor. She and her husband desire to eventually serve on a mission field. Montgomery has a degree in dramatic arts and communication and is a social worker in Nashville. He's been involved with Artists Community Theatre, writes children's material for Vacation Bible School, and plays Mr. Gummy for presentations of *It's Time to Get Smarter* on faithkidz.org. His reason for the name Mr. Gummy comes from when the triplets were younger. The girls couldn't pronounce Montgomery, and so they called him Gummy.

It has been a long winding pathway from Lanny's death, and raising triplets after that. As mentioned, there were times of frustration, anger, feeling overwhelmed, and questioning, but through it all I have come to realize that God can handle it. I have had my ups and downs and failures, but I've discovered that God is big enough for all that. I am blessed!

(BIO:) (Bonnie) Four years after Lanny passed I started dating Sherman Waters. He was a successful District Manager in the computer industry, but we both felt a call to ministry. He volunteered at a local church as a youth pastor, we got married in our second year of dating, and after that he went into full time ministry. He has risen within the ranks of our district and held several leadership positions. One church we were at was quite small and couldn't afford a full time pastor, so then Sherman became bi-vocational, again in the computer field.

Over the years I had been in the position of associate pastor several times, but then became ordained in the Church of the Nazarene, so now Sherman and I are co-pastors. We serve an older community, and in the course of 10 years conducted over 65 funerals. One thing I learned from my experience with Lanny's passing is that funerals are not about the one who died; they are for those left behind. As a result of my experience, I can do more than just sympathize; I can truly empathize with those in mourning, help them with questions they have, and assist them as they start to move forward.

CHAPTER 37:

LISTEN TO YOUR INNER BEING AND FACE YOURSELF
BRANDON THOMPSON

(Compiler's note) Brandon Thompson attended a small rural elementary school where, because he was so smart and ahead of his peers, he was often in trouble for not paying attention, etc. This frequently ended in him being sent to the principal's office. He was not mean or malicious, just bored, and there were no advanced classes where he could have been challenged at his level. One positive thing that eventually happened was an older teacher there, Audrey Barkman, recognized the problem and was allowed to spend time with Brandon giving him schoolwork more appropriate to his intelligence level. Naturally, Ms. Barkman became someone Brandon really looked up to.

One semester the fundamentals of theatre class at the University of Pikeville performed Shadowlands *by William Nicholson, the story of C.S. Lewis and his eventual wife, Joy Gresham. We had one cast member (Brandon Thompson) not in the theatre class to play the part of Douglas Gresham, Joy's son. As the Theatre/Acting professor I directed the production. Near the end of the play there is a scene after the death of his mother where Douglas breaks down and cries against C.S. Lewis, the character I was portraying. It came across as a very believable moment onstage.*

About a year after the performance, Audrey Barkman passed away. I went to a viewing, and saw Brandon sitting in one of the rows, so I went and sat down alongside him. It was a Deja vu moment as he turned into me sobbing. A theatre question frequently asked is, "Does art reflect life, or does life reflect art?" and in this case it I believe that it turned out a little bit of both.

(Now, Brandon)

The world and this experience called life changed dramatically around when I began kindergarten. I was finding myself in trouble at school, dealing with family turmoil at home, and longing for help in some way with all of the emerging perspectives in my life. My parents were in the beginnings of a violent separation. My sister and I were enduring different types of abuse from both family and caretakers. As a family we owned and operated a diner and arcade that was failing due to troubles with my parent's separation.

To add to all this, a friend of mine who would play at the diner with me after school, committed suicide in his bedroom. At a certain point I became overwhelmed and wanted to commit suicide as well, and even tried with an outlet at home after waking to find my father beating up my mother in the dining room with the same belt he would sometimes whoop me with. My attempt resulted in blowing the fuse and causing the breaker to reset, which scared me into joining my mother who, after the incident with my father, was sleeping on the couch. I laid there awake, faking asleep, and wondering how I could repair these broken elements in my life.

I went to school to find my answers. I begged my teacher Audrey, to contact me once she passed away in the afterlife if she was able, just to reassure me that I could go there if my life got too out of control. I took apart all of my toys at home to maybe understand them and invent new ones that could save us from financial troubles. I turned the vacant field beside our house into a farm and my treehouse into an observation deck. I built stone shelters in the woods and made friends with every animal I ran across in case I needed to run away. I entered a pool tournament with adults (against my Dad's opinion) and won the $700 winner's pot. My Dad was surprised that I won and in that moment he looked at me, handed me $75 and said that was enough for a little kid. I used it to buy a desk from Lowe's that I found in an ad. I really felt such a close bond to my family and felt as if it was my responsibility alone to hold us together.

When I was in elementary school I was regularly sent to the principal's office, and I specifically recall feeling like I wasn't the problem. I knew I was making mistakes, but I didn't feel that any one was there to guide or help me make better choices. Herman, the principal, seemed to me like an exhausted authority figure that would rather be playing his harmonica, or even putt-putt golf in his office, than dealing with my freckled face. He paddled me a few times which immediately caused me to never want to emotionally connect with him. I was torn in a strange way; I didn't want to be stuck in class where boredom was driving my bad behavior. I didn't want to be in the halls and run into a bully, and I definitely didn't want to be in the principal's office, that is unless he was planning to give me back the money he confiscated from me during my Crayola marker tattoo endeavors.

As Basil mentioned in his preface to my story, my teacher/confidante and strongest supporter Audrey Barkman died, and the only way I can describe what I felt is, FLAT. If life was a pop-up book it was as if someone had closed it shut. She taught me how to use an open mind and was my best friend in all matters. The thought of her passing still floors me today, and in her honor I remember her words and try my best to give that same magic back to anyone who will hear it. I still feel flat and disconnected from a frequency I had never encountered until I had her for a teacher. I will never forget that if I close my eyes, I can travel back into that classroom where I spent so many hours exploring and learning about a world I didn't know I would never be able to speak to her about.

(Compiler's note) About a year ago I was able to reconnect with Brandon and then a few months ago asked him about using his story. Along with the above, he sent me some of his journaling entries, both prose and poetry, along with permission to rework them into a format for this book (some things are dated, others not.)

(Brandon again)

So when I think of productivity, pulling my own weight, around the clock; do not dare fall behind! Overtime? All of the time, until the work is done and the door is closed. Then, you pay yourself, if your productivity produces free time, it's yours to keep, spend any way you want. Yippee! *-RBT, 1-11-2019*

I'm so grateful to be here. What once was a tomorrow, what will be a yesterday, is for now home.

I stay in my head a lot more at work now. Good thing the shifts aren't that long. I'm not bored, more like done thinking about these things … work, money, kids, etc. Silas is 11, Christian 9... and I'm 32. My mind would go on for days chewing on ways to better provide or considering this or that. I must release it with this pen over pizza at work. BBQ pizza. This way I am appealing to my senses (not like the cold, thick air, dry skin, bullshit, and arthritis. Those suck more and more each day.) *-RBT, 1-23-2019*

My Story! Who ever imagined a pizza place could tire you so quickly? I didn't. Most of the exhaustion is physical, once I learned how to stay in my 'zone'. Some of it is mental, but like I said, that part is avoidable. The rest is repetition, hard work, and getting along with coworkers. Make the dough so my family can eat. Sometimes it can feel lonely in the back of the restaurant, but my coworkers are quick to pick me up and out of the mud so I don't get down about it, plus, I like stretching pizza dough, well, as much as I like having a paycheck.

But I get tired, fast. My joints hurt and my body aches. I'm over eating pizza most days. I know this job is important; still I can't forget how I got here or why I remain. One, I must have income to support myself. Two, I found myself at a turning point in my life that caused me to decide to take an easier job that isn't destroying my body and mind. *-RBT, 2018*

Writing helps me. The truth does come out on paper. I'm tired, but not too tired to think; to think about how to not be so damn tired so often. Physical labor is a great way to keep in shape and can teach a person much about themselves and their limits. I have learned where my limits and barriers are. I can now push to break through them through understanding and observation. It is safe to say limits and barriers are only made real by lack of understanding. I expect a lot out of myself but, I also expect to learn and grow from my mistakes (which of course implies I need an outlet where mistakes happen.) Work isn't the place to learn. Yes, mistakes happen at work sometimes but normally the pressure and demands of a job don't allow for much thinking (daydreaming, perhaps?) So I need to give myself the required space to explore possibilities. This is essential, but unfortunately I feel like I am lacking in this area, and to fall short here causes me much grief; grief that bleeds into everything I do, and sharp enough to cut through my ability to function properly. I have the resources to expect all of these elements in my life, but they are unorganized and scattered among seemingly uncontrollable circumstances.

Or maybe that can all change with some smart rearranging of resources, time invested, and goals clearly set to be met. Why does art appeal to me more than building? Art is freedom. Work is income, skill, and dogged determination. Combining these two causes great results and opens up new ideas. It's hard to pretend I have found balance, harder even to think I should have to pretend. I want freedom of expression, ceilings lifted, and doors that open both ways. I need to enjoy rainy days. -*RBT, June 2018*

It has come to my attention, many times, that my determination blinds me from goings-on in my life. My focus on this or that goal, motivations and drive, ability and potential, have become rigid and somewhat desperate. I have lost relationships, abandoned achievement, left what elements of my life that didn't serve my goals and then suffered for it all. This has to change.

To transform these parts of my life I must not forget the lessons I am learning from life. Nowadays the lessons are as plentiful as the roads that brought me to them. Good thing I haven't lost my ability to dig for the truth, find clarity, reflect it in every direction and go at it again. I have so much love for my kids, my family and friends that my heart beats for them. I only hope I can make them proud. -RBT, 2019

Who am I? I have a job and coworkers I can depend on, free pizza and memes for days. I have an education I can build upon. I share friendships with others who share similar views and interests. I have a place to call home where I can relax and enjoy the company of those I love.

The seemingly out-weighing negatives are $7.25 an hour for drama, and a lot of aggravation. It has been 5 years since I thought I would go to college. To date; no credits or degrees. I also find that my views and interests change and affect others. As human beings, we choose what we want. Less experienced individuals are much likely to easily determine their wants, while needs are chosen typically by experienced elders. In my middle age, needs are obvious and wants are powerful. Of course I need food, water, shelter, and livelihood. -RBT, 2019

Mind-wreckers: Lazy Routines, Other's Opinions, Codependence, Nicotine, Inactivity, Overanalyzing, Poor Attitude, Giving into Anger, No Respect

Some mornings I get up to be productive. I put on coffee, toss out garbage and pick up the house. Two cups of coffee and ten cigarettes later I find myself settled into a kitchen chair with my notebook and there I sit milking out my enthusiasm while attempting to inspire and motivate change. Puff, puff, bored. These are the underpinnings to the lazy routines I've fallen into. So what caused me to slip?

I think it's safe to say I caused myself to slip. If the stepping stones I'm travelling are the only thing keeping me above water, then what are these stepping stones and how do I get back on them? As I'm writing this, others' opinions come to mind. You can lose momentum, lose touch, feel lazy, but you just need rest.

Dude... I've gone lazy. If I don't deal with my wrecked mind, it's only going to get worse. Like an old automobile that's too dangerous to drive due to lack of maintenance, sometimes there are places to be and this is my only ride. The radio works so I tune out the rest and go. I guess I'm writing this because that tactic isn't working and I have a responsibility to myself. Silas is still sleeping, and these morning hours go fast. My responsibilities to them and my family are also very real.

Bad dreams ARE the worst. They take our fears, uncertainties, and that's all our imagination needs to run wild with some blazingly horrible experience or scenario that has the ability to very seriously affect us to our core; sometimes we feel a constant flow of stress the rest of the day. At night, our minds often shuffle that back into another bad dream, hopefully creating an experience to learn from.

Fear says, "Oh you think you're tough? Here then, run terrified from these enormous tentacles that stem out from the sea to rearrange the sands and all that dwells on them." To make sure it frightens you on every front, fear throws in elements of any and everything you've ever experienced as bad or hurtful, aligned and in any effective order. Fear demands, "Face me and listen; not only is this world that you want ending, it is crumbling because of you ... because of this mistake, that failed relationship, (insert short-coming here), et cetera."

And all that holds us away from the direction we want to move toward is a loud call to our courage that we might even have to chase down. And the contrast; what a relief!

Courage says, "You are tough. Listen to your inner being and face yourself. We are one." And like a poorly timed escape from a cramping muscle, we feel it, we catch our breath. We see fear shudder in the presence of courage.

Fear in its frustration says... "I help you live!"

Courage laughs loudly at this and says, "I help you die!" The cramping subsides, the struggle is over and we realize that since we are living and one day must die, our fear and courage are only guidance systems for navigating this inevitable journey, and ultimately are only there to help us decide. They beg us to understand, but understand what? To understand we have a choice. To understand that just as we are capable of using powerful energy that creates our bad dreams, we have a choice to transform that energy and create our good dreams. If I can imagine great horrors, I can imagine the great joys of my successes in overcoming them. And now, I'm here. -RBT, 2019

It's heavy on my heart, what to do with my life. I can't decide on a career because I am unclear of my role in the lives of others around me. How could I focus on a career and still be present enough to raise my boys? Obviously I will need income to support them, but must I choose such a demanding position in a field I am uneducated in? I don't have the answers I need to be certain of anything other than I intend to be a present father, an asset to my family, and a kind friend. These must come first. -RBT, 2019

I hurry and get ahead of myself under stress. I accept the risk of failure and move forward prematurely under the pretense that you win some and you lose some. I suppose it only appears as a problem during a long losing streak.

Somethings you just do, one day it's hard work done smartly, another day it's hard assessments of the work done, closely examined. Either way is challenging. *-RBT, 2019*

I am sick with the flu or a head cold. I'm congested, aching, and feverish. Even though I'm feeling so poorly I still feel an overwhelming desire to think about my path to wellbeing. I want to live, ya know. Knocked out from medicines and writhing the sheets is living, yes, but I can aim higher can't I? Balance in well-being; I'm a pot-head cigarette smoking stress ball emerging from years of accumulated stress and unnecessary anxiety to face the truth, my truth, and learn to go on. That's fairly accurate. Wellbeing has been a learning path or my avenue to turn to when focusing on overall health. *-RBT, 2018*

Free-writing exercise. Life without my laptop is surreal and less interesting. I use it for nearly everything; journaling, typing papers, using email, passing time with a game, and even as an alarm clock. Much like some people are with their cellphones, I cling to my laptop; it is my link to the outside world. If I need to call my mom and dad at the same time, I can just open a hangout on Google+ and chat with them both from three separate geographical locations. On the contrary, if I want to isolate myself to the dingy confines of a dungeon in an online game away from all the rest of the world, I can. I use it for budgeting, keeping spreadsheets, and taking advantage of the calculator. My laptop is always close by in case I want to look at family photos, watch a movie, read an e-book, or simply explore the internet's infinitesimal realms of this and that. I may require glasses from the glare and develop arthritis from typing, but I will not be short on entertainment, productivity, and a true assistant. *-RBT, 11-23-2018*

Automatic Writing. Life moves fast like a pen. Like a sharpie pen, smooth, fluid, and easy to drive. My body doesn't move that fast anymore. It hurts. Drags, like an old ball point that has been resting on some sunny dashboard. Out of ink, sometimes it seems. -*RBT, 1-11-2019*

Dear World, My life is pretty cool. Whatever that means, I find myself consistently amazed with the unfolding events, surprises, and achievements that occur daily. That is growth, I think. -RBT, 2018

Isms. Optimism: Expand. I want to run a tight ship.

Pessimism: Contract. I want to hide away from being overwhelmed and sleep. -*RBT, 2018*

In the foggy morning I see that not a lot is as it was; even this cup of coffee grows cold on my tongue. Freely my words pour like water from a fountain onto my canvas of reality where all can see. Forth and back through the marks; rungs to knuckle my way up, off and into some dancing memory. Put your words to rest now. Even a fountain needs to replenish. -*RBT, 2019*

Under the Influence. Find anything to be satisfied in your life, but be aware of what you're asking for. Go into receiving mode. Timing and rhythm. Deliberate creation, reality maker. Sync up with the powerfully focused, non-physical part of you. There are rivers and streams of all kinds of things. -*RBT, 2019*

Create a port. Along the way you will find alongside and underneath, the rocks and pebbles, trees and vine, seeds and soil and substance that which is used to build bridges, posts, and dwellings. In the library where I work, I sharpen my observations on modern and traditional architecture. Though my whetstone employment is crude, I discover its sweet spots more and more often. It is there contained by high walls and drapery, the notion to step outside and rest for thought on the sidewalk. And when that is what I do, I suppose it's who I am. -*RBT, 2019*

Music

More and sometimes less
Understanding of life, depending on the
Station you're tuned into.
In harmony I believe music
Can be a sound friend

(because even when in stark contrast, all music does is help one better know who they are.) *RBT*

(BIO:) I'm a 34-year-old living in Pike County, Kentucky, a rural area on the eastern tip of the state. I'm a father of two young sons, Silas and Christian, for whom I want to mention are astonishingly kind and intelligent boys. (So now, life after pizzas.) Now I work for the county's public library district with a title of assistant technology coordinator— however serving the public means fitting many roles to fulfill a constantly evolving environment of culture, learning, and discovery. In my free time, I enjoy days off with my kids, reading, cooking, sharing the company of close friends, and exploring the wonders of technology and nature.

Recently I have had the opportunity to start teaching a class I devised aimed toward senior citizens who want to have fun learning useful computer skills. More than ever seniors are having difficulty keeping up with the rapid changes that come along with emerging technologies. I help them learn how to manage and stay in touch with common tasks like registering for vaccines online, staying connected with loved ones, among other important stuff that I feel passionate about! This is simply an idea to help out folks in my community who struggle to find assistance performing everyday tasks and keeping up with the Jones's. I hope it's a good thing – it's all mine and I have been preparing for about a year to roll it out. A little prayer, some coffee, and patience is my plan.

Learning is my true passion. Helping others do the same is my calling. One thing you should know about me is my advice to whoever is reading; go, out there, and live your life in a rampage of appreciation for having the incredible opportunity to be you.

CHAPTERS 38 – 40:
THREE OUTRAGEOUS STATEMENTS
BILL IRWIN, ABDUL SAMAD, AND
MEN AT WALKER STATE PRISON

(Compiler's Note) I discovered a few years back that, although our determination and courage are a large part of overcoming obstacles, our humanness, coupled with faith, also seem to come equipped with additional tools. I have learned this from observing and listening to:

Bill Irwin, at that time, the first blind person (there have been a couple more since then) to hike the entire AT (Appalachian Trail) from Springer Mountain, Georgia to Mt. Katahdin, Maine;

Abdul Samad, an Afghani who lost both hands as a young boy when the Russians were fighting in Afghanistan;

and, Several men who are or have been prisoners at Walker State Prison in Rock Spring, GA.

CHAPTER 38:
LOOK OUT AT, BILL IRWIN'S ON THE WAY.
BILL IRWIN

(Observations by the Anthology Compiler) The Special Events Committee at the University of Pikeville, then Pikeville College, had invited Bill, author of Blind Courage, to speak.

I was coordinator for the event, so I made arrangements for him at the Landmark Inn, and, upon his arrival met him there to bring him to the college dining hall for the evening meal before his speaking engagement. My oldest son, Ralph, was there to hear Bill, so I introduced them. After Ralph said hello to him, Bill's response was, "Ralph, so you are a little taller than your father." (Okay, six inches taller, what's your point?) But Bill was focused on what height the sound was coming from.

Before his presentation Bill was chatting with several different people that he was meeting for the first time, and during the question and answer session after his motivational speech, I noticed that he called a few of them by their names when they asked a question. When I asked him about that, also during Q&A, he replied (calling me by name) that after he lost his sight his sense of hearing became much sharper, and he focused in on vocal differences, much like we might pay attention to how people look, or what they are wearing.

Also, during the presentation, Bill said that after he lost his vision his senses developed to the point where he could walk down the middle of a hallway that had several doors and tell you which ones were open, and which were closed. It is amazing to me how our system automatically compensates for other deficiencies. Bill also described some occasions on the trail where he stepped out in faith, and later was told he had made the right decision. He added that losing his sight was the biggest blessing that God had ever given him.

All in all, I became much more aware that evening of the tools we are equipped with, not just in our body, but also in our mind and spirit. Bill was, and is, a powerful example of how we are fearfully, and wonderfully made.

In addition, he talked about falling down, and getting back up. Someone estimated that in Bill's nine-month trek, he fell down about seven thousand times. That sounded reasonable to me; in 2001, I was picking myself up from losing my balance or footing some three or four times a day on my 150 mile southern half of Long Trail backpacking hike. Had I been nine months at that rate, it would have been over five hundred falls, and that's with eyesight. But the point Bill was making was, when you fall, the only thing you can do is get back up and keep going.

Bill Irwin said, "Get rid of some of the baggage." In his presentation, Bill told of how he started out with everything he was sure he needed, plus extras, just in case. He was packing over one hundred pounds. After a few days on the trail, at a stop to replenish food supplies, someone went through Bill's pack with him and helped strip away unnecessary baggage. He then talked about taking the time in our personal lives to evaluate the loads we carry around in our hearts and spirits, and see if there is baggage we need to shed. He told the audience that, about things in our lives, to ask ourselves the question, "Is this item worth the weight?"

I believe that one of the things that makes it difficult to evaluate our load is there can be a certain sense of security from carrying baggage; it can evolve into a safe place where at least we know what the patterns and routines are. And there can also be fear that if we don't carry the weight around we will be in new territory which can be scary. Finding out who I am now can also bring along new responsibilities, and unknowns.

Baggage – too much? I know first-hand from my (short?) 150 mile backpack trip in Vermont what a relief it can be to get rid of extra weight. If you are still out on the trail, then you leave what you are shedding at a shelter as there may be someone coming along who will need it, or at least think he or she needs it. At one shelter, Kid Gore I believe, someone had left a rather heavy duty sleeping bag. I was experiencing a little chill at night with only the blanket I had opted to bring, as it was still getting into the low 40's. So I decided to pack it. About a half hour into the new day, headed north, I dropped my pack, and while Raj, my traveling companion for 45 miles, took a break, I hustled back to the shelter we had just left to leave my newly acquired, but short-lived, bag-mate for someone else to consider carrying. It weighed more than I wanted to add on.

I've discovered this with personal baggage too, be it fears, cautions, habits, memories, materials thngs, or other. Sometimes I can let little things start to add up and before long I'm starting to feel down in my spirit. I have discovered that if I allow adequate quiet time first thing in the morning, I can sort out the day, and it's easier throughout the day to stay on track. Personally, I can't just jump out of bed, shower, and rush out the door, without feeling weighed down in my core.

So, let's go back to a lesson we can learn from Bill Irwin. "I once could see, but now am blind; am blind, but now, I see." This is a common theme in literature, and with good cause. Sometimes there are things we can't see until we can't see. We are so bombarded with messages, visual and aural, that sometimes we don't take time to reflect on what is important. Many of us are familiar with the saying to the effect of, "We spend a lot of money buying things we don't need to impress people we don't even know or like." For me, this is another example of where we can see all the things around us, but are blind to what we are doing.

I have seen on Facebook where someone lost a family member or friend and they post, "Hold those you love tightly; things can change quickly." They may be in effect saying, if we can spend more time in reflection, blind to the things of the material world, then we can start to find out what and who the really important things and people in life are. And after a life changing experience we might also start to discover who we are now.

March 1, 2014 Bill Irwin died at the age of 73.

CHAPTER 39:
LOSING MY HANDS;
THE GREATEST BLESSING OF MY LIFE
ABDUL SAMAD

Abdul Samad is another person we were able to invite to Pikeville College as a part of the Special Events Program. Abdul joined the Freedom Fighters against the Russians fighting in his country as a young Afghan boy. Back in the 1980's, he left off from fighting when the small village he lived in was destroyed, and Abdul had no idea where his family was, or if they were even alive. Later, he saw something shiny in a field, and, thinking it might be some kind of toy, picked it up. It was a landmine, which exploded, blowing off both of his hands. Eventually he wound up in the United States and enrolled in school. He was near graduation from a local community college the first time he spoke to our group.

Abdul didn't particularly like his prosthetic hands; instead he learned how to do just about everything anyone else could do with his arm stubs. He drove with specially designed cups on the steering wheel, ate pizza slices as well as anyone, and basically lived as normally as he would if he had hands. Abdul told the audience that having his hands blown off was the greatest blessing of his life. He elaborated that he would never have received an education, or learned just how much he was capable of had the incident never occurred.

(BIO) Abdul Samad works at the Bread of Life café in Casey County, KY.

CHAPTER 40:

COMING TO PRISON: THE BEST THING THAT EVER HAPPENED TO ME
SOME PRISONERS AT WALKER STATE PRISON ROCK SPRING, GA

I heard on several occasions some men incarcerated at Walker State Prison say, "Coming to prison was the best thing that ever happened to me." I was a volunteer instructor and mentor at Walker State Prison in Rock Spring, GA, for almost four years; I stopped after both my and my wife's health started going downhill at a little faster pace. I taught a Communication course, and a journaling course using my book War Wounded: Let the Healing Begin as the springboard. I heard many speeches, and engaged in a lot of discussions, and a recurring theme I heard was, "I don't know where I would be, or if I would even be alive, if I hadn't come to prison."

Walker was the first totally Faith and Character based prison in Georgia, and men had to apply to be admitted to a two year program. Faith based means acknowledging help from a higher power to get out, and stay out, of prison. It does not involve any requirement to belong to this particular faith over any other. I had men in classes who were Protestant (a variety of different denominations), Catholic, Jehovah Witness, Muslim, Jewish; I once had a Wicca in class. It is noteworthy that with men who completed the program and got out, the recidivism rate was less than 2 percent, pretty much unheard of elsewhere (ABC News Channel 9 (Chattanooga), March 30, 2018.)

While instructing and mentoring there I made the decision to send financial support (call it my tithes if you will) on a monthly basis to both the Veterans Group and Lifers Group in the prison, and got invited on five occasions to special dinners they were able to sometimes have. On three of them I was able to eat in a room with over thirty men with life sentences, no guards or counselors around, just me and them. I felt as safe and comfortable during those times as I do sitting at home with my wife (that's a ten on a ten scale.) I've had men with life sentences tell me that even if they never got out they would rather live with peace inside than be constantly looking over their shoulders, worrying, wondering. They have truly experienced life changing events and are engaging in a positive process of discovering who they were.

By the way, an exercise I assigned some of my classes at Walker State Prison was a reflective exercise, looking back over their life and trying to narrow down the following:

A Good Exercise 10/7/5

- 10 Defining Moments
- 7 Critical Choices
- 5 Pivotal People

When I first read about this idea, I found it very difficult to determine what the 10/7/5 things were. Try this. I found it was a good way to try and get some things in perspective, even start to see the bigger picture enroute to discovering who I am now; and the life changing/forming events, choices I have made, and people in my life who have had an impact on all that.

During class discussions, and other conversations with some of the men at WSP we talked at times of being on the guard's and Warden's schedules, and related that to life in some ways where we didn't always see the bigger picture. Another thing we discussed was the idea that someone may be on a 1000 (or 10,000) step journey through life, and we may enter their life long enough to help them get from, say, Step 482 to Step 483, and then we are no longer there for them and someone else takes over. But the fact could be that that person being helped might not have made it to the next step without our assistance.

CHAPTERS 41 – 44:
ADDICTIONS THAT HELD; MOVING ON
WEST CARE PROGRAM (NOT THEIR REAL NAMES)

(Compiler's Note) The local jail facility in Pike County has a rehabilitation program that inmates can volunteer to go through. Bill Baird III, a long-time University of Pikeville board member, works with a ministry through the program and makes weekly visits to the jail. In 2012 (before my retirement from the University of Pikeville) Bill invited me as a guest speaker to the group a few times, and later I asked Bill if he would see if there were any inmates who might be willing to talk to me about the role addictions played in their situations. Four men talked with me; these are their stories.

CHAPTER 41:
I NEVER THOUGHT IT WOULD BE LIKE THIS
TOM

(When he walked into the room for the interview I was a bit surprised. He wasn't my age, but he's getting there. After we shook hands and introduced ourselves, we sat down and he began to talk.)

It wasn't my upbringing that was a factor in my being here. I was raised in a strong, traditional family; my parents are still married. They sent me to a private school, a good Catholic one. They made sure I got a good education, stronger than most. It was in 1986, after college that I enlisted in the Air Force. My test scores were high enough that I could have been an officer, but I've always been more of a hands-on type of person, so I chose to go into the enlisted ranks. I did my job well, and overall had what I guess you would call an un-eventful career until I was deployed to Saudi Arabia in 1990 and 1991 for operations in Desert Storm.

I volunteered to be with a crash recovery team; we would go to where a plane or helicopter had been downed, and, after certain items were retrieved that could be used, made sure the rest of the aircraft was destroyed so it couldn't be used or studied for information, by the enemy. One time, when we came under fire, it was the first time ..."

(Tom stopped, clamped his lips tight together, and fought back tears. He was quiet for a moment before continuing.)

It was the first time that I killed someone.

I was right there with him in that moment as I recalled to my own experience of being aware that I was responsible for taking the life of another. I told him that in the book I was leaving with him (Poetic Healing; A Vietnam Veterans Journey from a Communication Perspective) *there was a poem I had written about the same feelings and questions. We looked at each other, college professor and jail inmate, with the bond of brotherhood that combat veterans understand as he paused again, regrouped, and then continued.*

"And, there was a warehouse that was hit by a scud missile in Saudi Arabia with over 150 TCN's (Third World Nationalists) caught in it. The sight, and smell, of those bodies was awful. I guess now they'd say I had PTSD but it wasn't really talked about during that war, not like after Vietnam, or Iraq, or Afghanistan. I started to have night-mares, and I started to use alcohol, to self-medicate.

Meanwhile, my military service progressed along until budget cuts enacted by Congress in 1994 brought it to an end. I planned on making it a career, but in 1995, after 9 ½ years, my time on active duty ended due to downsizing, but eventually I was able to serve in the Re-serves.

However, things started to fall apart at home. My drinking was causing problems, and my wife left and moved away with our only son, and I thought I had hit bottom. My boy and I didn't have contact with each other for a long time, although we are close now.

I asked Tom about other turning points either positive or negative and he paused and smiled before continuing.

I've had several. For a while after I thought I had bottomed out; I guess you could refer to it now as my first recovery, I remarried, started going to church, and thought things were getting better. I became active in the VFW, and, in 2004 I bought a motorcycle; I was drawn to the allure of it. But, I started to hang out with the wrong group of people, some unsavory characters. I started drinking again, which created a lot of friction with my third wife.

Our house burned in 2006, and, later, I was raking through the charred remains trying to see if there was anything salvageable, any kind of mementos or keepsakes. I was by the refrigerator, and there were some steaks that had burned, and while I was raking up those charred pieces I had a flashback to that warehouse in Saudi Arabia. Then the dreams started back, and I got back into the cycle of drinking. I tried to justify it by saying that I had to in order to get to sleep. Then in August 2008 I broke down and was committed to the psych ward at the VA. I spent some time there, got out, and went back to the same cycle.

Things got worse with me and my wife and there was a divorce. I was at the bottom again. I had a good job, and was getting ready to start another tour at Fort Knox with a salary upwards of $125,000. I had all the toys, but they didn't mean anything, and I was ready to end it all. I went through several days of debating whether or not to take my life. I wanted to talk to my ex, but she didn't want me there. The police came, and I resisted arrest. I grabbed a 12 gauge shotgun and pointed it at the officer, so, of course I was charged with a violent crime. I understand all that, and I was in the wrong; my world was just collapsing around me.

Tom thoughtfully paused again, and then went on.

I never thought my life would be like this; the way it has been. But it's okay, I'm at peace now. Ironically, one of the areas I received training in while in the military was counseling, and I have had jobs as a counselor. Now I'm a player instead of being the coach. But this has been good for me; a turn-around. Actually, after I get out of here, and go through the follow-up programs, there is a good chance that with my background I can get into the program as a counselor. I've worked before as a counselor following the basics of the Twelve-Step Program. This program is faith-based, and it has helped me get back to a place of spiritual peace with who was once my first love, my Lord."

I asked him if he had any words of advice to pass on to others. Again, the thoughtfulness, and then he said:

It's okay to cry; that's the beginning of healing. Too many people try to maintain a tough attitude. Crying about things that have hurt deeply help purge; give you a clearer perspective; help you move on to the next step. When I say I'm at peace with my Lord, I'm not talking about being churchy; I'm talking about a one-on-one relationship, that's where the real peace comes from.

When we talked about a bigger picture in life, he said:

Although it's hard to see sometimes, if we can learn from everything that happens, even though it may be a result of some poor choices we have made, there's hope. Like I said, even though I never thought my life would be where it is right now, it is okay, because I have found peace and a hope for the future.

CHAPTER 42:
MY ADVICE; DON'T GO DOWN THIS ROAD JACK

I'm forty-two now; it's been over twenty-five years since I heavily start-ed using alcohol. I was sixteen when I let a buddy of mine take my car. A little later I was with another friend in his car and we were going down the road when we saw the wreck. It was my car, and when we got out and went over, the ambulance crew had already covered the body with a tarp; my friend who had borrowed my car.

I wish now I had never done it, but I lifted the tarp; one arm and his head were nearly cut off. I wish I had never seen that. I wish I hadn't let him use my car; I've always felt guilty about that. He might still be alive.

When I was about six, I remember my mom and dad bought some property and cleared all the trees and brush off it, and we built us a home. I took about four years, but we moved in when we got enough of it done that we could. I remember those years as a good life. Still, and I don't know why, I was just always in trouble most of my childhood. When I was younger, me and my brother got a BB gun for Christmas one year, and we sure got in trouble because we were shooting BB guns at a telephone repairman who was up working on a line. We were just mean. We shot at him five or six times each before he got down from the pole. We took off running for the house and he followed us there and told my mom. We got a bad whippin for that.

We had to walk about a quarter mile to the bus stop, and there was this big bee's nest of yellow jackets. I could not walk by them with-out throwing a rock, and every evening I would try to throw to tear their nest down. Every morning they had it built right back up. I got stung three to four times a week and my mom kept telling me to leave them alone and they wouldn't bother me. But I would not give up; I had to get even with them until one day I got stung about thirty times and had to go to the hospital with big red welts all over me, and get a shot. I guess that learned me the lesson to leave them alone like my mother said.

Later when we were older, I was about eight, me and my brother got in trouble in school because we hung two guys; we didn't kill them, but it scared them. They were going to tell on us for something we did, and we didn't like snitches, so we hung them. I felt sorry for them and let them down, but we still got in big trouble over that. We had to go to court and the judge asked me what part I had to do with it, and I told him, 'All I did was hold the rope.' He said I was just the one he wanted to talk to, and suspended me and my brother from school and my mom had to take us to an alternative school for a year.

I would see a lot of people come and go as I grew up. I remember everyone would come to my dad's to party. I made a good friend, and me and him would get into his dad's beer and take some, find a place to hide, and drink them. We did this every weekend for a long time. When I turned sixteen I thought it was party time so I got me a car and a driver's license.

It was after my friend was killed in the car wreck that I was shot with a .357 Magnum. That was after I got in trouble in school for smoking pot so I had quit and moved away from home. I had a pretty good job at a factory, and there was plenty of money, women, and pot. I grew a lot of pot.

I had a fight with a neighbor one night and I whipped him. The next day I was coming home from work, and when I started down my driveway I heard what I thought was firecrackers, and then I heard my back window bust out. I realized someone was shooting at me and I felt one hit me in the back. So I floored the car, got to my house and got my gun. I loaded up and started firing. He was running back to his car but I hit him a couple times. Then I got in my car and drove to the hospital. The cops were all over me there. They didn't arrest me while I was in the hospital. I was there for a month, but as soon as they released me, a cop was waiting to give me a court date. I served time for attempted murder and wanton endangerment. That's the first time I got in trouble with the law for drinking. The bullet was still inside me, and I drank a lot then because it helped kill the pain. I still have the bullet inside me.

I've had a lot of wrecks from drinking, and a lot of DUI's. On some of those arrests I would try to fight and got arrested once for assault on a police officer.

In 1998 I was hurt at work. We were working on a dozer taking up the slack in a chain with a binder. It broke and hit me; broke a disc in my lower back. I began drinking even more; again saying it was for the pain. I quit drinking once for quite a while but then was hurting, and got prescribed some 30's and Xanax. But then I got to feeling like I could handle a six-pack, so I started drinking all over again. I got into these loops. I'd quit drinking for a week or two, then I'd have a bad day.

I've spent ten to twelve years of the last twenty-five in jail. I wrote the parole board I needed the S.A.P. (Substance Abuse Program). I've got five kids; my first two were with my first wife; she died of an overdose. I realize now I've robbed all my kids of so much. They've had a dad who's been living lifestyles of the not so rich; and dumb. I'm surprised that I'm not on America's Dumbest Criminals.

He paused a moment, started taking about his children again, and brightened a little.

My kids are doing well; one's graduated from college, another's started college, and a daughter, after her grandmother died, she wrote a poem about her, and it was published in a poetry book. I'm real proud of her. I got my GED while here in the program, and I want to try and make some things up to my wife and my kids. I've been married twenty-two years, and my wife is waiting for me. She's hoping, like I am, that this program is my big turning point. I've got to make good choices and make it work.

I'm a good worker. I always worked hard when I wasn't in jail. I like to read a lot, and fish. I like to work with wood; I make some real nice birdhouses. I'm thinking that now I have my GED I will go to school for auto mechanics or auto body work. I like to do both of them.

West Care has been a major turning point for me; it's helped me step back and look at all the things that brought me here, and see the things I need to avoid so I don't get here again. It's changed my way of thinking. They say insanity is doing the same thing expecting a different outcome. That was me. I'm open now to all suggestions. I'm forty-two and there's got to be more to life than what I've been doing. I've got three grandbabies now and I think that's going to help too.

When I asked him if he had any advice for others, he thought a moment.

My advice to others is, don't go down this road. Deal with life as it happens, on its terms. Don't be afraid to talk about what's bothering you. I might have been a lot better off earlier if I had talked to someone about what was bothering me. I never really could get away from the sight of my friend when I lifted that tarp, or the guilt I felt over letting him use my car.

But, you know, I come from a small town where a lot of people have died of overdoses; a lot of drugs. I thank God I'm alive. I want to try and help others now because of what I've been through.

I want to try and make up some things to my kids, but I do have to say, because of where I am now, in this program, I'm at peace. I'm the happiest I've ever been.

CHAPTER 43:

IT'S ALL IN THE CHOICES YOU MAKE
STAN

I was twelve when it happened. My sister and I came in from school and saw a note on the table. My older brother John, he was sixteen, was upset because he was being grounded. We hear a pop from his bedroom and ran in there; he had killed himself. I saw him; it was a mess. It took its toll on the family. I started sneaking and drinking my dad's beer, and smoking weed when I was thirteen.

When I was sixteen, I started drinking even more. One day my dad was home in Edmonton working on his car and I was supposed to help him. However, I chose to go with a couple friends to Bowling Green and get drunk instead. When I got back I was told I had to go to the hospital; my dad had had a massive heart attack while he was working on the car that I was supposed to be helping him with.

I was a freshman in high school, and I quit. That was when I started taking acid and crank; I'd cook crank. I was in jail from when I was eighteen to twenty-two. When I got out I stayed straight for a while; I had two kids. Then I started substituting illegal drugs with legal so I thought it was better. I didn't see it at the time as hurting anyone, but it was; I was taking from my kids to support a $200 a day hydrocodone habit.

My mom's on probation. She gets off pretty soon. She's clean now, too. We worked together at the same time on meth; but never in front of each other though.

I'm a repeat offender. I've got several felonies against me; violent crimes, stealing, fleeing and evading the police. I've made some real bad choices. I was caught for possession, and was put on probation for five years. I was two months away from getting off probation when I was arrested for shoplifting. That put me where I am now.

I enrolled in the West Care Program because I want to change. I think being here will help me do that. I've got three kids, two biological, an eight-year-old son and a twelve-year-old daughter, and a fourteen-year-old step-daughter that's the same as mine. My goals are to stay off drugs and support my family. I love logging; that's what I want to do when I get out. My grandparents and my mom between them have several hundred acres I can log enough off of to support my family.

When I asked him if he had any advice to pass on, he was quick to reply.

It's all in the choices you make. For me, things started to snowball, and then I lived almost fifteen years in a blur. I was trying to get away from pain, mental pain, but you've got to deal with it. My sister, who saw all the same stuff I did, made different choices with her life and she's doing okay. She moved to Florida right after our father's death, made good choices, and today she is a dispatcher in a County Sheriff's office.

Me, I've lost my wife due to all this trouble and drugs. I plan on supporting my kids still; it's just that now it looks like it is going to have to be from afar. It's going to be hard to make it all right with the people I hurt, but I can, with different choices than the ones I've been making. But I can do it better without drugs, I know that.

CHAPTER 44:

I DON'T WANT A LOT OF MATERIAL THINGS; I WANT A FAMILY
HANK

(Compiler's Note) After we introduced ourselves and I explained what the interview was about, he started talking with a pained look.

The hardest thing I've ever done was hold my mom in my arms when she died of cancer. It took me a long time to come to terms with that; I was real angry at God. I had a lot of anger toward my two brothers, too, because they weren't there for Mom when she died. They've spent a lot of time in jail; I don't talk about them much. But one thing about this program is it has helped me realize I can't stay angry at people.

When my uncle died, he was my best friend, I was real angry at God and other people. I worked in the coal mines, but I had also started selling pills. I was all the time running around; I never even thought that my family would rather have me than the money I was bringing home. I didn't really see the pain I was causing others; I had fifteen or more years go by in the blink of an eye, that's what it seems like. My ex-wife told me that she dreaded every time there was a phone call, because she thought it would be about me in trouble again; another problem. If I'd kept going the way I was, I'd a probably been in the graveyard in two or three years.

I asked him about the West Care program he was in, and how it was helping him. He took a deep breath and started:

When you've been living like I have, you've got to change your way of thinking, got to start doing things differently. I think God's letting me be here for a reason. I've lost a lot in life, lost a lot of relationships. I'm not mad at my ex; I don't blame her for leaving. I used to think I knew it all; now I know that I don't.

I have some regrets over things I did; choices I made, but I can't dwell on them, I've got to start thinking ahead. I've got to learn from my bad choices and go on. I was always searching for something, and I didn't know I had it, a family. They were right there in front of me, and I lost a lot due to dope. If I hadn't been on dope I could have spent more time with others. With my ex, I wish I was here in this program eight or nine years ago; things might have turned out different. But I can't change that. She got someone new, and he's good to the kids. I'm glad for that, but it still hurts that it's not me there.

I am proud of what I'm doing here; it's helping me look at life in a bigger way; I can see a reason for everything that's happened; it's helping me learn a lot. I'm trying to change for the better; it's gradual, but I do see I'm changing. I like this new way that I'm thinking. They've taught me here that I've got to take care of myself before I can take care of others. Trying to get a lot of material things isn't important; I want a family. I need to repair relationships with my kids. I was married thirteen years and I have three kids, fourteen, eight, and four. When I look back, I realize my best times were with my children. I'd like to be a good role model for them now. I want to prove to others I can do it.

I've taken classes here on anger management, and parenting. I need to re-establish relationships, and I think what I have learned here can help. I want to show love toward my brothers; stay sober. A real man needs to see his children, provide for them, and set an example.

We talked about how much time he had left in the program and he said he had almost completed it, and was getting out soon.

I love my children, and I want to see them again, but I'm nervous and anxious about it too. I've got some goals. I want to get a job in the mines again; I loved working in the mines; I love to work. They told me where I used to work that they liked me as a worker, and that if I would get help with my drug problem they would give me a job again. Having a job offer helps; a lot of people don't know what they'll do when they get released; it helps to have a job to look forward to.

I've always had a good bond with my daughter, and I want to spend time with her. I miss seeing her and the things she does. She's a cheerleader. I have an aunt that's always been close to me, and she keeps me in touch with my kids. That's my mom's sister. She's always stuck by me. She tells me she's so proud of me in this program, and that means a lot to me. I look around at other guys in here, and a lot of them don't have family; I need to do some work to fix some things, but I do have family. If you do the right things, family can help keep you on track. Like I said, my best times were with my children.

I thought I was having fun with my friends, but they weren't really friends; none of them have contacted me in here; said they hope I do better. Real friends don't throw you out as soon as they're done with you.

I asked him if he had any advice to offer others who might be in a similar situation as he, or headed down a path in that direction. He paused a moment before speaking.

If something is bothering you, find someone you can talk to. Seek professional counseling if you need to, even go into rehab. If you go to church, find a friend who can help you. Don't try to be alone. If I had put as much time into trying to get help as I did into getting high, I'd have been a lot better off. Pick your friends better. Enjoy each day; it might be your last. Think about your choices; I never thought I'd be here.

I really do want to be a blessing to my kids, not an aggravation. I hope that when I'm out I can help someone who is headed down the wrong path. I'm in the stage of the program here now where I'm helping teach responsibility to some of the guys just starting in it. I really like the way I feel when I'm trying to help someone else. I hope some will listen. Everything we do, we can say 'yes' or 'no'; it's our choice. Like I said earlier, I like this new way I'm thinking; I'm starting to feel a lot better about myself.

(Compiler's Note) You may find, like I have found, your heart weeping for people who want to do the right thing, but will find, especially upon release that they are going to have to fight like never before in their lives. Choices carry their consequences, and gullies worn over time will take even more time to get filled in with positive choices, actions, and directions. My heart and prayers go with these men as they fight back against their earlier life activities and travel the road of discovery of who they are now.

CHAPTER 45:

A TRULY LIFE-CHANGING, MOST POSITIVE, CLIMB EVER
BASIL AND CORA CLARK

I'm ending this anthology with one of my life changing events; many of the negative ones have been told elsewhere (*Poetic Healing: A Vietnam Veteran's Journey from a Communication Perspective*, and, *War Wounded: Let the Healing Begin.*)

I saw an article about Seneca Rocks, WV, in *Backpacker* magazine, and knew from that moment on I was going to get there someday. My opportunity came while coming back from a trip to Vermont the summer of 2008. I not only was able to get a good picture, but I knew that as soon as I got to the top I would be able to get a photo similar to another rock depicted in the article that caught my attention. There was an observation platform near the pinnacle where I took a few pictures and enjoyed the view.

So I was sitting atop Seneca Rocks, WV, reflecting, pondering, and a bit lonely. But I was used to the loner role; I'd spent most of my life there. As I left the observation area to continue my climb, I encountered a sign which, along with a warning to not climb to the highest point, said that the view from the observation platform was just as good as the view from the top. Two things; (1st) I thought the warning was an invitation, and (2nd) they lied; the view from the top was much better

However, I could not see the rock pictured in the *Backpacker* article. I decided to have a snack, and then after eating, I looked around the summit a bit more. While peering over an edge I inadvertently relaxed the grip on one of my trekking poles and it slipped out of my hand and fell downwards. My frustration was short-lived though, as I saw the pole lying on a ledge just a few feet below my location. I climbed down to where it was and recovered it. And from my new location I saw it; I had a clear view of the rock from the article; a picture I could never have gotten had I not climbed to the top and then accidently lost my trekking pole over the edge.

However, the most significant trivial action that turned out to be a life changing event occurred as I was leaving the top of Seneca Rocks. In a spur-of-the-moment decision, I decided to hold my camera phone at arm's length and take a self-portrait (Selfie, I guess.)

A few months later when I decided to go on e-Harmony.com I used the image for my profile picture. Cora said the picture was what caught her eye, she read my info, and decided she wanted to "get to know a little better this university professor who wears a do-rag." The rest is history.

She decided to take a chance and come out from her loner-shell-role, contacted me with e-Harmony guided communications, which was eventually followed by lengthy phone calls. January 2009 was our first face-to-face meeting, and then over two years of six-hundred-mile round trips almost every weekend before our March 2011 marriage.

"So your sons will marry you."

This is taking a verse out of context, but sometimes that can be fun when it fits something else. The NIV translation of Isaiah 62:5 includes, "... so will your sons marry you." Cora and I have to smile at that one because between us we have three sons: Troy gave her away, Rocky was my best man, and Ralph officiated at his first wedding. What can we say?

So who are we now? Two connected loners, and definitely, no longer lonely. I thank God daily for the most incredible blessing he has given me, and, since she contacted me first, I guess I really can say, indeed, she is a gift from God.

By the way, I didn't retire from the University of Pikeville until 2014, so there were still a lot of 600 mile trips (in five years around 120,000 miles on our vehicles), giving my Elvis Gospel CD's a workout, and coffee, and potato chips, and sub sandwiches, and coffee, and ... And, all because I climbed up to rocks where I wasn't supposed to go, and took a spur-of-the-moment picture. I guess this is just reinforcement to my firm belief that *life turns on a dime.*

The Missy Mae is the name we have given her; our 2008 Burgundy ragtop. One of the things we enjoy when the weather allows is taking the Mazda Miata out for a ride with the top down. My first time driving it was over The Tail of the Dragon in western North Carolina, touted as 318 curves in 11 miles; fun. We had a get-together with some family, Easter 2010. Cora drove over. I still smile recalling her words as she shifted through the six gears, "You'd think we'd get too old for this; but we don't."

In the 80's, the contemporary Christian musical group White Heart released a song *Convertibles*, and one of the refrains is

God made convertibles.

My response is, "Let us worship!"

THE TREE
(2012) by Basil B. Clark

Have you ever looked at a tree
Twisted by the winds of time
And wondered about the storms it has weathered?
Put yourself in its place.

When life's squalls came against it
The tree swayed as it was pummeled by violent winds.
Still, it held its own and survived.
Put yourself in its place.

Many bent trees still put forth beautiful flowers,
Some still produce an abundance of fruit, and others
Provide much needed shade for those exhausted by the heat.
Put yourself in their place, and then ...

"Go forth, and do likewise!"

ABOUT THE COMPILER

Basil B. Clark is a retired associate professor from the University of Pikeville where he taught public speaking, voice and articulation, interpersonal communication, political communication, mass media, and fundamentals of theatre and acting.

His interests lie in writing, art, and enjoying time with his wife Cora and their two cats, Scooter and Little Bit

In 1983 he won grand prize in the performing Arts Repertory Theatre (Now TheatreWorks, USA [NY]) for his play "Change of Exchanges." In 2001 his story "The Town Drunk" was included in *The World's Best Shortest Stories* published by Quality Paperback Book Club (NY), and in 2005 he co-authored *Poetic Healing: A Communication Journey From a Vietnam Veteran's Perspective,* (Parlor Press). He is also author of *War Wounded: Let the Healing Begin* (Waldenhouse Publishers), *Barabbas: Son of a Father* (Waldenhouse Publishers), and *Massacre at Hill 303* (Waldenhouse Publishers.)

He served fourteen months as an Infantryman with the 1st Air Cavalry Division in Vietnam where he received the Silver Star, two Bronze Stars (one for Valor), and a Purple Heart.

In 2008, he wrote a DVD script for use by 4th grade teachers, "Mars Invasion 2030: Coal Camp to Space Camp." The curriculum was approved by the KY Department of Education and coordinates with the Mars Invasion program at the Challenger Learning Center of Hazard, KY. The DVD is on Cedar, Inc. – Homepage (www.cedarinc.org)

Also, Basil has developed and performs several monologues where he presents as the character ranging from twenty to forty minutes in length:

- Presidents Abraham Lincoln, U. S. Grant, James A. Garfield.
- Biblical: Adam, Moses, Jepthah, Naaman, Job, Jonah, Mordecai, Micah, King Solomon, Nebuchadnezzar, Barabbas, Peter, and Paul.

- Historical: Dr. Thomas Walker (early Kentucky Explorer) and, Daniel Boone.
- Other: Cpt'n B (Pirate).

Minion Pro and AR Darling on LSI crème white
Type and Design by Karen Paul Stone

CPSIA information can be obtained
at www.ICGtesting.com
Printed in the USA
BVHW031450231121
622345BV00005B/108

9 781947 589445